Altars
in the Street

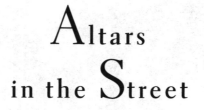

Altars
in the Street

A Neighborhood Fights
to Survive

Melody Ermachild Chavis

Bell Tower
New York

For Jarvis,
and for the children.

My hope is, you'll read this someday and you'll think: "Yes,
she got it just about right. That's what it was like there in
those days."

And for Carolina.

Contents

Acknowledgments

I have had two steady partners. The devotion of my husband Stan has made possible everything good in my life. My literary agent Ann Rittenberg has shown me the way, with her generosity of spirit and editorial brilliance. She recognized the conception of this book in my essay "Street Trees" and then became its midwife and godmother.

A deep bow to my Buddhist teachers, Sojun Mel Weitsman, Maylie Scott, Reb Anderson, Eric Meller, and to my community at Berkeley Zen Center and the Buddhist Peace Fellowship.

My gratitude and affection to each member of my writers' groups, talented women all, and central to my life.

And to my dear friends, Carol Emory, Tova Green, Susan Moon, Karen Payne, Jan Sells, Barbara Selfridge, Pamela Siller—a loving circle.

Many teachers have helped me to find my voice: Ellery Akers, Tracy Baxter, Tom Clark, Friedel Dilloo, Reese Erlich, Naomi Epel, Wilma Friesema, Lee Glickstein, Leroy Johnson, Wendy Johnson, Martha Richards, Josie Segal-Gallup, Jane Straw. Toinette Lippe, my editor at Bell Tower, has shaped this work wisely with Manjushri's sword into a book crafted with Avalokiteshvara's care.

I owe thanks to Blue Mountain Center and Ragdale Foundation for the gift of time.

The members of the Berkeley Community Gardening Collaborative have sustained me throughout the labor of this book with inspired passion for growing food, nourishing children's spirits, and feeding the hungry.

My everlasting admiration for the city of Berkeley employees we could always count on, the ones who do their jobs from their hearts.

I have changed the names of my neighbors and dear friends in Lorin to give them privacy, and so it makes no sense to reveal them now by thanking them personally. I thank you each and every one for giving me the only real home I have ever known.

When people praise me for something
  I vow with all beings
to return to my vegetable garden
and give credit where credit is due.
                              Robert Aitken Roshi

Altars
in the Street

CHAPTER ONE

Skye's House

My house on Alma Street was my sister Skye's gift to me, but she never knew that.

Like a lot of young people who die without meaning to, Skye went into a downward spiral and just got too low to get up again. She was working in Alaska as a "bull cook," oil pipeline talk for a kitchen worker, one of twelve women in a camp of a thousand men above the Arctic Circle on the North Slope.

Skye's troubles started when her boss tried to get her to sleep with him. When she refused, he reported her for not working hard enough. Three times Skye refused him, and three times he wrote her up, until she was fired and forced to leave camp. She phoned me from Fairbanks, alone and out of work in the middle of winter.

In the days before Skye died, I talked to her on the phone several times, calling her at the one-room wooden cabin she had rented on the outskirts of Fairbanks. Our other sister Naomi phoned her too, from her home near Fort Ord in Monterey. Naomi and I conferred on the phone about Skye. There was no one else we could call. Our parents had died years before, and there was nobody but the three of us to figure out our problems.

Raised together as army brat migrants, we three sisters knew the feeling of knowing nobody in a new place. We all grew up too soon, each of us out on her own by seventeen, and we scattered. I'd left in trouble, pregnant, feeling suicidal, and headed for a home for girls. Skye's and Naomi's teenaged years had been equally rough. We didn't get together much, maybe because we were all running away from the same hard place, but we held on to a feeling of helping each other get through life. An invisible triangle, mostly of phone lines, tied us together.

Before the pipeline, Skye had worked as a waitress, but really she was a weaver. She had a big handmade loom stored with her stuff in California, and she knew how to take an unwieldy, dirty sheep's pelt and wash and card and spin the wool, dye it with colors she made from plants she gathered, and weave it into intricate warm blankets.

Working on the pipeline, Skye made four times each hour what she made in cafes in California. When Skye was fired, Naomi and I begged her to come home, but Skye was determined to stay and get her job back. She'd filed a grievance with the union and was waiting to get a hearing. She said she didn't really want to be in Alaska any longer, but she wanted to prove that she had done her job and show that the man who had driven her out was wrong.

She sounded so low, though, on the phone, we kept telling her it didn't matter, let it go, come on home. Then when we tried to reach her, she didn't answer, day or night, for three days. In Fairbanks, just before Christmas, those were long, dark nights with only a few hours each day of weak sun low in the sky.

The second day, I called the police, but they told me a missing person had to be gone for three days before they would do anything. My boyfriend Stan called them back, but they told him the same thing. We didn't know anyone in Fairbanks.

I couldn't sleep, imagining Skye frozen outside someplace. It was far below zero up there. The afternoon of the third day, Naomi told me on the phone that she had convinced the police to drive the miles out to Skye's cabin and check on her.

That evening, we still hadn't heard, and a worried Stan took the kids out for pizza. I fell asleep for a few minutes on the couch next to the Christmas tree. When I got up, I decided to take a shower, and I stood under the water without any thoughts, pressed down by dread.

I stepped out of the shower just as Naomi opened the bathroom door. She didn't say anything. It was the look on her face that made me kneel down naked on the pink bath mat and curl over, not wanting to get up again in a world without Skye. But then Naomi started to cry. I've always been the big sister, and I got up.

The police had broken the door in and found Skye's body. They said she had been drinking alone and had passed out. An open bottle of tequila was on the table. Her head had hit the base of a lamp when she fell, and she lay facedown until she inhaled the contents of her stomach and died. She was twenty-seven.

I didn't sleep for the next two nights. I stayed awake walking and crying, because if I fell asleep and Skye was still dead when I woke up, that would make it true.

The third night after she was found dead I finally slept. I dreamed of Skye talking to me. She said, "I'm okay, Melody."

I arranged everything by phone. After I learned how much it would cost to send Skye's body back to California, I told the mortuary to cremate her body and send her ashes to me. They arrived in a black plastic box.

The morning of Skye's memorial service, I got up while everyone was still asleep and sat by myself, holding the black box on my lap. I remembered standing close to our mother's elbow in an army base kitchen at Fort Bliss, Texas, while she gave six-month-old Skye a bath. Skye, fuzzy blond hair slicked down, lay on her tummy in the enamel dishpan, flailing her plump arms and legs and smiling at me, showing one white pearly tooth floating in drool in her pink bottom gum.

A person's parents are supposed to die before she does, but not her younger sister. I felt as if the floor of my life had dropped away. If my baby sister could turn into a box of ashes, I could too, any time.

The next summer, Stan and I flew up to Fairbanks and retrieved Skye's things: two duffel bags stored in the property room in the basement of the police department. As I pulled her clothing out of the stiff green canvas bags, the limp emptiness of her musty-smelling jeans and T-shirts and long-skirted dresses were another way for me to know she was gone.

The man who owned the cabin where Skye died let us pitch our tent in his backyard while we spent several days erasing Skye's name from the bank and the union and the human rights commission where she had tried to fight her wrongful firing case. Skye's union told me that every member had $10,000 worth of life insurance, and Skye had named me and Naomi as beneficiaries. This was a complete surprise.

In the landlord's backyard with our tent lived a mother dog, half husky and half wolf, with her litter of frisky, roly-poly puppies. The last thing Stan and I did before leaving Fairbanks was to trade Skye's heavy arctic parka and boots for a fuzzy part-wolf husky puppy, white with black markings around her eyes like mascara. We named her Alaska.

On the long trip home, I thought about Stan, sitting next to me on the plane. We had met at a teacher's conference where I had been instantly attracted to this tall, slender single father, good with kids. We had been together, but not married, for six years, and in my experience, six years was a likely time to break up. Instead, Skye's death seemed to bring us closer. Stan had been steady and devoted to me, feeling Skye's loss almost as much as I.

At the time Skye died, I was splitting the rent on a small house in Oakland with a woman friend. She had one of the two bedrooms, and my kids shared the other one. I slept on a cold sunporch. My mirror was on the back of the kids' door, so if one of them opened it while I was brushing my hair, I had to jump back to avoid a bump on the nose.

Stan lived with his son Neal and a male roommate about a mile away. In our six years together we had tried various living arrangements. At first, both of us low-paid teachers, we had lived in a crowded apartment with our kids, Amina's little bed in the corner of a hallway and the "big kids" squeezed into a room they divided into a boy's side and a girl's side with bedspreads hung from the ceiling. Stan and I put our mattress on the floor of a sunporch.

Then we lived in a hectic commune of a dozen people with a child care center on the ground floor and almost no privacy for us as a couple. Now we had a women's house and a men's house, and a schedule: we schlepped the kids, their sleeping bags, favorite toys, and homework from one house to another several nights a week in order for Stan and me to get to sleep in the same bed.

On the nights we spent together we got up early and while Stan fed everybody breakfast, I packed a whole row of brown bags with lunches.

We dropped off Amina at day care and the older kids at school and made it to our classrooms before our students started coming in.

After a long day teaching children, we picked up our own. After dinner, there was usually a meeting to go to—if not PTA, then a political group. We were both activists, opposing apartheid in South Africa and working for nuclear disarmament. Our schedule required such incredible stamina, it was sometimes easier to do it apart than together.

We were in love, but our juggling act kept us out of balance. Our relationship seemed stuck in a cycle of fighting, making up, making love, and starting all over again. I didn't see how we would overcome the ambivalence that beset us. We'd both married young, and divorced young. I'd married and divorced again. I felt as if I hadn't learned how to be married, but I'd learned how to get divorced.

Stan was an army brat too, and it always seemed easy to both of us to move on. As kids we'd learned never to unpack completely, never to let ourselves get too attached to friends or a teacher. I lived ready to say good-bye, with stuff I never took out of boxes, always looking for a better deal on a cheaper apartment, say, or maybe even a better boyfriend.

On that plane ride, leaving behind Fairbanks where my sister had died alone, there was nothing under my feet but air. Stan's hand was warm on top of mine, and I knew I wanted to try to stay with him.

Back home with the kids and our new rambunctious puppy Alaska, I thought about what to do with my half of Skye's insurance money. Five thousand dollars was the most money I'd ever had at once.

My teaching job, in an alternative co-op elementary school, paid so poorly I got food stamps. The hardest bill for me to pay was always rent. No matter where I moved, the landlord got nearly half my paycheck.

Stan had quit teaching to work as an auto mechanic. He'd learned to fix cars from his dad and granddad when he was a teenager, and he was good at it. Even fixing cars with his friends at a makeshift garage in a backyard, he made more money than I did teaching school.

I looked at the $5,000 check and I thought, "I'll get a couch, a TV, and a used car."

I told that to my teacher friend Elyse at school, and she said, "No couch, no TV, no car."

Elyse and I had adjacent classrooms, and we were good friends. It seemed as if we didn't have a lot in common, since Elyse was single and had no children, but we were close. She taught dance classes too, and I always enrolled. I loved to watch her, moving to music like a lion, her mane of thick blond hair swirling around her face. Elyse is so pretty, some people immediately think "dumb blond" and can't take her seriously, but she has a strong sensible side.

Elyse said she'd read an article that said that a person who didn't have a house should try to buy one before making any other investment. Home ownership was a revolutionary idea, and I liked it.

My sister Naomi's husband's family had money, and they owned a home already. Naomi offered to loan me her half of Skye's insurance money. So I had $10,000—still not enough for most down payments, according to a realtor I talked to.

Stan's commitment to me at that point didn't include buying *anything* together, let alone a house. Besides, he didn't have down payment money to contribute. But with Skye gone, I felt suddenly tired of running through my life as if I were about to be transferred to a new army base. I wanted the life I really wanted, now. The family I'd been born into had never been very happy and now it was nearly gone. I had learned how to be independent and take care of myself and my kids on my own, but I always felt shaky and insecure. I wanted to make a family for myself, and a home with as much love in it as I could have. I determined to try.

My daughter Rosemary's sharp eyes saw the house first. She was fourteen then, and she and I were doing errands in the car. We were driving along Alma Street when she pointed. "Look! There's a sign on that house."

I pulled over, but I couldn't see any sign on the enormous yellow wooden house on the corner. It was two stories tall, with a steep roof and a lot of Victorian gingerbread trim. Then I spied a small card taped to a post on the front porch. We got out and walked to the bottom of the staircase. In blue ballpoint pen ink the sign said FOR SALE.

The neighborhood didn't seem much different from those we had always lived in. Most of the people we saw on the street were black. We saw white people too, and brown. There were lawns and trees and the occasional corner store. Big old houses like this one were mixed in with smaller, newer ones, and several large stucco apartment buildings punctuated each block.

Standing on the front porch, I could see a huge yard to the side of the house, half hidden behind a tall hedge. I started to want this house and its yard right then.

The elderly man who answered the door was tall and broad shouldered, with red-brown skin. Mr. Hightower introduced himself and said he was the owner. The price was only $62,000—low for the Bay Area, but at the usual 20 percent, it would require too much down payment. In his Louisiana accent Mr. Hightower asked me, "How much money do you have?"

"Ten thousand dollars," I said.

He invited us in. There was an entry hall with a window of amber-colored wavy glass over the huge mahogany door. I wanted to live in the glow of that window forever. We sat down in his neat, old-fashioned kitchen, and Mr. Hightower asked me about my job as a schoolteacher and about Stan and our children.

"Well, I'll tell you what I'm going to do," he said. "I'll sell you this house for $10,000 down and carry the note myself."

It turned out that Mr. Hightower was retiring from a long working life as a painting contractor. He owned three houses and he was selling the two in Berkeley and moving into his favorite one in Oakland. He said he wanted my children to have the house to grow up in. He preferred to hold the note himself so that he and his daughter would get the payments directly. Mr. Hightower said he didn't believe in bank mortgages.

I didn't either, and even if I had, I would never have qualified for one. Neither of us had a realtor. We went together to a title company and asked for all the papers to be prepared. We signed and the deal was done.

The next Sunday morning, I invited Stan out on a special date, a hike on Mount Tamalpais across the bay. From the top of the mountain, we could almost pick out the area where Alma Street was in the flatlands of Berkeley. We had brunch in a waterfront cafe in Sausalito where I made a proposal: I asked Stan to move in with me and make a family life in the house I'd just bought. He said he wanted to try.

Moving day was terrifying. All on one day we were blending ourselves into a living-together couple, and our kids into a family. I had committed myself to payments that would be hard to make, even with Stan helping. We reminded ourselves we had been paying rents to landlords without fail for years. The realization that there wouldn't be any landlord to call when things broke down scared us too.

The house had three apartments, two upstairs and one in the basement, all of them too small for us. The first carpentry Stan and I did together was to knock a hole in a wall joining the two upstairs units back into the big home it originally was. When we broke apart the crumbling plaster we found it was mixed with horsehair, something Victorians used to bind walls together. The house was older than our parents, even older than our grandparents.

The children ran excitedly from room to room, picking out bedrooms. All the rooms needed paint jobs, but every kid had one to call his or her own. And for Alaska, there was the big side yard.

We had lived in some crummy apartments, but the house on Alma Street was in the worst shape of any place we'd ever lived. We had our choice of two dry-rotted kitchens, both with scary old wiring, no cupboards, ugly fake-wood paneling on the walls, and scaling layers of decades-old linoleum on the floors.

We chose the kitchen with a big window looking out on the yard. Somehow, we all ended up gathering near that window, and it was obvious it was the heart of the house. Out of it you could see up the middle of the block and admire the big old trees in the backyards. I set up stacks of orange crates for cupboards and started cooking.

We planted trees right away: apricot, plum, lemon, apple, and a row of firs to screen off the apartment building behind us. Each tree was just a thin little stick, but we had hopes for them.

The house was made of redwood, thick planks of siding outside, and true two-by-fours inside the walls. It was built in 1885, when the old-growth redwoods were being logged. I liked to imagine that our whole house had been made from a single huge tree.

Stan and I were complete novices at renovation. Luckily, not far from the house was a library branch with how-to books and a tool-lending project where the tool librarian gave us advice on tile grout and toilet installation.

It was hard for us to do this kind of work together. Besides our size and strength differences, there were our opposing temperaments. We acquired construction nicknames for each other: Mr. Meticulous in partnership with Ms. Slapdash. We had our own political slogan, as if we were a couple of prisoners of construction: Free the Alma Street House Two!

While we redid the kitchen, we put the refrigerator in the living room and parked Stan's old hippie school bus out back so that we could cook on its stove. For five rainy winter months we ran up and down the back stairs, slogged through mud to the bus to eat crowded around its tiny table, and carried our dishes back upstairs to wash them in the bathtub. We were so fed up with each other by the end that we joked about the whole family getting a six-way divorce.

Before we started construction each day Stan and I stood in the middle of the mess and held hands to say a kind of incantation we'd made up. We called it "The morning chant of the house builders." It went: "Women and men everywhere are builders of homes! Men and women everywhere make shelter! Today, I will work with you, brother! Today, I will work with you, sister!"

This was supposed to inoculate us against fights. Of course it didn't always work that way. But for the times it did, I wrote in my journal: "When it goes well, our nails go in like drinks of water."

We became experts at demolition, calling ourselves archaeologists as we peeled off layers of misguided fifties and sixties paneling and wallpaper to find the Victorian core. We uncovered fascinating old newspapers sealed up in walls. In the attic, we found a little girl's brittle penmanship book, the yellowed pages filled with careful penciled letters, the date 1897, and the name Catherine Payne on the cover in her neat hand. I framed the book and hung it over our couch.

The house looked like a lifetime project, but we had our whole lives ahead of us. I hung Skye's photo in its frame in the front hall and covered the ugliest walls with her weavings, and we were home, in the house she had given me. I would always think of it as Skye's house.

Now, how to pay the mortgage? I set out to find a new and better-paying job.

CHAPTER TWO

Everything I Needed to Know
About Being a Private Eye
I Learned as a Kindergarten Teacher

After seven years of teaching school, I could feel the heat of burnout. I loved the children in my classes, but too many mornings, I could hardly get out of bed to face them. I kept a photo of four cute kids in my class taped to the wall by my bed. Every morning when the alarm went off, I would look at their expectant little faces and read the caption, hand-lettered by me: "Come on, Melody! Get up and teach us for another day!" But my own children were getting older, and I longed to rejoin the adult world and earn a full-grown salary.

Soon after I bought Skye's house, I met a real-life detective when she enrolled her daughter in my class. Sandra Sutherland told me how she made a living investigating cases for attorneys, and she encouraged me to give it a try.

The hot summer I was nine I had read every single Nancy Drew mystery in a small-town Arizona library—a whole shelf of them. I lay facing the back of the living room couch, trying to make my sweating body invisible, ignoring my mom and my sisters, substituting Nancy's family for mine.

I wanted to be a detective like Nancy, mostly because she worked for her wonderful father, the rich attorney. All I had of my father was a few photos of him in his army air corps uniform taken before the Nazis shot his plane down when I was a baby. My stepfather was a soldier who was gone to Korea so long that when he returned I hardly recognized him. Nancy Drew's debonair father was always around.

My Nancy Drew days came back to me as I talked to Sandra Sutherland about becoming a private eye. It seemed as if I might have the skills she said were important: the ability to write reports, to talk to practically anyone, and a lot of nerve.

I enrolled in night school law classes to prepare myself. Stan loaned me the tuition and cooked more than his share of dinners for the kids that year.

Eventually, Sandra hired me to be a "stringer"—an on-call part-timer—for Palladino and Sutherland, the agency she ran with her husband Jack.

Investigations was definitely a man's field. The form for joining the California Association of Licensed Investigators asked me to fill in the name of my wife. I wished that I had one.

Ninety percent of private detectives were former law-enforcement men who got state licenses easily after a few years on any kind of police force. To get my license I had to work for an agency for three years to accumulate enough on-the-job training hours to apply.

It was my good luck that the agency I joined up with was an exception to the all-male ex-cops rule. For one thing, the female partner Sandra was one of the best investigators in the state and a wonderful role model for me. For another, no one on the staff had been a cop. We were a new breed of investigators, a mix of overeducated actors, writers, and veterans of the civil rights and anti–Vietnam war movements.

Until I was hired, the staff were all men. A highly competitive bunch, "the guys" at the agency liked the idea of being "dicks." I knew they pictured themselves getting middle-of-the-night phone calls and rolling over to answer, "Yeah?" while lighting up a cigarette—even though most of them didn't smoke.

When I joined them—not only a kindergarten teacher but also a mom who dished out oatmeal before coming to work—I could tell I was completely blowing their tough detective images. I knew, though, that not much could be tougher than classroom teaching and parenting teenagers.

Not long after quitting my teaching job, I graduated from glorified gofer to a full-time staff position and was given my first murder case: to investigate a defense for a man who had left four corpses rolled up in rugs piled in a basement. I was appalled by the autopsy reports I had to read and the photos I had to look at, parts of my job that I've never gotten used to. I had to endure my colleagues' endless bad rug jokes—"Roll 'em, Melody!"—while I made myself go back out night after night to find witnesses.

After a while, though, I realized that all the sick humor around the office was a laugh-to-keep-from-crying defense against the continual horrors we had to read and talk about. I had wanted a job in the adult world; I ended up studying all the worst things human beings are capable of doing.

As I did more important assignments in tougher neighborhoods, I began to believe I could be a good interviewer. For one thing, I already knew how to talk to children—by listening. For another, both men and women like to talk to a woman.

My chameleon-like background as an army brat was a definite asset. When strangers open the door to me, I automatically start reflecting them—a physical attitude, or a slight inflection I mimic in their speech. I have the usual female antenna for social tensions, but I was also raised by an unpredictable, sometimes violent mother, so that I learned early to be hypervigilant for the slightest signs of shifts in mood.

I began to be assigned to interview people who were expected to be hostile. One of my male colleagues was once chased off at the point of a shotgun by an irate motorcycle gang member. My boss sent me out to the biker's trailer on a Southern California desert ridge. I drove out there, saw how remote the place was, and drove miles back to the nearest pay phone.

"Listen," I told one of the guys at the office, "I'll call back in a couple of hours. In case I don't, here's my rental car license number." Then I drove back up that ridge. The man was perfectly sweet to me, even though he lied about everything.

It was Sandra who taught me how to handle myself as a woman on this job. You could call what we did "using feminine wiles," but she and I are both feminists. She showed me how to use other people's sexism to get what the case demanded. Many times, I put away my notebook at the end of an interview and *then* asked the important questions. The man I was talking to would make the mistake of thinking that even though I was still there, it didn't matter, since he was just chatting with a woman, maybe trying to impress me. The fact that I wasn't writing didn't mean I wasn't listening. It didn't occur to him that he would see me later, repeating what he'd said on a witness stand.

After I got my license, Jack asked me to stay another year, to get what he called "a master's degree" by working with him and Sandra, and I'm glad I did. We parted friends when I left with Barry Simon, another of the staff members, who joined me to start our own successful agency together.

The house gave us low payments and a stability that allowed me to start my career while Stan went to law school. Stan had never wanted to spend his future lying on his back under cars. He worked his way through law school, at first fixing cars in our driveway and later clerking at the public defender's office.

My memory of Stan during law school is of him hunched over his desk, reading late into every night while the family swirled around him and vacations passed him by. When Stan ripped open the envelope to find out he had passed the bar exam on his first try, the three of us celebrated: Stan and I and our mailman Percy. He had been watching for that envelope, and we danced around together on the sidewalk in the rain.

I felt like the woman who lived in the shoe, our battered boot of a home, all of us pulling ourselves up by the straps of it. We got extra income and made new friends from the basement apartment we rented out, and we usually had a foreign student upstairs with us too, in the biggest bedroom, the one with its own bath. The house financed my private eye license, Stan's law degree, summer music camp, and braces for the kids.

At about the time I started my investigations career, the same swing to the right that took funding away from education brought the death penalty back to California. The gas chamber was reinstated by popular vote in a ballot initiative in 1978.

Even if we hadn't been convinced by the studies that showed capital punishment does not deter crime, Stan and I were sure that giving the government the power to kill people was a mistake. My teacher friend Elyse said she dreaded the day they gassed someone and she had to explain it to the same students she was always asking to find nonviolent solutions to their problems.

When we voted against the law, along with all our friends, I never dreamed my life would come to be dominated by the death penalty. The first death penalty trial I worked on, the case of Freddie the rug killer, showed me that in every case there is a door I can find and walk through, a door that leads into the room the accused inhabits. Inside that room are not excuses, or even legal defenses, but root causes.

I walked through that door when I met Freddie's mother, a tired, thin, graying blond woman. She told me how she had tried to get help for Freddie as he had become increasingly mentally ill. She finally was able to commit him to a hospital after he cooked a dead dog he found along the side of the road and ate it. A few years later, when doctors wanted to release him from the hospital, she begged them not to; not long after, Freddie stopped taking his medication, got his hands on a gun, and shot and killed four people in the space of a few days. Freddie's mother loved her son, and she showed me photos of him as a sweet-looking little boy. On that case I learned that people like Freddie's mother are hidden victims of crime. Thoughts of the dead victims haunted me too.

I worked very hard on Freddie's case, since I didn't see the sense of killing him in the gas chamber. Freddie was psychotic, and his death could not bring back his victims. Fortunately, Freddie's lawyer was a good one, and the jury listened carefully to the evidence about mental illness. He was sentenced to life in prison without parole instead of death.

The best part of my job on that case, the time when I possibly did the most good, was when I researched schizophrenia and gave Freddie's mother a book about it. She said she had always wondered whether Freddie's illness was her fault until she read the book and we discussed it.

As was the case in Freddie's trial, the danger of freeing a guilty man is rare, since the evidence in most capital cases is convincing. Freddie had left a wide swath of clues that led from those bodies in the rugs to himself. The question most often is the sentence—whether it will be life in prison or death. Over the years, I saw others as mentally ill as Freddie go to death row if they had less diligent lawyers or more punitive jurors.

People vilify lawyers, and I've seen my share of vile ones. I've always refused, like my former boss Sandra, to work for anyone who mistreats me. The beauty of being self-employed is the freedom to fire obnoxious people who hire you. But most death penalty defense attorneys are dedicated and selfless people I admire.

For the years of our partnership, Barry and I made good livings doing personal injury and medical malpractice cases and wrongful firing and discrimination in hiring cases, finding runaway kids, checking assets and reputations, and defending all sorts of criminally accused, from conspirators peddling every illegal drug to computer-chip burglars and crooked diamond merchants. Among all our cases, the human drama of the death penalty defense work was what most fascinated me, and after some great years together, Barry and I amicably dissolved our partnership, he to continue his broader practice, me to specialize in capital cases.

I worked alone for a few years, and then joined up with my new partner, Pam Siller. We found each other when we both appeared on a cable TV show about female private eyes. Pam had been a licensed investigator for years, mostly working for insurance companies. Right away, I loved her strong, deep voice and her open, frank way of talking. She phoned me after the show for a lunch date and told me she was interested in going into criminal defenses. She was the first and only African-American female investigator I'd ever met. I jumped at the chance to have Pam as my partner. For years I'd wanted to see more black investigators. Because of the ex-cop backgrounds of most of us, private eyes are nearly all white. I felt I did all right working in the black community on behalf of my clients, but I knew Pam could do better, and we were both determined to change the all-white legal defense teams for black defendants.

As we got to know each other, Pam and I found an amazing amount in common. Linking us across the racial divide is the fact that we're both part Cherokee, with ancestors from Oklahoma. Pam was raised in the

U.S. Army too, and her father, like my stepfather, retired as a sergeant first class. We'd both been teenaged mothers, and when we met, we were thrilled young grandmothers. We nicknamed our partnership "GWA" — Grandmothers With Attitudes.

The role of the investigator is to come along after things have happened and try to make sense of them — to try to understand, for instance, what has brought a human being to the moment when he will kill another person. The answer is always a long one, because whole lives have led both the victim and the perpetrator to that moment. Pam and I investigate not so much crime scenes as vast webs of history and experience into which crimes are woven — what a Buddhist would call "Indra's net" — the whole interconnected expanse of creation around an event.

People who ask me about my job always hope I'm defending someone who is innocent. Sometimes I am. If somebody is wrongly accused, it certainly is up to me to try to find that out. Among the scores of men on death row whose cases I know well, there are several about whose guilt I have more than reasonable doubt. My secretary, typing my reports about such cases, cries out, "Oh my God, this guy didn't do it!" Those cases keep me, and her, awake at night in anguish because of the hopelessness of most appeals. More common are the many people who have done something wrong but not exactly what they're accused of, and they need an investigator to prove it.

The truth is, though, defending innocent people isn't the real heart of my job. The people who really need help are the ones who have done something terrible. The challenge of my job is to work hard to help the innocent, but also unstintingly to befriend the friendless.

The most troubling moral issue for a defense investigator is not whether the defendant deserves an investigation, but rather the trouble the investigation can bring to the innocent people who get sucked into the whirlpool of the case. An interview with me can result in a subpoena and a newspaper story, or the recurrence of nightmares about something someone has tried hard to forget.

To do this job, I've had to learn not to take rejection personally. I've had countless doors slammed in my face. I've been shoved a few times and screamed at too. One evening when I was trying to interview a juror who had sentenced my client to die, the irate woman shouted after my hastily retreating back, "I wouldn't have your job for a million dollars!" I only wished, at that moment, that it *paid* a million dollars.

Most Americans have a very wide and generous helpful streak. For every person who sends me packing, ten others will open their doors, and five of those will invite me in and start making me a cup of coffee. At times it seems as though the person I'm talking to has been waiting years for me to show up and ask them for their version of the story.

As an investigator I've learned more about child abuse and neglect than I ever wanted to know. Without exception, every one of my death penalty clients has had a childhood full of trauma.

It's clear to me that the human beings I meet on the other side of a pane of glass in a jail are still developing. That doesn't mean they should get out of jail, but it does mean that whatever growth they can achieve should be fostered. There has to be a reason every person is alive.

CHAPTER THREE

A Sense of Place

At the end of my workday, like a pigeon, I fly straight home. I'm not in the house five minutes before I'm out on the back steps in a sweatshirt and jeans, pulling on the soil-clogged, worn-out running shoes I keep by the back door.

When we moved in, there was a gate in the fence between my garden and the one next door. Mrs. Wells, a woman in her sixties, lived alone there in her two-bedroom house. She opened the gate often to give me ferns and bulbs and seedlings from her garden to put into mine. She had a jowly face that rarely smiled, and she would wave away thanks with her callused hands.

"Call me Ti," she said.

"T? Like an initial?" I asked.

She spelled it. "T. I. Ti."

Ti grew food crops on every inch of her lot, even her front yard. My kitchen window looked into her backyard full of beds of closely planted beans and tomatoes and greens like collard and kale. Early every morning, sitting at the window sipping my coffee, I would see Ti's sturdy form bending into her plants as if she had grown there with them. She exemplified the adage, "We come from the earth, we return to the earth, and in between we garden."

Ti gave most of the food she grew to people in the neighborhood. She made sure that Saul Schwartz, the white carpenter who lived alone

and I wanted to know the history of the people who had lived in Lorin before me.

I found clues in the ground. I was always digging up white plastic mouthpieces Mr. Hightower had dropped when he finished smoking one of his small brown cigars. I found a 1926 penny, and then a perfect obsidian arrowhead! I knew there was no local obsidian, and that this piece of sharp black glass flaked to a slim point was probably carried to the edge of the bay from one of the volcanoes a long walk to the northeast, maybe Mount Lassen or Mount Shasta.

If I walked fifteen minutes toward the bay from my garden, I came to a street named Shellmound where a hill of oyster and clamshells was piled up over centuries by Ohlone villagers. They lived where a creek emptied into the bay and gathered mollusks in the vast tidelands that were there before the marshes were filled in for the freeway.

I had read about the Ohlones, and I knew that they had been able to see each other's fires around the bay on clear nights. They had lived here so long, the paths between their villages were worn two feet deep.

Our house stood in what had once been an open meadow of native bunchgrass, very different from the European grasses that came later. The native grass stayed green all year, great oaks gave the people acorns, and along the creeks lived the redwoods, giant drinkers, their feet in the water. I often looked out my kitchen window toward the hills and imagined elk grazing and bears pulling at berry bushes along the creeks.

Once, driving around looking for witnesses on my job, I found the Ohlone cemetery among suburban houses just west of the Fremont Mission. I stood a long time with my fingers laced in the metal of the Cyclone fence, looking at the sign marking the grave of four thousand people, not one named.

Near a busy intersection between my house and Shellmound Street are clustered a large African-American Christian church, a black Muslim community center, and a Hindu ashram. Someone put a cement statue of Buddha in a vacant lot near there behind a junkyard, and people built a wooden shelter over it. Walking by, I came upon that Buddha by accident one day, and I sat down on one of the benches within the little shrine. Vines grew over the wood-slatted roof, and some flowers were planted in beds inside the fence. I wondered what it was about this city corner that invited prayer, as if the land itself held memory that people could feel.

I knew that in 1820 the Lorin area was granted by the Spanish king to a family of cattle ranchers who kept it for only two generations, because within a few years of the Gold Rush in 1849 the Spanish land grants were overrun by squatters.

I was often at the county courthouse looking up records, so I researched the old deeds to my house. A man named Harmon had come by a piece of the Spanish land. Harmon's was one of several sizable pieces out in the country between the then-small towns of Berkeley and Oakland.

The oldest homes in the Harmon Tract, Victorians like ours, were built about 1885. The Ohlone shell mound was hauled away after 1900, the shells crushed and used to gravel streets. The creeks were channeled underground.

I had to run up and down a flight of stairs to go out to my garden because the Victorians liked to live as high as possible above the dust and mud of the streets where horses were always passing, and the barnyards with cows and chickens.

Directly across from us, there was a wood-frame house built at the turn of the century with a small warehouse added on to it. Every afternoon, Mrs. Sanders, a rotund little dark-skinned lady with round eyeglasses, opened a Dutch door in the warehouse so that she could chat with passersby.

Mrs. Sanders was joined every day by Pearl, thin and fashionably dressed, with marcelled hair. The two of them put chairs out on the sidewalk and sat discussing everything that went on in the neighborhood.

Mrs. Sanders told me she had been born in 1925 right there in her house, which had belonged to her parents. Some African-American families like hers settled in Lorin long before World War II. Mrs. Sanders' father had owned a company that distributed African-American papers and magazines. She showed me pictures of delivery trucks standing in front of her house, among big trees cut down long ago.

The streets near our house were named Harmon and Woolsey,

both farmers, Mrs. Sanders said. "My father told me that Prince Street, the one next to Woolsey, you see, was the lane to Farmer Woolsey's barn," she said, "and when it came time to pick a name for the street, he called it after his favorite horse, Prince."

After the earthquake of 1906, thousands of refugees from San Francisco tripled Berkeley's population, but, Mrs. Sanders said, Lorin remained a rural area and the fancier people moved away when they left farming behind.

In the 1920s, when Mrs. Sanders' parents had come, the doors to immigration were opened to Japan, and quite a few Japanese families came to Lorin too. "There were laws in Berkeley then," she explained, "prohibiting the sale or rental of property in white areas to anyone non-white. Lorin was the sticks, and it was given to what they called colored people."

In 1964, with a baby in my backpack, I had knocked on doors with other students to register people to vote on behalf of a ballot measure called Fair Housing. Eventually the kind of open racial discrimination in housing Mrs. Sanders talked about was outlawed.

Mrs. Sanders had a book that showed the exclusion order of April 21, 1942. It told how 1,300 Japanese Americans had been forced to gather at the First Congregational Church on May 1, 1942. By that evening, there were no residents of Japanese descent in Berkeley. "All over the neighborhood," Mrs. Sanders said, "their homes and their churches were boarded up." Mrs. Sanders told me that war workers, mostly African Americans from the South, soon moved in, but she didn't know how the property was actually transferred under the law.

There was a whole group of people Mrs. Sanders' age who remembered when African-American people had prospered in Lorin, building many churches and businesses. When we came, a pharmacy, hardware store, cafes, cleaners, beauty parlors, and antique shops were still there. If the older people's children were successful, though, they did not stay. The irony of racial integration was that it ended the time when African-American lawyers and doctors lived in the same neighborhoods with workers. Mrs. Sanders said a superior court judge had grown up on Harmon Street, but he had moved away.

Mrs. Sanders had a photo of her father the news distributor with

C. L. Dellums, the organizer of the Brotherhood of Sleeping Car Porters, and the uncle of our United States congressman, Ron Dellums. Mrs. Sanders sighed, looking at the portrait. "I don't know what things are coming to," she said. "Children today don't even know about what those men went through."

A more cheerful neighbor was Mr. Howard, who ran the small grocery across the street from our house. His big Victorian house, originally built with a store in it, was even older than ours, and so well preserved that a photo of it, with its water tower, appeared in a book Stan bought for me on the architectural heritage of the East Bay. In the photo, Mr. Howard stands smiling in front, wearing his shopkeeper's apron. In his youth, Mr. Howard had been a shipyard worker, and later, a schoolteacher and a salesman. Now a handsome man with a shining bald head fringed by white hair, he sat at his cash register all day and sold milk and meat and soda pop.

Mr. Howard liked people to stop and talk to him. When he had come from Missouri to find work in the shipyards, he said, "Nobody knew the first thing about building warships." In fact, many had been sharecroppers from the South. "The majority of them didn't know how to do anything but chop cotton." Within a year, Mr. Howard said, those thousands of men and women had turned themselves into one of the greatest industrial workforces ever known. "We built a whole ship every few days," he said. "Nobody had ever seen anything like it."

A steady stream of people came and went from the store all day, starting the moment Mr. Howard opened the door in the morning to children on their way to school. After school, they came back to buy snacks. Mr. Howard was a person who set standards, and he made them mind their manners in his store.

Mr. Howard lived with his wife above the store, but she wasn't well and rarely appeared. He knew everyone's name and everyone's business. I loved having easy access to last-minute quarts of milk and cubes of butter. At first, when I walked in, if everyone in the store was black, it seemed as if the conversation would pause momentarily while people registered my presence. I worried, with my army brat's hopes for acceptance in a new situation, that we might never feel that we belonged, because we were white. But after I had walked into the store a dozen times, that pause stopped happening. People learned my name and greeted me. The older people all treated me like someone young and sweet, calling me "honey" and "sugar," although I, in my thirties and a homeowner now, felt very grown up.

I had quite a bit in common with the other mothers my own age I met in Mr. Howard's store. Most of the women I worked with in the legal profession had delayed motherhood. But many of my neighbors had been teenaged mothers like me, and their families, like mine, had long traditions of close-together generations. I was fated to be a young mother and grandmother; I had known my own great-grandmother Viola well, a tough and gruff Texas homesteader who had not passed away until I was nineteen.

I became friendly with Camille, a bighearted woman whose oldest son was about the same age as my daughter Rosemary. Camille suffered from diabetes and worked as an aide for the school district as much as her health allowed. Her husband Elliott was a laborer at the Port of Oakland. Camille was a short, plump black woman with a lot of freckles. Whenever she and I met on our way to the store, we stood talking on the sidewalk, often about the schools.

There was a group of older men who liked to congregate at Mr. Howard's store. I called them the "Sidewalk Superintendents" because they would watch me working in my garden. One of them, Hiram, walked around the block every day. He would take twenty minutes to pass me by with his halting steps, lifting the aluminum frame of his walker ahead of him, and he loved to talk.

"You're just like I used to be," he told me. "Always pushing and pulling on something."

Hiram read the newspaper every day, and so did I, and he loved politics. I took to following along at his snail's pace so that we could keep on complaining about the government.

Hiram, with his bad teeth and shabby clothes, did not look like most people's idea of an intellectual, but his parents had been schoolteachers, he told me, and it showed. He even followed the legal news about court rulings on the death penalty, and he opposed it. He also kept up a running commentary on American race relations. Rigid black and white categories did not hold for Hiram, whose father had been black and Christian and whose mother had been white and Jewish. Hiram was "black," even though his eyes were hazel like mine and our skin was close in color, because, as he said, "In America if you're *some* black you're black. The biggest secret in America is that the peoples have mixed together from day one."

"Where are your people from?" Hiram asked me. "Texas, North Carolina, Tennesee, Oklahoma," I said. "I don't know too much about them, because my parents and grandparents passed away."

"I mean your ancestry, your background. Who were they?" he asked.

"I'm Irish, mixed with other things," I said.

"What kind of other?" he persisted.

I couldn't tell him much. My granddaddies Arthur Chavis and Bill Sherley were both drinkers who'd left my grandmothers before I was born. I'd phoned the Chavises in phone books all over the country, and they always said they were black, or Creole, or Lumbees, Indian people from North Carolina who mixed with black and white. On my mother's side, her granddaddy Blackman Sherley was part Cherokee.

"You're probably a little bit of everything like I am," Hiram said.

"But I've always been socially perceived as white, and gotten all the benefits of that, so I'm white," I told him.

"Well there's no such thing as a *white* person, you know."

"Which box do you check on forms?" I asked him. "Like on the census?"

"I check 'em ALL," he said.

My other main sidewalk friend was Skeeter, a man younger than me whose age was hard to tell, because he was almost as wide as he was tall. Skeeter functioned as Alma Street's news service and clown. He had all the gossip and he joked and laughed and teased the children. He wore blue denim overalls and trundled around the neighborhood doing odd jobs—washing cars and mowing lawns—and carrying tales to and from everyone.

Skeeter would try to wheedle work out of me, but if I said no he took no for an answer. I often hired him to help me with heavy garden work. Not that he was stronger than I was. Skeeter was not only obese, he had diabetes and a drinking problem. He was so unhealthy, he would wheeze from exertion. Between the two of us, though, we could usually wrestle garden supplies out of my station wagon or dig a hole for a tree.

One day Hiram was across the street by the store talking to Skeeter and the other guys while I was pulling weeds out of the roots of my hedge and Stan was washing his car when I heard them all break into laughter. They seemed to be looking at me, so I crossed the street and asked, in a friendly tone, "What's so funny? Are you guys laughing at my weeding style?"

Skeeter was still laughing, and he said, "I just was joking that the white folks used to sit on the porch watching the black folks working, and now here we sit looking at all y'all."

"Texas, right?" I asked, pointing at him with an index finger.

"Yeah, I'm from Texas," he said. "How'd you know?"

" 'Cause my mother was from Texas and I know Texas is the place where the plural of 'Y'all' is 'All y'all.' " That really made them laugh.

Stan and I agreed that our children were growing up differently from how we had, and better in a lot of ways. They had a hometown. They could walk to the university campus to skateboard, up to the hills overlooking the bay to the public swimming pool. They went to high school with kids they'd known at preschool and summer music camp. They belonged.

They walked and skateboarded, rode bikes and went out with friends in cars. Crime was not our biggest issue. The burglary rate when we moved into our neighborhood was probably average for Berkeley. On weekend nights Stan and I were sometimes awakened by noisy voices in the street around the time the bars closed. In a few minutes, the talk would subside, and we'd go back to sleep. We weren't aware of a lot of crime.

When we moved to Alma Street, our oldest kids were almost in high school, and Amina was just eight. I told the kids it was illegal to grow taller than me, but they did it anyway. It happened so fast: it seemed as if one day the kids were following me around with their little faces tilted up, questioning me with their high-pitched voices, and the next day they were standing over me, looking down at me, giving mumbled answers to my questions.

A Sense of Place

I left a note in my drawer in the bathroom. "Ask yourself the following questions: Is your name Melody? Are these cosmetics yours? Did you ask Melody if you could borrow them? If the answer to ANY question is NO, close this drawer. Thank You." Someone printed in pencil, "Hey, I just use the hairbrush occasionally. Is this allowed? Anonymous."

For a few years there was a huge wooden structure that looked like a wildly tilted ladder as tall as the house in the backyard where Jonathan and his friends practiced rock-climbing moves. In another part of Berkeley, this monstrosity would have provoked litigation, but our tolerant neighbors just watched, bemused, as Jonathan and his friends played on it.

Teenaged boys stood in the open refrigerator door holding half-gallon cartons, tipping streams of milk down their throats.

My old teaching partner Elyse was my main advisor on adolescence. She had become a psychotherapist and was a counselor at a junior high school, coping with the problems of teenagers in crisis every day. We stayed close because both of us have front-line jobs that are hard to do without support.

Elyse and I had a standing date to talk while walking our dogs on familiar trails up in the hills. I drove over with my white husky Alaska in the back of my station wagon and we started off from Elyse's art-filled apartment in the foothills with Cricket, her little red corgi.

"What is it with the *milk*, Elyse? And why won't they close any doors?"

"Graduate students are researching these questions," she told me, "but the results are not yet in."

"Just think, Elyse," I told her, "the whole of psychotherapy is about just *two people*: Mom and Dad. Nobody wants any kind of mother but perfect, all-giving, loving, wise! How am I going to be all that? Especially with *my* mother for an example?"

"One day at a time," she said.

Because of the spread in our kids' ages, for more than a decade our living room furniture sagged under adolescent bodies, and teenagers' cars pulled in and out of our driveway. There were parties and proms. Young men slammed in and out of the house, always on their way somewhere, it seemed.

Steering a family ship through Berkeley's troubled waters was truly a challenge. Some of us countercultural parents cooked up interesting educational experiments such as a junior high school that had classes only three days a week, leaving the other days free for "creativity." Some kids hung out and smoked dope on the nearby "Avenue," frequented by erstwhile hippies the kids called "burnouts."

Stan's son Neal, who fondly nicknamed me his "wicked stepmother," almost disappeared for a couple of high school years into that Avenue's scary subculture. We could barely get him to come home, let alone go to school. Neal came to no lasting harm, mostly due to a lot of counseling and some luck. There were quite a few kids adrift from families where no one seemed to be at the helm, and we half-raised several unrelated youngsters along with our own.

I was perpetually unprepared. When the big kids were almost finished being teenagers, Amina started. I remember coming home from work one day when Amina was eleven and collapsing onto the couch opposite her, where she was sprawled in a chair. I looked at her pert face with her famous dimples in her round, irresistible cheeks, the braces on her teeth showing through slightly parted lips as she focused on reading through the mascara gooped on her eyelashes. She wore black tights with a black T-shirt pulled down over them as a miniskirt, scuffed tennis shoes, and a jean jacket. One leg was over the arm of the chair showing a stretch of the crotch of her tights. Her fingers holding the book she was absorbed in had dirt under the nails, but they were polished with shocking pink lacquer. My baby. My youngest. I was about to turn thirty-eight and I remember thinking, "I'm not ready for this."

Fortunately, we had a lot of co-parents. Extended families formed by multiple divorces are common in Berkeley. Stan's first wife's boyfriend's son and Amina called themselves "brother" and "sister," and it made perfect sense to their friends. What we called "The Big Family"—our whole complicated group of former spouses and half-siblings and stepchildren—gathered in the house for kids' birthdays and co-parenting conferences in times of trouble. Our whole group of co-parents had strong shared values: we tried to suppress whatever strained feelings there might be in favor of what was best for the kids.

We did family counseling like other people flossed their teeth; we probably paid for enough of it over a decade to send two therapists around the world.

Stan and I called ourselves "matrimonially delayed." It wasn't that we didn't want to get married. It was that we never both wanted to at the same time.

We enrolled in parenting class where we learned to make clear "I" statements, as in: "*I* don't *want* to drive you over to Jennifer's tonight."

Our kids grew up on proletarian Alma Street, and they had friends in wealthier areas, and friends of all races. I was proud that they were comfortable in a wide range of social situations. This is what we had wanted for them, and it was working.

There was definitely racial tension, though, at the high school. There was only one high school in Berkeley, so it was integrated, but like their parents, the kids remained mostly segregated socially. There were a dozen separate cohorts, each with a nickname, a dress code, and a place to eat lunch, like the preppies and nerds, and the hippie granolas, black kids from the hills and black kids from the flatlands, and sets of Latino and Asian kids, some born in California, some from every South American and Asian nation.

Our children had their share of racial problems: there was the time several black kids pushed Amina under the water in the school pool until she was crying; the time some Chicano girls threatened Rosemary because they were mad she was dating a Chicano boy, and the time Stan's son Neal had his backpack taken away by black boys.

Berkeley High had lots of positive interracial mixing too, and so did music camp. When we went to our children's music performances and team sports events, we could be proud; every kind of family would be there, and we would think, "This is the best part of raising kids in Berkeley."

Car pools, evenings of homework, nights of childhood illnesses, and wild slumber parties, our child-raising years rushed along like a train of overloaded freight cars running downhill with no brakes, giving no hint of nostalgia about themselves while we were living them.

I do remember pausing sometimes to give thanks, and I'm glad I did. Sometimes, at the end of a day, while I was cooking, when all the kids were in the house, and Stan too, everyone busy, the sounds of them coming to me at the stove, I would tell myself, "Now is a good time. This. Tonight."

We raised our children to be independent, and so we had no one to blame but ourselves when Neal moved to Hawaii at eighteen, and Rosemary to far Northern California. Stan took a photo of me holding on to the back bumper of Rosemary's loaded truck, pretending to try to keep her from driving away.

Elyse had been right. We had done it one day at a time. We'd had our good parenting days and our bad. "We made lots of mistakes," Stan said, "but everybody survived."

I was still unprepared, and my emptying nest surprised me. It had all gone by so fast. Half a dozen times, setting the table absentmindedly, I put down too many plates.

It was hard to keep track, because Skye's big old house never completely *emptied*. Our kids made leaps out into the world, but still attached, they bounced back, like jumpers wearing bungee cords, to stay in the house again between jobs, apartments, and relationships. Thus our generations ran together. Amina was still in high school when I started baby-sitting my new grandson, Jonathan's son Benji. I was forever giving baby showers and doing duty as birthing coach for friends my own age whose offspring made great playmates for my grandson. There was never a year when I seriously considered getting rid of the high chair or the dog-eared copy of *The Cat in the Hat*.

My little blond grandson Benji drew a kindergarten picture for me of Skye's house, showing me standing in the doorway, a little boy coming up the front stairs, and the caption, "My Grandma loves me when I get there."

The other white families who had moved onto Alma Street were a lot like us: Marty, a carpenter, and his wife Beth, a public defender, and Sue and Barb, a lesbian couple, one of them a teacher of sign language and the other a waitress in a woman-owned restaurant. There was Jim, a classroom teacher, married to Libby, a drug counselor. Everybody had children, and nobody had much money. All of us, white people moving into a mostly black community, were part of "gentrification." But wherever the real gentry lived, they weren't on Alma Street.

Sometimes, a greedy little voice inside me wished for gentrification to really happen. We read about neighborhoods in San Francisco where property values soared after high-income people moved in. We had some ingredients that might have attracted yuppies: big old homes, big trees, a subway station nearby.

A few blocks away there was a row of bars where you could hear good live jazz and blues. Stan and I danced at one of the clubs fairly often and had a good time in an interracial crowd. There was Stubby's too, a pool hall with a Skid Row atmosphere we never braved. Stan used to tease me, "Wanna head down to Stubby's for some pool?" I joked that someday maybe we'd be able to order cappuccinos at Stubby's. But it wasn't to be. The neighborhood had too much of what yuppies disdained: apartment buildings with black and brown people in them.

We had a rent control law in Berkeley, something Stan and I had voted for because we'd been renters most of our lives. The idea was to slow the rise of rents in a crowded university city that students could hardly afford to live in. Rent control kept low-income people from being driven out, and it stopped speculation in housing property. The Black Property Owners Association, though, complained that rent control hurt them. Property values and rents in Lorin had never been high, and when they were prevented from rising, owners had a hard time keeping their buildings up when their costs rose.

If yuppies had arrived, I wouldn't have welcomed them, really. I didn't want high property values as much as I wanted a home. I had never lived in an all-white neighborhood and didn't want to, and I didn't want my low-income neighbors to leave.

But the demographic shift that was taking place in Lorin was hard for some of the African-American people who felt they were losing ownership of a place that had been theirs for thirty years. Not only white people came, but people from Mexico, Vietnam, and Ethiopia.

Wherever we came from, however we had come, we were all here now. We were like the world: more people of color than white, more poor than rich, and like the rest of the world, we had to learn how to get along.

CHAPTER FOUR

Soul Food

The first really bad thing that happened after we moved into the neighborhood was the robbery of Mr. Howard's store, in 1984. A young black man grabbed the butcher knife Mr. Howard used for cutting meat, forced the old man to lie down on the floor behind the counter, and took money from the cash register. Whoever the robber was, he was never caught.

All the next day, people gathered in the store to talk about it. When I was there, Mr. Howard kept shaking his shiny bald head. "I don't want to go through something like that again. Next time maybe it'll be my life." Mr. Howard was so shaken by the experience he closed the store for good.

After that, we had to walk two blocks to a much newer corner store everybody called the "Arab store," because it was owned by a family from Yemen. That was the same year that we first saw clusters of furtive-looking people half hidden under the pepper tree next to Mr. Howard's store. From our bedroom window, I would see a match flare, briefly illuminating people's bent heads. I thought they were lighting cigarettes until I heard about freebase cocaine and realized they were lighting pipes.

That year too, I learned all about cocaine psychosis, doing an investigation for Roscoe Thomas, a black man who started out selling heroin for an Oakland syndicate and ended up on death row. The witnesses I talked to said Roscoe had stayed awake inhaling freebase almost constantly for three weeks before he shot his crime partner, pulling the rings off the dead man's fingers to sell for more of the drug.

The furtive people I saw lighting up freebase pipes under Mr. Howard's tree were not teenagers. They were adults five to ten years younger than me — in Roscoe Thomas's age group — my younger sister Naomi's generation.

What I hated about drugs and alcohol was feeling out of control. I got drunk exactly once, at age nineteen, and it reminded me too much of my out-of-control parents. If I was addicted to anything, it was to staying sober to make sure nothing was going wrong. For the same reason, I hadn't liked marijuana either. One of the few times I smoked it, I was a young mother. When I couldn't remember where I'd put the diaper pins, I thought, "I don't like this," and I passed it up after that.

The dangers of cocaine turned most people I knew against it. But many didn't get away from it until they reached bottom — their marriages and bank balances broken.

That's exactly what happened to my sister Naomi.

It took me a while to catch on. Naomi and her husband had always had more money than we did, and she gave nice gifts to me and my kids. When she stopped sending gifts and started asking me for money, I gave her several loans she never paid back before I let myself admit what was happening.

Naomi denied she was using cocaine, but then one afternoon she phoned in tears and admitted it. Like a lot of people who had trouble handling alcohol, she was also vulnerable to cocaine. I called all over to find out about treatment facilities. There was a hospital in San Francisco, expensive, but it sounded good. I offered to take care of her three kids while she and her husband went there. But then she said, "Everything's okay, Melody. There's no problem, all right?"

I've tried to forget our horrible cocaine Christmas, but I can't. While I was basting the turkey, Naomi and her husband kept disappearing into the bathroom and out onto the back porch. First they were maniacally happy, then irritable, and finally fighting with each other. After a tense dinner, with them drinking too much wine, they went out into the cold garden. Stan's son Neal, home for Christmas, followed them outside and came back in to report that they had offered him cocaine.

After that the fight expanded. We confronted them, and they denied everything. Stan wanted to throw Naomi and her husband out, but I wanted them to stay, because I was scared they would kill themselves and their kids driving home drunk. Then Naomi insisted on leaving. Stan offered to drive them to a motel, but they refused. There was a screaming scene in the front hall, Naomi and I pulling a set of car keys back and forth, our watching kids standing close together looking pale and shocked. Finally I gave up when it seemed as if Naomi was about to hit me.

All the way down the front steps she hurled curses at me that sounded as if they came straight out of our mother's mouth. When I talked to Naomi on the phone the next morning, she said she didn't remember any of the words she'd screamed at me. This was just like life with Mother. I would remember for the rest of my life, and she didn't remember the next day.

As the big sister, I specialized in rescues, but I couldn't figure out how to reach Naomi. Telling Naomi that addiction was bad for her and for her kids could not help; already, she did not want to be addicted. I knew she hated herself for it.

Naomi didn't want help, but I knew I had to have some. At the hospital Naomi wouldn't go to, I went to a workshop for relatives of addicts and learned about denial, intervention, coaddiction.

The workshop leader was Judy, a soft-spoken young woman who was one of the least judgmental people I'd met in my life. "The souls of addicts are starving, as if they have a huge hole inside," Judy said. "That is why they pour 'spirits' into themselves. They are trying to feed their souls, but with poison. You can't rescue an addict, but never give up faith that they can recover. A soul can sicken, it can be wounded, but it can never die. When the poisoning stops, if the person's soul finds food, it will be healed." That food, Judy said, can be creativity, or spirituality, or love of self and others.

Loaning Naomi money and picking up the pieces with her kids was enabling her addiction, Judy said. When she said that the best thing to do was to cut off contact until my sister was clean and sober, I wasn't sure I'd be able to do it.

I felt as though Naomi were drowning and I was her big sister standing on land telling her she would be okay if only she would just swim to shore. But I knew that if I dove in and got too close to her, she would drown me too.

When I picked up the phone to Naomi slurring her words, or Naomi screaming epithets in her voice like our mom's, I steeled myself to say, "I'll talk to you later, Naomi, when you're not high," and I hung up.

Sometimes Naomi called at dinnertime, and when I came back to the kitchen with a tense face, someone would ask, "What's wrong?"

"It was Naomi," I would say, and I'd sit down, my dinner ruined, thinking, "Why her, but not me?" All my joy in the warmth around my table drained away because Naomi was shut out of my circle.

My worry about Naomi got worse when I had to face addiction every day in my neighborhood. Freebase was quickly replaced by crack. It seemed as if the moment we heard about crack—the cocaine for poor people, only $5 a hit—Stan noticed it in his law practice representing children in foster care for the county. Many of them had moms on crack.

One night our doorbell rang, and I found a woman on our front steps almost in tears. "I'm Cherie," she said. "Don't you know me?" I didn't, but she said she lived in the big apartment house up the street everyone called Green Gables. "I'm Camille's friend, but Camille isn't home. My baby is having an asthma attack," she said. Cherie needed $20 for the baby's medicine. "I'll pay you back tomorrow morning," she promised.

I hesitated, but then I reached for my purse. When I closed the door, I felt kind of foolish. "Well," I told Stan, "no one would be so bold who didn't really need the money."

Cherie didn't come back the next day, or the next, and when I asked Camille, she shook her head. "Oh, Cherie," she said. "She probably used the money on drugs."

That wasn't the last knock on our door with that phony medicine story. I learned to say, "I want to help you, but I don't have any cash. I'll drive you to the pharmacy, though, and pay for the medicine with my credit card." Somehow no one ever took me up on this offer. People stopped asking us once they knew we would not give them money.

On my job, I was right on the front line when the opening shots in the War on Drugs were fired in the mid-1980s with the federal racketeering prosecutions. I worked on one trial after another with lawyers who were defending members of drug-dealing organizations. Black and Latino gangs dealing drugs on city streets were easy targets for the feds because they could readily pick up youths out on street corners and turn them into government witnesses to get to their bosses. Somewhere not very far above those bosses, the drugs came from white hands, but whoever *those* people were, they rarely appeared in court or in prison either.

When I met my client Felix Mitchell, the famous drug lord of Oakland, I was impressed—and saddened. Even in an orange jumpsuit in a cell, Felix was a commanding figure, so intelligent he could have been the CEO of a corporation if he had gone to Yale instead of the "street academy." He *was* the head of his own corporation, which sold millions of dollars worth of cocaine and a kind of heroin nicknamed "China White." A whole group of snitches the Drug Enforcement Administration had turned out of Felix's gang into the federal witness protection program were ready to testify about numerous murders ordered or known about by Felix.

What made me sad about Felix was how he used his talent, selling drugs in the same housing projects around Sixty-ninth Avenue where he had grown up. Felix wasn't hard to arrest: he drove a long black car with the license plate "69 MOB."

Not long after he went to federal prison in 1987, he was murdered by another inmate. Felix was given a hero's funeral that made the national news. His casket passed through the streets of Oakland in a horse-drawn carriage, the sidewalks lined with mourners, as if he had been a great leader.

He was hardly Robin Hood, but Felix was missed in East Oakland because he had given a little bit back—basketballs and trips to Disneyland for kids. I had interviewed people from run-down housing projects who had ridden in Felix's limousines and gone to his parties. Yet that horse-drawn hearse at Felix's funeral symbolized to me how drugs had replaced hope in the twenty years since Martin Luther King's funeral.

It seemed to me that it was after the breakup of Felix's organization that drug dealing came out into the open in our neighborhood, as if Felix's demise made room for lots of small entrepreneurs to start up.

The first crack dealing that we were aware of started in the driveway of a small apartment building. It was a good spot, very dark at night, with bushes to hide behind. We couldn't see it from our house, but driving by, we noticed people standing around there at night. Cars parked in the street while young men came up and leaned in the car windows. This was alarming. I knew plenty about shootings associated with crack.

I decided to go across the street and talk to Mrs. Sanders and her friend Pearl about it one afternoon. Mrs. Sanders wore a threadbare housecoat and sat with one hand on top of her cane, but Pearl always dressed up to come out, with her shiny black hair done up in tight waves. The two of them sat side by side on chairs just inside the doorway, discussing everything that went on around them, including current events. Pearl was fond of saying, "Oh, that is terrible. Just *terrible!*" about most of the news on TV.

Mrs. Sanders and Pearl told me they both knew Mrs. Jackson, who had lived in the building where crack was being sold, for fifteen years, raising her two sons there as a single mother. They were grown and had moved away, but now the Jackson brothers, Carl and Charles, had come back to make the driveway of their mother's building their drug sales territory.

Mrs. Sanders said she had talked to Mrs. Jackson about her sons. "She said there is nothing she can do. She can't do one thing with them."

The two ladies had also found out that other tenants in the building who were afraid of the drug dealing had moved out, and a girlfriend of one of the Jackson brothers had moved in, giving them access to the building without using their mother's apartment.

"It's just *terrible,*" Pearl said.

It was Saul Schwartz, the white contractor who lived on the other side of Ti from us, who suggested that we meet to talk about what to do. He said Potter Woods, the bearded African-American longshoreman who had sent a daughter to Harvard from his home a block away, wanted to get together too.

Saul invited Ti Wells and Mrs. Sanders, but they didn't want to come. "I've done my share of meetings," Ti said firmly, and she couldn't be budged. Mrs. Sanders was afraid to go out at night. Pearl wanted to come, but she was afraid she would be seen by the Jackson brothers going to a meeting, so we all agreed to meet at a pizza parlor downtown. As Stan and I passed Pearl's on the way to the meeting, we saw her inching her big sedan out of her garage, headed for the same place we were going.

Looking around the pizza place table, I was impressed with the amount of talent we had. Saul Schwartz and the longshoreman Potter Woods were there, and Louis Sandoval, a Latino bus driver who lived on our block, and Louis's wife Manuela, a cook.

Libby the drug counselor who lived half a block from us was there too. I had always liked Libby, a freckle-faced skinny blond with a ponytail, for her wide grin. She worked at a halfway house, and she was an artist. Her living room was like a runaway gallery hung with big oil paintings and festooned with colored streamers, homemade papier-mâché masks, and pinatas. You had to pick your way across the floor strewn with toys and children—her little girl Aurora, and usually several from the Green Gables apartments, all hard at work on art projects. A lifesized cardboard Spock from Star Trek leaned against the wall.

"Dr. Spock," Libby would introduce him. "We're raising Aurora according to his advice."

At that first meeting, the group decided to send Saul and Potter to meet with the police to demand action. As Potter said, "This wouldn't be allowed in front of the mayor's house! The police would chase them off in two minutes!"

Libby and I both said we would go door-to-door talking to other neighbors, to invite them to the next meeting. "There's strength in numbers!" Louis the bus driver said.

That's how I met Addie and Joe Josephs, who lived right next door to the drug dealing in a Victorian house as old as ours, with huge old plum trees in the yard. "Call me Mr. Joe," he told me. He had worked for thirty years in an auto plant, and I had seen him for years working around his house, fixing cars and appliances and selling and trading them.

Mr. Joe's wife, Addie, was a petite light-skinned woman with Asian-looking eyes. She kept chickens and grew vegetables in their backyard.

From the Josephs' front window filled with Addie's African violets, you could look right down into the drug dealers' driveway. Addie had a bad back, and she didn't like to sit at meetings, but Mr. Joe, who had been a union man, was eager to join our group.

"I'm not afraid of them," Mr. Joe said. He was a big man, very dark skinned, calm, and dignified. "I've seen much worse than them in my life." When I left their house that day, I carried a carton of fresh eggs.

There were a lot of people who turned me down. Many were too busy, or too afraid. The committee we formed was not a majority of the people on our street, but we were a committed minority, and that, I reminded myself, is what had always changed America.

Libby had recruited Marty and Beth Timson, a white couple with two children. Beth was a public defender and Marty a contractor. Libby also invited her friend Ruth Hinson, a black woman who was a full-time mother of three.

When I first met Ruth, she hooked me right away because something about her reminded me of my dead sister Skye. Tall, with shiny copper skin, high cheekbones, and a dignified strong jaw, Ruth was a handsome woman. She had the same big-boned, loose-jointed way of moving Skye had had, and she smiled with a kind of friendly sunny quality that I missed, not having Skye. I often heard Ruth's deep voice outside, calling to her kids, or her chuckling laugh as she talked with the neighbors. I thought she would be a strong leader for the committee.

At the first meeting Ruth Hinson came to, she and I were surprised to discover we each had a daughter with the same name: Amina. Ruth's Amina was a baby, and mine was a young teenager.

A policeman came to our meeting, the result of Potter's and Saul's trip to see the chief. "Call 911," he said. "Report drug dealing."

"We've been calling," Saul said. "The police drive by, the dealers scatter and come right back as soon as the car is gone."

"And when I call," Pearl complained, "the lady who answers just says, 'What are we supposed to do about it?' She is rude!"

"As soon as they hear Alma Street," Ruth said, "they don't take us seriously."

Using my investigator's skills, I had found out that the owner of the building where the Jackson brothers were dealing drugs was a man named Wallace with a home in the Oakland hills who owned a dozen other properties. We decided to write Wallace a letter demanding that he fence his building, install lighting, cut the bushes, and evict his drug-using tenants. We got no answer, and no action from Wallace.

Because of our meeting, police raided the driveway of Wallace's building the next week. They found crack, but it was in some bushes out on the public sidewalk, not on anyone's person. They had no cause to arrest anyone loitering in the driveway, because they were guests of tenants on private property. After the raid, the dealers came right back.

A few days later, Mrs. Sanders handed me a copy of the letter I had typed to Mr. Wallace the landlord. "Mrs. Jackson gave me this," Mrs. Sanders said. "The landlord put copies in the mailboxes of all the tenants. Now the Jackson brothers know about the committee."

Luckily we hadn't put anyone's name on the letter, just "Alma Street Neighborhood Committee." Still, everyone was scared.

But if the drug dealers were scared of our committee, they didn't act like it. They kept right on, all night every night, and getting bolder, they also started selling during the day.

Then one day while my son Jonathan was playing ball with his son Benji in our garden, the ball went into the hedge, and trying to retrieve it, Jonathan put his hand into a cache of bullets.

I brought the bullets to our next committee meeting, and we decided to take them to the city council meeting. There were eight bullets, and it so happens we have eight council members, counting the mayor. I taped one bullet on each of eight cards, and labeled them: "Found on Alma Street, where children play every day." As Potter Woods spoke at the microphone, I handed one bullet to each council member. They were nonplussed. No one knew what to do with them. A police officer finally took them away. Libby, Saul, Stan, and Pearl stood up at the back of the council chamber holding a sign: "South Berkeley Demands Action."

Potter, a stern presence with his short gray hair and wide chest, told them, "Apparently drugs are legal on our street. They're being sold with impunity day and night. We rarely see police in the neighborhood. When they do drive past, the dealers stop their activity and stand and stare at the cops. Nothing more happens."

The council members were clearly uneasy with this news, unsure how to react. Most of Berkeley was still in a sixties mentality in which drugs were semi-okay, and the police were not to harass the citizens.

Potter continued, getting more vehement. "When I was young," he said, "if I had dared to commit even an infraction, I would have rotted in jail for a long time before anyone even investigated what had happened to me. I don't want to go back to those bad old days, but I simply cannot understand why drug dealers are not arrested immediately."

No one had anything to say in reply. The mayor just thanked us, and the meeting went on. It was clearly easier for the council members to deal with the next agenda item, hills people talking about trees blocking their views, than with cries for help from our corner of town. We left the meeting that night feeling very alone.

Meanwhile, Jonathan decided to do something on his own. He found Nathan out on the block. Nathan had a little son with one of Rosemary's high school girlfriends, and he knew everybody on Alma Street. He promised Jonathan to tell the guys not to hide any bullets— or guns, or anything dangerous—in our yard again, because of Benji. That was how we learned that we could communicate with the dealers, at least by sending messages.

At our next meeting, we talked about our city council visit. "I realize now we can't wait for somebody to come and solve our problems," I told the group.

"No one cares but the people who live here," Potter said, "not the police, not the city government."

Ruth and Libby reported that there were dealers now loitering at the Green Gables apartment building too. Ruth lived next door to the Green Gables, and she said she knew a couple with kids who lived there who both had become addicted to crack, first the husband and then the wife. "She cries all the time, it hurts so bad when she tries to quit," Ruth said.

The couple used to get along, but now they had screaming fights almost every night, and their children were going unfed. Ruth, and sometimes Libby, were feeding the children whenever they could. Ruth knew about the pain of addiction because she was a recovered alcoholic. "I chain-drink Pepsis, and I smoke," she said, "but I'm working on quitting those too."

At the courthouse, I found out the owner of the Green Gables was an elderly black man who lived twenty miles away in Martinez, an oil town. The gossip from Pearl was that the owner's son was taking money from the dealers, and if the women tenants who were addicted couldn't pay their rent, the owner's son took sex from them instead. Pearl didn't use those words: "He makes them do—*you know*," she said, until I got her point.

My friend Hiram who walked around the block on his walker confirmed Pearl's gossip. "That landlord's son is probably using that crack stuff too," he said.

One item always on our committee's agenda was speeding cars. The sound of the squealing tires was one of the worst hazards the dealers brought with them. Ruth was a big booster of closing off one end of the street with a barricade. "Sooner or later, one of the children is going to be killed by a car," she said.

Pearl disagreed. "This isn't New York," she complained. "Why should they play out in the street? Their mothers should keep them inside." But Ruth pointed out that we had no park close by. She wanted the street barricaded so that the children could play ball and jump rope safely. In the end, our committee voted to ask the city for street barricades, never realizing we would have to go to a dozen meetings and hearings to get them.

One day I heard the roar of a chain saw. When I rushed out to the garden I saw a young man lopping branches off Ti's beautiful old Norfolk pine. It stood in her front yard, blue-green and stately, and she was standing next to it, watching the cutting with her arms folded across her chest.

"Ti, what are you doing?" I cried.

"I'm cutting this tree down."

"Why? Oh, Ti, I love that tree!" It was too late already. Too much of it was gone.

"I want to see what they're up to," she said. "I want to be able to watch out for those drug dealers from my front porch."

On a cold night in November 1987, while our committee was still writing letters and going to meetings to get street barricades, a car sped up Alma Street just as Stan was walking Rosemary out to her car. Automatic gunfire burst from the car as it passed a group of guys standing on old Mrs. Burley's front lawn halfway up the block. Stan and Rosemary both threw themselves down flat on the sidewalk.

We found out that the shooting was the result of a dispute among dealers for control of Alma Street. No one had been killed, but several young men had wounded legs. We saw one guy hobbling around on crutches with his leg in a cast. It was the first of three drive-by shootings that winter.

Telling the story to our friends, Stan kept saying, "I saw red flashes spurt out of the gun barrel."

"How can you live there?" our friends from other places asked. It was hard to explain that there was never a day on Alma that was bad all day. The violence came in quick bursts, exactly like bullets from an automatic weapon.

At last a traffic barrier was installed, three heavy cement bollards like big, ugly, steel-reinforced flowerpots. Little kids came out to play in the street, and we planned a block party.

I saw an article in the paper quoting African-American professor Harry Edwards, a famous athlete. In the article, he said, "Crack is the greatest challenge to our community since slavery." Libby, Ruth, and I all painted the quote on a bedsheet in big red letters outlined in black and green, working on Libby's living room floor, shooing Libby's baby Aurora and Ruth's baby Amina away from the paint. We wanted to string the banner across the street between two phone poles for the party.

I asked Jonathan, my rock-climber son, if he would hang it up for us with one of his old ropes.

"Oh, no problem," he said. "I'll just go out there like the Lone Ranger and take a stand all by myself against crack while you guys party." He had a point.

We made a plan: when the time came to hang up the banner, all the members of the committee would surround him, so it wouldn't look as if it were all his idea.

That Saturday before Halloween dawned warm and sunny. I wore my good witch outfit, a black dress with a pointed hat and a wand. Quickly the street filled with kids decorating trick-or-treat bags and dunking for apples. Mr. Joe brought a bag of popcorn the size of a four-year-old, and Mrs. Sanders came walking up the street with a big plate of corn bread and took a seat on a folding chair. As soon as she did, Ti came out and sat down beside her.

When we had enough people, we executed our banner-hanging plan. Libby, in her gypsy dress, snuck it out of her house in a shopping bag, and we rounded up ten people to gather around her and Jonathan with his climbing rope. Nathan the part-time drug dealer came over to help. "Oh, hi, Nathan, how about giving me a hand?" Jonathan said, smooth as molasses. We all walked in a tight mob to the bottom of the phone pole, and Nathan boosted Jonathan up to the first peg. Jonathan tied it, but we all kept our hands raised as if we were tying it too. We repeated our charade on the other side of the street, and voilà!—it was up, and no one was singled out as the hanger-upper.

People looked at the banner, and some nodded their heads, but no one talked about it. I was serving baked beans when a woman held out her plate and sneered, "This party should be for the *community.*" I got her drift: the *black* community. But Potter, who was standing right next to me roasting hot dogs, waved his barbecue fork and declared, loudly, "Don't pay her any mind," and winked at me. "She's been drinking," he whispered, after the woman went on down the line.

"Thanks, Potter. I know there's no point in trying to communicate with somebody who's drunk," I said, thinking about Naomi.

I thought about what that woman had said, though. Our banner said crack was a challenge to "our" community, in the sense of those whose ancestors had been slaves. Or it could mean that we were all challenged to end crack the same way all our ancestors had been challenged to end slavery.

To our surprise, the Jackson brothers and their pals joined the party, helping themselves to hot dogs and corn chips, potato salad and cake, and standing around nonchalantly while members of our committee gave them either furtive glances or fake smiles. Guys their age and younger, though, gave them high fives and slaps on the back, and pretty young girls flirted with them. Nathan ostentatiously hung around next to the Jackson brothers, but he talked to Rosemary and Jonathan too, and helped Stan, dressed as a farmer in overalls and a straw hat, who was roasting marshmallows.

Three cops, one white, one black, one Asian, walked around nodding to people and giving everybody tight, uncomfortable smiles. They each accepted a hot dog and stood together, solemnly chewing. None of us wanted to be seen standing around talking to the police. Nobody knew the cops, but practically everybody had known the Jackson brothers, and their mother, and their cousins, for years.

I noticed one guy who seemed about twenty years old, a heavyset muscular black man with a loud voice and an unnerving way of constantly grabbing his crotch and rearranging himself in his pants. He stood to one side with a beer in a paper sack and yelled rude comments to some of the girls. I heard him say, "Hey, bitch," to Virginia, a Chicana student who lived alone in a studio apartment.

"Who is *that* guy?" I asked Ruth.

"That's Mrs. Burley's grandson Wilber—he lives in Richmond, but he comes over here sometimes," she said. "Don't you remember? He was out in front of Mrs. Burley's house the night those guys got shot?"

"No," I said, scanning Wilber's face for a minute so I could try to remember him.

"His dad was killed when he was young," Ruth went on. "He's been in jail."

Camille's tall husband Elliott, his goatee lending credence to his vampire outfit, helped set up a volleyball net. Most of the games were casual, with no rules, little kids and overweight mothers batting the ball back and forth, old guys playing with one hand, the other cupping a cigarette. But one serious, all-male game developed, with Saul and Jonathan, Stan and Potter, Jim and Elliott, two cops and several drug dealers and the firemen, all rotating to serve. They laughed a lot, loudly, and at the end, sweaty and out of breath, they all shook hands.

"This is like a Christmas truce in a war," I whispered to Libby, "when the soldiers come out of the trenches and sing songs."

When it was time to "dedicate" our new barricade, Ruth rounded up the kids and Libby made a little speech:

"This shows we can make our street a better place. People in other neighborhoods have flowers in their barricades, and so will we."

Libby had brought some geranium shoots from her garden, and we handed out soupspoons so that every child could help with the planting. Ruth spooned dirt with one hand, holding her toddler Amina on her hip with the other. Ruth's son Dondi solemnly took part. A newspaper reporter was there, and Dondi gave her a fervent statement. "We're planting the flowers to make our street nice, because we don't like drugs." The reporter scribbled it all down in her notebook while the smaller kids, including Dondi's shy little brother Jamal, their noses just reaching notebook height, watched her pen closely.

The local paper printed a photo that showed the kids smiling next to the geraniums and the sign they had made: "Bless Our Street."

After the party, business was back to normal. I sat with Ti on her front porch, watching the dealers, and she said, "I'm sorry now I cut my tree. I wish I hadn't done it. It's better not to see what they're doing. Some of my foster children gave me that tree twenty years ago."

The next day, I stopped at a nursery and bought the only Norfolk pine they had, one about two feet tall. Ti and I hefted it out of the car together and put it, in its pot, on the stump that was all that was left of the old tree in her front yard.

Ti liked the little tree, but she stopped sitting on her front porch.

CHAPTER FIVE

Way-Seeking Mind

One sunny afternoon, while rock climbing happily with my son Jonathan, I jumped down and the gravel under my feet slid and sent me sprawling. I got up with scraped hands and a bloody elbow, and it took me a while to realize that my left foot would no longer obey me; it flopped helplessly. I learned that my Achilles, the thick, tough tendon that connects the heel to the calf, had ruptured completely.

It's hard to treat a severed Achilles. It can be stitched together, or it can grow back on its own inside a cast, but either way, it takes months. I decided to try a cast, because the sports medicine doctor said surgery might make my tendon forever short and stiff. I liked running, rock climbing, and dancing too much for that.

I found myself with a big foreign white object on my leg, my foot pointed straight down like a ballerina's. I was unable to put even the slightest weight on my left leg.

The first weeks on crutches were filled with frustration. I railed against my situation and grieved for my foiled plans. I remember throwing my running shoes and climbing shoes violently into the back of my closet and weeping with rage.

Lil, my Buddhist friend, gave me a handmade sympathy card, "This just IS," it said. Lil is a writer who does layout on the night shift at a newspaper for money. I first met her in a writing class for women. She'd practiced at the Zen center for twenty years, all through single motherhood, raising her two sons, now grown, alone. She sat down on the edge of the couch where I was lying, pushed her wild, gray-streaked brown hair back from her face, and said, "Melody, I'm so sorry."

"Lil, I feel like Job, not Achilles," I said, feeling sorry for myself. I didn't really like her card much, but I taped it to the wall next to my bed.

I was worried that I couldn't work, because I had taken a new case not long before. My assignment was to prepare for the trial of a twenty-three-year-old black man in maximum trouble. He was Jarvis Masters, an armed robber who had come to San Quentin at age nineteen, gotten involved with a prison gang, and was going to be tried for taking part in the conspiracy to murder a guard who had been stabbed to death.

Jarvis stood a very good chance of getting the death penalty, since most jurors were going to wonder what else to do with an inmate who was involved in the death of a prison guard. It was my job to talk to him and find out who might testify on his behalf. I had seen him only a few times before my accident.

Jarvis had come out to our first visit wearing dark glasses, a sullen expression behind them, and a blue knitted cap pulled down to the top of the glasses frames. Just below his left eye was a crude amateur tattoo: "255" in fading blue numerals about a half inch high, done in ballpoint pen ink.

"What does 'two-five-five' mean?" I asked.

In a tone of voice that said it was none of my business, he informed me, "Two-five-five's a street where I used to hang in Harbor City. A dead-end street," he added.

I told Jarvis I would need to go out and interview his family to prepare for his trial. He refused to tell me anything about them. I knew that with someone as young as Jarvis, born the same year as Jonathan, my oldest, there would be a period of testing, so I decided to concentrate first on gaining his trust.

On one of our early visits, Jarvis looked skeptically at my feet in navy blue pumps.

"You can't go out and find my family," he said, teasing me. "Your shoes aren't strong enough for walking."

"I can run a mile in these," I said, and he laughed.

Now I had disappeared from Jarvis's life; all I could do was send word with his lawyer that I was disabled for a while.

Jarvis's lawyer complained, "Melody, please, *rock climbing*? Can't you just vacation like other people, maybe check into a nice hotel somewhere and relax?"

Every three weeks, the doctor removed my cast to see if the ends of my tendon were knitting. After nine weeks, no progress.

"I'll give you one more chance," he said. "If it doesn't grow in the next three weeks, you'll have to have surgery." Surgery would be like starting over, because afterward, there would be more months of casts.

I didn't tell him how terrified I was of surgery, how my mother had died at forty-seven, of complications from a routine operation.

The doctor said I needed to slow down and concentrate on growing my tendon. "Pretend you're a lizard growing a tail," he said. "Visualize that tendon in there, making new tissue." He suggested meditation.

The very next day, my eye caught the word "Healing" on a bright turquoise flyer in our mailbox, addressed to a student who had lived with us five years before. It was from a Tibetan Buddhist center in the Berkeley hills, and classes started the next day. I phoned. Yes, a nice-sounding man assured me, someone could help me negotiate the stairs.

I'd first seen Buddhists in 1966: three yellow-robed Asian monks who sat meditating cross-legged on the ground up against the fence of the Oakland army base. I was with the picketing, chanting demonstrators trying to block the gate because soldiers were being flown from there to Vietnam. Curious about the monks, I walked close to the fence and tried to peer into their faces. I wondered how they could sit so still, and I wondered what good they thought they were doing there.

The only real Buddhist in my life was my peace activist friend Lil, who had years of rigorous meditation under her belt. When Lil talked about becoming calmer and paying attention, it sounded good, but I said, "I'm too busy to meditate. I couldn't sit still for five minutes if I was tied down."

I had never learned anything about any religion. My "real" father's family were Catholics, but I didn't know them very well, and my mother never looked back after she got away from the small-town Texas church she called The Dragons of Christ. She said she didn't believe in God, but on her bad days, she said she hated him.

"Well, I don't think of Buddhism as a religion," Lil said. "It's a *practice*—meditation keeps my heart open." So when I called to say, "Guess what? I'm going to try meditating for my leg," she encouraged me.

"I hope your leg likes it," she said.

The Tibetan Buddhist center was not a monastery—it was like a college, except happier and more colorful. The building was painted yellow and orange and blue and green and purple, and in the garden there were red and gold prayer wheels turning, flags flying, and huge orange and white fish hiding under blooming water lilies in a pond. Eric Meller, the teacher, was a regular Berkeley white guy about my age, with a beard and a wardrobe stuck back in the sixties.

The early morning two-hour class was rigorous: an hour of silent sitting followed by discussion, then a lecture based on readings, and more sitting. I could not believe how hard it was to sit still, trying to focus on my breathing. My mind planned, argued, dreamed, and fretted.

"I've been here for an hour," I told Eric, "but I only *meditated* for two seconds."

"Two seconds are good," he said. "You can expand them into your whole life."

It was obvious that I was trying way too hard. I was angry at my leg, and frightened by it, and my attitude was to will it to heal. I had been focusing on the one tiny broken spot on the back of one ankle. When I sat down and paid attention, I realized my legs both felt dead, as if they had been amputated. Very little blood was flowing down through the dark interior of my cast to reach my toes, which looked swollen and unhealthy.

Just sitting still in a quiet room, I was as frightened as I had ever been, staring in the face the fact that I didn't really control my own body, or anything else about my life, or my death.

"I thought this was about becoming *calmer*," I complained to Eric. "I feel panicky. I'm not sure I can keep on doing this."

Eric assured me that the way out of any kind of pain was through it. "Try to stay with the feeling, and I promise you, it will shift. It will change into something else."

Way-Seeking Mind

That was true. I couldn't stay panicky any more than I could keep my mind on my breath.

Eric told the class that meditation would loosen our grasp on what we thought we wanted. I saw that before the accident, I had wanted things. After the accident, I couldn't have them. Immediately, I wanted some other things, among them, a healthy leg.

Eric asked me to practice thinking of the surgery as something that would be okay. "Any path can be a good path," he said.

My terror of being physically weak had to do with scary childhood memories of having polio. I was spending time each hour of meditation back in 1949, unable to walk, lying sweating in a metal crib in the sweltering olive drab barracks that Fort Bliss, Texas, used for a hospital, crowded that summer with sick soldiers and children. My mom had baby Skye to take care of, and much of that time in the hospital, I was alone.

Eric said that the feelings my mind had attached to my memories were "stories," with nothing permanent about them. "Just bring yourself back to your breath," he said. "You'll realize that nothing bad is happening right now."

I had spent a long time as a five-year-old holding on to parallel bars, summoning the determination to obey adults who coaxed me to try to take a step. All that postpolio physical therapy had cultivated a strong will. Once I learned to walk again, it was hard for me ever to sit around.

Paradoxically, it was that same determination that helped me to go on sitting, even though what was in my mind was so hard to face. I found there could be a little gap, a tiny space no bigger than a wisp of breath, where I could have a choice about how I felt. Some part of my fear relaxed, and my legs felt warmer.

Driving me to the hospital to get my cast off, Stan asked me whether I thought my tendon had attached or not. I said I didn't know, but I knew I was ready to have surgery the next day if necessary. "Every path can be a good path," I said, quoting Eric, and I almost believed that could be true.

While I held my breath, the saw whirred through the fiberglass and gauze on my leg. My doctor's face broke into a big grin. "Oh, there it is," he announced. "All attached! It looks great!"

My doctor prescribed a new series of casts, changed each week as the tendon lengthened and my foot returned to its place flat on the ground, and he gave me a letter to take to the prison, stating that my cast was real and not a way to smuggle in a weapon.

"You have to give me the prize for dedication," I told Jarvis as I swung myself and my new walking cast carefully into the visiting cell. I could tell that he was glad to see me. We resumed our struggle over my need to contact his family to get ready for his trial.

"You're just a stranger, why should I want you to go see my family?" he asked. "You'll write your reports, and I'll never see you again. I've been on that trip before."

He was asking me to promise to be his friend.

I felt that I was effective in my work with criminal defendants because of my leave-no-stone-unturned doggedness on their behalf. But Jarvis was right, my posture was "professional"—I maintained the distance of a social worker or attorney.

Until I met Jarvis, I thought I had it all down pat: during visits I bought soft drinks for my clients, I sent occasional Christmas cards, or phoned their wives or mothers for them. We were friendly, but not friends, and that seemed to work well. Nothing more was required. But as Jarvis's trial grew closer, a friend was exactly what he needed. He didn't want a girlfriend or a mother in me, but he insisted on a real bond.

"You're just another social worker," he said to me. "You're *professional*, but you don't care. You don't *really* care."

When I met Jarvis, not one person had visited him in the four years he'd been at San Quentin. He wasn't sure of his mother's address, or whether his father was living. The file on Jarvis I got from Los Angeles County showed nine foster placements, starting at age five when police found Jarvis and his sisters and brother alone without food. His mother's maternal rights were eventually terminated after she missed court dates and visits with her children. For four years, Jarvis was placed with an elderly couple he loved, but when the social service agency decided those parents had become too old to care for him, he was taken away from them, at the age of nine. After that, Jarvis ran away from several foster homes. He kept finding his way back to the elderly couple's house.

So then he was sent to the county's large locked facility for dependent children, and later some more group homes. Once he stayed with an aunt for a while, but he got in trouble at age twelve. Then he was in and out of juvenile halls and camps and boys' homes. The files were full of papers about Jarvis, all signed by people who dealt with him and then passed him on to someone else.

The State of California had raised Jarvis, and like bad parents, we had abandoned him, not once, but a score of times, leaving him friendless.

At the age of seventeen, when he was a very angry young man, Jarvis was released from juvenile hall, and he went on a crime spree, holding up convenience stores and fast-food restaurants until he was captured. He never shot anyone, but he was definitely scary.

When Jarvis arrived in San Quentin in 1981, right away he got involved in what the prison system calls a gang. Blacks in those days passed on black history and militancy from older men to younger inmates. The group gave Jarvis a sense of family, but it was a hierarchical and violent family.

In 1985, a prison guard named Sergeant Burchfield was murdered by an inmate who stabbed him in the heart by thrusting a prison-made spear through the bars of a cell on the second tier of a cell block. At the time, Jarvis was locked in his cell on the fourth tier.

Although many inmates were suspected of conspiring to murder Sergeant Burchfield, only three were tried, Jarvis among them. One was accused of being the "spear man"—of actually stabbing the sergeant. Another, an older man, was accused of ordering the killing. Jarvis was indicted for sharpening a piece of metal which was allegedly passed along and later used to make the spear with which the sergeant was stabbed.

"But how could he be eligible for the death penalty?" Lil wanted to know. "I thought you had to actually kill someone." I explained that conspiracy to murder carries the same penalty as murder, and killing law enforcement personnel is a capital offense.

I had a question for Lil: "If Buddhists accept suffering, does that mean they just accept injustice?"

"No," she said. "Buddhists' job is to respond generously to others, and that means opposing injustice. But we try to do that without a lot of self-delusion. Buddhists try to be compassionate the way trees give off oxygen."

What would it mean to my life to be a friend to Jarvis? My main feeling was fear. There was a lot of cynicism among legal workers about "manipulative" inmates. Jarvis wasn't being manipulative — he was perfectly clear about his needs, and asking me up front to help him. But I felt embarrassed to make friends with an inmate. What about my "professional" image? More to the point, I was afraid of promising something I couldn't fulfill. And what if Jarvis were sentenced to die?

"This isn't a *game*," Jarvis kept saying. "I'm a *person*."

Jarvis's words followed me to my meditation classes with Eric. I wanted to meditate, but it continued to be hard. I felt as though I had been busy all my life running around on top of an inner volcano, and as soon as I sat down, it blew up. Years of unfinished grieving erupted: Skye, lying dead on the floor of her Alaska cabin; my lost dad, killed in the war when I was a baby. I sat as if I were in hot lava, burning with anger about my mother's violence and my stepfather's complete failure to protect me from it.

The pictures on the wall of the meditation room depicted mythical Buddhist worlds like the Heavenly Realm, and here I was in Marlboro Country with my parents. When I meditated, I felt as if smoke were coming out of my ears.

It was all right with Eric if people cried quietly while meditating, and I did that every hour for many months, tears rolling down my face and dropping into my lap, while I snuffled as quietly as I could.

On our dog walks in the hills, Elyse was one person I could joke with about all this.

"This stuff's okay, Elyse, but I hate being so *trendy*. Everybody's getting in touch with their inner child. I feel as though I just stumbled into my inner day care center!"

I told Stan I was grateful for his understanding. "I don't think I'd get many responses if I ran a personals ad saying I wanted to meet someone to support me through a major midlife crisis," I told him.

Memory seemed to be stored in my muscles and bones, not just in my mind. Eric taught his students to balance their breathing, the in-breath matching the out-breath in duration and amount of air. Whenever I tried, my throat would seize up. I would have a tremendous need to swallow, but I couldn't—I felt as if I were choking. I'd have to gasp and then swallow with an embarrassing noisy gulp.

I asked Eric about it. The neck, he said, connects the head and heart, the mind and body. "Maybe a lot of tension gathered in your neck long ago in your life. Maybe someone didn't know how to support your head carefully when you were an infant."

You don't know the half of it, I thought, and in my mind I watched my mother who for years grabbed my shoulders unprovoked and shook me, whipping my head back and forth, snapping my neck until I was so scared she was about to kill me that I went deaf to the sound of her yelling voice, and just stared, paralyzed, into her big spitting face.

Eric said that I could imagine myself in a safe place from which to watch that scene, and then I could give myself the help I needed in that situation. I kept at that meditation, breathing space and light into memory until, as Eric promised me would happen, the images began to lose their power.

Then Eric suggested that I send my mother the help she must have needed. I gulped and I tried. Slowly, my throat opened.

Eric said meditation would open up some space around our hearts by loosening the concepts we were grasping. I asked him the same question I'd asked Lil: what about the danger of accepting injustice? I didn't want to lose my ability to act with urgency against things that were wrong.

Eric said the difference between being an awakened human being and not was the difference between reacting and responding. "When we react, it's already too late, we are out of control. When we respond, we are choosing." He added, "Another word for enlightenment is relaxation . . . relaxing the hairsbreadth boundaries between self and others, love and hate, heaven and hell."

Who was I to hold my "professional" self away from Jarvis? Why cling to the barriers that divided me from him? We were different in age, gender, color, and incarceration status, but Jarvis was right—he was a real person and so was I. There was no other time to be real than now, sitting on my cushion, or on the hard plastic chair in the San Quentin visiting room opposite Jarvis.

Into the new space around my heart flowed friendship. I told Jarvis I would do my best to stick with him, whatever the verdict in his trial, whatever the outcome of his appeals, as his friend.

What he had in mind was a two-way relationship. He wanted to *be* a friend, not just get one. I told him about Skye, and he was sorry. When Jarvis was four, his mom Shorty had given birth to twins, a boy and a girl. Shorty had "given" the girl to Jarvis's five-year-old sister to take care of, and the boy, she had told four-year-old Jarvis, was "his." All Shorty's kids were often left alone, sometimes for days. One day while their mother was away, the boy twin, the one Jarvis loved so much, died in the twins' crib. I couldn't determine if the baby had died of sudden infant death or of neglect, but Jarvis knew what it was like to be the "big" one, and have the "little one" die.

Slowly my leg got stronger. A year after I fell, I was walking up the hill to Eric's class. And I was driving around the state working on Jarvis's trial.

When I found people who had known Jarvis in foster care and institutions, most of them did remember him. I wasn't the only one who thought Jarvis was special. He had left an impression on foster mothers and juvenile probation officers. They remembered a good-looking, smart, and articulate youngster with a sense of humor. They also remembered he was wild with rage.

I finally met Jarvis's mother Shorty. We sat talking for hours together side by side on a couch while her grandchildren played around our feet. "I'm not going to lie to you," Shorty said. Her life had been about heroin all the time her children were growing up. Jarvis's father had been addicted too. He had been violent to the kids, and she had thrown him out. He was still alive, but hard to get in touch with. The love of Shorty's life, also an addict, had died in prison.

"I can't stand a prison," Shorty said. "I never want to see my babies in a prison." She didn't think she would be able to come to see Jarvis. She said she would try to come to the trial, but her health wasn't good.

She looked a lot like Jarvis, a handsome, dark-skinned woman. She cried, talking about her children. Sipping wine from an aluminum water glass that afternoon, she reminded me of photos of Billie Holiday toward the end of her life, worn out and sad, but beautiful. Shorty's failures had left Jarvis feeling like a motherless child.

Like Jarvis, Shorty had the gift of language. In her throaty drinker's voice she told me, "I know I didn't do right by my children. I don't know why, but God has kept me alive to have a chance to be a better grandmother than I was a mother."

I took a picture of Shorty with Jarvis's nieces and nephews he had never seen, and I told him everything she had said. Cautiously hopeful, he sent her a card but got no answer.

"I'm sorry, Jarvis," I told him. "You know Shorty's not the writing type. But I know she's glad you wrote to her."

Things were going well with Jarvis, but in my meditation practice I was full of doubts. Had I been trying to help people all my life just to prove that I was a good person? Had it all been nothing but compensation for a hard childhood? Was there a way to do my job as a Buddhist? I consulted my teacher.

"Maybe I should quit my job," I told Eric Meller. "I think I've been trying to forgive people who have done terrible things because I've never forgiven myself."

"Maybe there are shadows in your motivations," he said, "but if you notice them, you'll be able to do your job better than ever, if it's what you still want to do."

It made sense to Eric that I worked in a life-or-death job. "If you had become a doctor, you might have chosen the emergency room. It's good to have a broken heart—it makes it easy to recognize another one."

As his trial approached, Jarvis became more and more terrified. He had a recurrent dream about the trial. In these dreams the jury foreman stood up and pronounced the sentence and Jarvis was always guilty. The foreman was always Jarvis himself.

The trial kept being postponed. Jarvis would prepare himself, and then it wouldn't happen. "I'm going nuts," he said. "I can hardly go back in my cell, Melody. What can I do?"

"Jarvis, all I know to tell you is what is helping me," I said. When I offered to teach him to meditate, he said he wanted to try. So I passed on Eric's instructions from the Tibetan Buddhist Institute—straight back, even breath—and Jarvis tried it in his cell, sitting on the floor on his folded blanket. He said he liked it, but I had some doubts.

"Are you sure you don't want me to find some other kind of teaching for you? Maybe there's an African-based tradition you would like better."

"Well *you're* not from Tibet," he said. "I want to do whatever works, and this is helping me."

And so we meditated together, keeping each other going. We set up times to "meet" on our cushions, him in his cell and me in my room at home. He "joined" Eric's class, and Eric gave me some books and a picture of Tara, the symbol of compassion, to give to Jarvis.

Jarvis's greatest problem was finding quiet in the clanging, howling cell block. He was also reluctant to be seen meditating, worried his neighbors might interpret it as a sign of weakness, which could cause him problems. But despite all these difficulties, Jarvis pursued Buddhism on his own with impressive dedication. He sent for books by a Tibetan lama and started corresponding with him.

Even in the security housing unit, simply paying attention had benefits for Jarvis. The window opposite his cell was broken. "Melody, the beautiful smell of the fresh air coming in is like a gift," he said.

As his defensive shell broke away, Jarvis's handsome face emerged. He stopped wearing his stocking cap and dark glasses, and expressive light began to shine in his eyes. "Jarvis, you look more like a college student now than a gang member," I teased him. As I gave up my "professional" cover, he was giving up his "gang" cover.

Together we read the foot-tall stack of police reports from his brief one-man crime wave as an armed robber before he came to prison. All this would be used against him at his trial. I had to find and actually interview the people he had robbed, since they might testify against him, and we needed to prepare for what they would say.

"I sure am glad *I* wasn't in this taco shack when *you* came through!" I told him. Jarvis's eyes widened as he pictured me and my children in line for tacos, cringing on the floor and crying while he waved a gun and took the money from the till. It was a learning moment. He put his head down on the table. "I did all this. I hurt so many people."

Not long before the trial started, the prison chaplain appeared at the bars of Jarvis's cell to tell him that Shorty had died suddenly of heart failure. She had never filled in the forms I'd given her to arrange a visit to Jarvis.

Jarvis was so despondent he could barely talk above a whisper. I insisted that he send a message to Shorty's funeral. "You've got to be there somehow," I begged him. "I know you'll regret it if you aren't."

Word by painful word, he dictated a message of love for his mother that I would send by telegram to his sister. As I left San Quentin, the noisy motorized gate slid back to let me walk out into the breeze blowing off San Francisco Bay. I passed by a stone marker in the grass near the main gate carved with the names of ten officers killed on the job in California prisons since 1952. Sergeant Burchfield's name was etched there into the granite. As always, I nodded my head in a brief bow to the officers' memorial stone.

There are no models for a friendship like mine and Jarvis's. Like so many people, we both came wounded to a spiritual life, carrying so many losses that in different ways our cushions—his a folded blanket, mine a traditional round black pillow—felt like the last stop. Jarvis and I just sat down, helpless, together.

"Sometime, somehow, a person has to give up," Jarvis said, "and sit down to meet their self."

At home, I planted a magnolia tree for Jarvis in a corner of my garden. Putting it into the ground, I felt afraid. If for some reason it failed to live, Jarvis would feel worse than if I hadn't planted it at all. I meant the magnolia as a symbol of hope, but if Jarvis were executed, it could turn into a memorial instead. Alma Street was having so much trouble, planting another young tree there was flying in the face of despair.

Eric had said, "Live without hope or fear." I mailed Jarvis a photo of Stan and Alaska and me, standing next to his magnolia tree.

All kinds of people still asked me about my neighborhood, repeating the same old "Why do you live there?" refrain. I decided to relate to that question on the ultimate level.

"Why *do* I live here?" I asked myself. "Why am I living?" I decided to roll up my sleeves and see what I could do.

CHAPTER SIX

Hunger

Our block committee had outgrown the pizza place, and I thought maybe more people would come if we met right in the neighborhood. I noticed that the South Berkeley Community Church a few blocks away on Fairview Street had started offering a free lunch to hungry people twice a week, and the city's HIV-testing truck parked there on those days. A sign in front of the church announced a new minister's name: REVEREND CLARA MILLS, PASTOR. If we could meet there, I hoped, the drug dealers might think we were a church group, and people could feel safe.

I went inside on one of the free-lunch days. A dozen long tables were crowded with people eating spaghetti and salad on paper plates. They were mostly men, some of whom looked homeless, but quite a few women were also eating, most of them mothers with young children. The door to the minister's study was open, and when I knocked, she stood up behind her desk and offered a slim, manicured hand and a firm handshake.

Reverend Clara Mills was not what I expected in an African-American minister—or any minister. She looked more like a fashion model or a news anchor. She wore expert makeup, and her hair was turned up in a soft, shoulder-length curl. She wore a clerical collar with an impeccably tailored suit, shoes with heels, and a gold cross on a chain around her neck.

On her desk were photos of her children: a little girl about eight, and a handsome young man in an soldier's uniform.

When I explained our committee and asked her if we could meet at the church hall, she welcomed us. "Please call me Reverend Clara," she said. "Now, look here, look out this window. This is affecting our attendance at church, because they are out there even on Sunday mornings."

From her desk, Reverend Clara had a perfect view of the corner, occupied as we spoke by several young men loitering, waiting to offer drugs to the people eating lunch when they left the church. We sat together for a while and saw several transactions, the furtive hand movements, the buyer rapidly walking away.

"How do you feel about people eating a free lunch and then buying crack?" I asked her.

"I don't like it," she said, "but I know most of them would still buy the crack, but they wouldn't eat. It would be easier for me to minister to a congregation where I never saw people who were sick and poor and despised. But these are the people Jesus talked about.

"We must find something better for these young men to do," Reverend Clara said, looking out the window. "I know it's hard to resist or recover if drugs are on every corner. But we are suffering mainly from poverty of the spirit. The only real answer lies with God."

Reverend Clara said she was writing her thesis for her doctorate in theology. I told her I was a student of Buddhism. "Reverend Clara, I believe people need to feel connected to a community. I'm learning Buddhism, but I think it can be any faith that supports us with love."

She gave me a key to the church that barely worked. I had to arrive early to struggle with the lock and set up the folding chairs. The building was a fading Spanish stucco beauty. Inside, a large redwood-paneled space was divided by big doors that could be rolled up. Half was the sanctuary with stained glass windows, while the other half was a social hall where the lunch program took place and where our block committee met. The dimly lit hall was too cold in winter and too hot in summer. An old refrigerator hummed, and in order to hear each other during meetings, we had to unplug it.

Reluctantly, I chaired the meetings. It didn't seem right for me, a white person, to chair, but the only other person who ever wanted the job was Louis the bus driver, and he went off on too many tangents, giving passionate speeches against Reaganomics instead of keeping the discussion on our immediate problems.

Emotions often ran high at our meetings. So much was at stake: safety and home and in many cases our money, in the form of property values. We were growing. Reverend Clara usually attended meetings with one or two church members who lived in the area. Dave and Jeff, an attorney and an artist who were renovating a Victorian house, had joined the group, and an older black woman who owned a beauty parlor nearby. Sid and Pauline, a white disabled couple who shared a tiny apartment, came. Sid was a big man with a booming voice who was legally blind and walked with a cane. Pauline was a diabetic who used a wheelchair. When Reverend Clara saw Sid and Pauline, she said, "If they have hope of making things better, who are we to ever be discouraged?"

Looking around the room at our meetings, I realized that we had years of combined experience with every tradition of American political action: union organizing, legal recourse, religious activism, political pressure and protest. When I looked around at the faces of our neighbors, all of them willing to help each other, to me they looked like the salt of the earth and food for my soul.

We started to talk about suing one of the slumlords. In the opinion of Potter Woods, there was no point. "Even if we move crack out of the Green Gables, they'll just go somewhere else."

"You're right," Libby said. "But I think we should see if we can make the dealers move out of one building. For the sake of the children and old people, we should try."

Mr. Joe agreed. "Why should we let the dealers get comfortable? We should keep them moving."

"Let's set one goal and see if we can accomplish it," I added.

We decided to sue. There was crack in quite a few buildings, but we chose the Green Gables because we had the cooperation of several of the tenants who lived there. Dave the attorney volunteered to handle the suit. Small-claims court was the way to go, he found out, asking for damages because the landlord was maintaining a nuisance. Dave kept sending us papers to sign.

We had gotten absolutely nowhere with Mr. Wallace, the landlord of the Jackson brothers' drug-dealing driveway—the one who had passed our letter along to his drug-involved tenants. Conditions were so bad there that the Jackson brothers' mother had even moved out. Wallace, outrageously, had rented her apartment to a girlfriend of the dealers.

I tracked down Wallace's home phone number and called him. To my surprise, he agreed to come to a committee meeting. He turned out to look like an aging hippie—he had wild gray hair and rumpled khaki pants, and he defiantly refused to do anything about his property.

"It's a police problem," Wallace asserted. "I can't keep these people away. They're guests of my tenants. What they do is none of my business. If they are breaking laws, call the police."

That was one of the angriest meetings we had. Everybody wanted to argue with Wallace. He became extremely belligerent and irrational, and I thought he was going to slug Libby's husband Jim. "You people have no right to tell me what I can do with my private property!" he shouted.

"Your irresponsibility is ruining our lives!" Jim shouted back in his loudest schoolteacher's voice—the one he probably used out on the playground.

As chairwoman, I repeatedly asked the landlord to leave and Jim to sit down, and finally both did as I asked.

The police had made little progress with the Jackson brothers, who had recruited several young men my kids had gone to high school with. Nathan, the young guy who had helped Jonathan with the bullets, seemed to be working for them, and so did Nathan's younger cousin, CJ, who as a boy had enjoyed coming over to hang around our driveway talking to Stan and watching him fix cars.

It was terrible to see kids we knew slouching in that driveway. When I drove past, I averted my eyes. If I saw CJ in the Arab store, he still smiled at me and said, "Hi, Moms," the generic greeting for mothers on our street, because he had known me as Amina's mother for half his life.

Visiting Jarvis at San Quentin, I tried to describe what life was like outside. "You just wouldn't believe crack, Jarvis," I told him. "If you got out right now, you wouldn't know the world."

He said he couldn't believe the shape some newly arrived prisoners were in. "They are pitiful, Melody, thin like skeletons. And they talk about all the things they can make a woman do for crack! Yheeew." He shuddered. "I can't tell you what they say, Melody, it's too disgusting."

"Like what?" I pressed him, always having to know everything. "Come on, tell me."

"I'm warning you, it's cruel. This guy said a woman came in a crack house and he was in there with six guys selling it for ten bucks and she only had nine, so the main man said if she gave every one of them a blow job, right around the room, he would give it to her for nine dollars."

There was a pause while my mind had to see that picture, and I imagined stuff like that going on in apartments on Alma Street.

"And she did it?"

"Yep. The guy said she was crying the whole time."

"Oh, God, now I wish I hadn't heard that." I cringed. "You want to hear what my neighbor Camille told me?"

"Probably not, but go ahead," Jarvis said.

"She said she knew of a woman who had nothing left in her apartment but the mattress her baby slept on. The woman traded the mattress for a piece of crack, and put the baby on the floor."

"Oh, no, I don't want to know about that!" Jarvis cried. "Now I'm sorry you told me."

Anything about child abuse drove Jarvis wild. Whenever pictures of hungry children or children in war came over the television in his cell, he turned it off immediately.

Jarvis's theory about why prisoners hated child abusers so much was that almost all of them had been abused themselves as children. "In the showers, you see the scars on most of the men, and if you ask them, they say they got that way from getting hit, burned, cut when they were little. And they don't even think that's abuse!"

"That's slavery, coming right down to today," my investigator partner Pam said. "The whipping, the killing, nothing healed, everything just going on and on."

Jarvis said he spent a lot of time thinking about this, and when he meditated, he sent loving kindness to suffering children.

He loved to hear stories about my neighbor kids. There were lots of children on Alma Street who had been a part of the continual pack of three- to six-year-olds who loved my garden and my dog. They had a secret place under the canopy of a purple-blooming cinanothus shrub that dominated one corner of my yard. I would bend down and hand a paper plate of crackers and plastic cups of juice to them under there for their tea parties. My dog Alaska would scoot in on her belly to join them.

"Call Alaska, Melody!" they would cry. "Call Alaska! She's trying to eat our crackers!"

The children liked to troop down the path that ran along the fence Ti and I shared, stooping down to go under the apple branches, brushing past the scratchy raspberry canes. They froze, hardly breathing, when they saw a hummingbird hovering in the fuchsias. Their favorite thing to do was "work." When I had time to play with them, they always wanted to help. I paid them a penny apiece for pulling dandelions, and I let them plant seeds. Water was magic elixir to them. I would take off their shoes and roll up their pants legs and give them the hose with the water barely running and let them take turns aiming the stream wherever they wanted except the sidewalk. Their favorite "work" was bathing Alaska. She would sit in my big old washtub trying to look dignified while they rubbed suds into her fur and then solemnly poured cups of water over her like priests baptizing a baby. "Shake, Alaska, shake!" they would cry when she was released, and she would oblige, spraying us all with doggy drops of water.

The children came into the garden when they were ready to leave their mothers' sides and make their bonds with the wild world. I could remember being that age, spending afternoons under a certain bush up against a Texas army barracks, where I stirred water into dirt with a stick and tried out eating ants.

"What if," I thought, "instead of a welcoming world, they met nothing but danger? How could they venture into it?"

They craved the apples, apricots, and plums, but I couldn't get them to try the purple figs, orange-red and seedy inside. I struggled with the children to teach them when the fruit was ripe. I found bitter knobs as hard as crab apples all over the grass, each green plum or apricot with a set of little teeth marks in it. I tried leaving notes on the garden gate in big kindergarten printing. "Dear kids, The apples are not ready yet. Please do not pick them until school starts again." And, "Dear kids, Please ring the doorbell and ask me before you come into the garden. Love, Melody."

Stan scoffed: "That will never work!" But it did. We could hear them out there by the gate deciphering the writing and discussing it. Once we heard a bossy little girl say, "No! Melody said *not to!*"

The children learned to accept the times I said, "Not today," or, "Not right now," and when I wasn't home, they did not go into the garden.

"See, Jarvis," I told him. "It's hard to explain our neighborhood. It's like that nursery rhyme: when it is good it is very very good, and when it is bad it is horrid."

"That's not a very Buddhist rhyme," he said. "I guess the neighborhood is whatever it is, moment to moment, just like this prison. It's hard to explain too."

I drove up to that prison one day and to my surprise, I recognized Jarvis's sister in the parking lot. She had picked a freezing winter night to borrow a car that had no heater and drive it through a storm all the way from LA, with her three kids wrapped in blankets in the backseat. She hugged me and said she'd had a fight with her boyfriend and had decided on the spur of the moment that she had to see her brother. Lucky for me, I happened to be in San Quentin to see another client, so I was standing in the crowded phone-visiting hall when Jarvis's ten-year-old nephew Dante took the phone receiver and held it upside down like it was a microphone and he was a singer. Dante looked into

Jarvis's eyes on the other side of the glass and belted out his a cappella rendition of "You took a fine time to leave me, Lucille," and brought down the house.

I sat in my darkened living room late at night watching the drug-addicted wraiths slipping by outside, and I remembered my teacher Eric Meller talking about the Hungry Ghosts: "They live in a realm of perpetual craving," he'd said, showing the class a painting of the Tibetan Wheel of Life with the six realms of existence that we all experience. The Hungry Ghosts have protruding bellies and gaping mouths, but their throats are too narrow to allow more than tiny bites to pass, and so they can never be satisfied.

I watched the Hungry Ghosts wander on the other side of the window glass and worried about my sister Naomi. I wanted Naomi to be different than she was, but that could only be up to her. I knew she had to find something larger than herself to hold her safe before she could fill the void inside with something besides drugs and drinking.

Buddhism was that safe place for me. I took refuge in the teachings, sometimes imagining myself climbing up and resting in Buddha's ample lap.

When I sat meditating, I often felt my own self-loathing. I could hear a voice inside berating me for my failings, mad at myself just for saying something stupid or dissatisfied with myself for not meditating more. What must it be like, I wondered, for addicts to look at the empty bottle, the used syringe, the crumbs of the whole cake eaten?

I knew that just because I realized I was doing something I would rather not do, I couldn't always stop, or stay stopped. When I looked at my addiction to doing too much, to trying to "fix" everybody around me, I saw that I was filling my own hungry belly with spirited activity while Naomi filled hers with spirits. In my unawareness I gave away my life hour by hour, abandoning myself just as much as Naomi forsook herself by drinking.

The more dangerous the street outside became, the more Ti and I took refuge in our gardens. One morning we met at the rather flimsy wooden fence between our yards and found some boards snapped in two.

"They jumped over here and broke this," Ti said, disgusted.

Everyone always referred to the faceless people doing mischief as "they," whether it was the government or the drug dealers.

Ti and I made makeshift repairs to the fence with some wire, threading it back and forth between us, and then I went to the nursery, where I bought a Cecile Brunner rose, a fast-growing and very thorny climber. Ti and I planted it where "they" took a shortcut through our yards, and it acted like pink-blossoming barbed wire. "No one's ever going to run through here again," Ti declared.

CHAPTER SEVEN

Skin

Sleeping alone in our bed one night when Stan was away, I was awakened at 5:00 A.M. by a big wind. I put on my slippers and robe and went into the kitchen. It was late November, a month after the block party, and still dark at that hour of the morning. When I tried the kitchen light, I realized the power was off, and looking out, I saw the streetlights were out. The wind was gusting so violently down the driveway between our house and the apartment building next door, I was afraid the fir trees would blow down. I stood in the window watching them toss and bend alarmingly.

Suddenly, a dangerous, acrid smell sent me running down the hall. Amina had awakened too, and she met me at the front door.

"Do you smell smoke?" she asked. "There's a fire somewhere." We ran out in nightclothes, Amina barefoot. Blowing trash was scooting across the pavement and pushing up against the buildings in jumbled piles.

When we reached the middle of the street we could see flames filling the downstairs windows of a house half a block up the street on the other side. I knew the fire was in the ground-floor apartment where Ruth lived with her husband Michael and three children, Dondi, Jamal, and Amina. We heard sirens approaching. Just then a white man I didn't know stopped his pickup truck in the street and jumped out. We ran toward the fire, and the man ran with us. The flames and smoke were too fierce for me or Amina to go any closer. The Good Samaritan, though, found a board and fearlessly began to break the front apartment windows.

In a moment we saw a fire truck coming, but the Samaritan's pickup was blocking its way. The fire truck's driver blared his horn. Amina ran to the pickup, and she steered while a young black man pushed it aside. The fire engine drove up, and firemen rushed out.

We stood together while one of those fire scenes you see on television developed: firemen pulled hoses, and people watched, helpless, while other people screamed. More fire trucks and ambulances came. In seconds, water turned the flames to dirty smoke. The Samaritan sat on the curb, his face black with soot, coughing, while a fireman pressed a plastic oxygen mask to his face. Closer to the house, everything was confusion, people running, shouting.

I kept my distance, standing alone in my slippers, my arms wrapping my robe closer around me, staying far out of the way across the street behind a fire truck, trying to get away from the smoke, which was gusting everywhere.

I thought of going back home, since there was nothing I could do. Then I became a witness to something I never wanted to see. A young fireman came walking quickly toward me, a small bundle in his arms cradled close to his chest. He shifted it to one arm to open the driver's side door of the fire truck, and I saw that he held the completely charred, lifeless body of a small child. No part of the baby was left unburned. She was blackened. Her almost fleshless legs flopped as the fireman lifted her up onto the front seat.

The young fireman slammed the door fast, and I understood that no one was supposed to see. The fireman was hiding the baby's body from her parents and the crowd. For one second the fireman rested his head against the truck door, the brim of his hat leaning on the metal. Then he ran back across the street.

I spun around and bent over, close to fainting. This was the first dead body I'd ever seen. I hadn't wanted to see it. I wanted something to take that image away. I knew this was an extra thing to carry, always.

Skin

I was almost sure the dead child was Amina, Ruth's adorable toddler who shared the same pretty name with my own daughter.

Turning, I saw the young fireman walk to an ambulance that was pulling up and speak to the driver. He gestured with his head toward the truck and shook it, meaning, "Don't take her away now, while the people are still here."

People were saying that because the power had gone off, Ruth had lit a candle so she could see to tend to the baby. The flame had set some curtains on fire.

More ambulances came and took away the Samaritan, Ruth's husband Michael, and her little boy Jamal. I couldn't see Dondi, but I assumed he was all right somewhere, since no one said anything about him. The wind had died down, leaving behind the blackened, water-soaked apartment and trash strewn around the street. The morning had turned out cold and sunny, and most of Alma Street's people were still outside, talking in small groups.

Ruth was sitting on a wall in front of the apartment building next door to the fire-damaged house. Several black women were around her, holding and comforting her. I walked to her and stood for a moment outside the circle of women. Ruth was rocking her body back and forth, sobbing, tears streaming down her face, saying, "My baby, my baby."

I knew, in common with her, what it is to give birth to a child. Now Ruth had crossed over to another place. I knew she was living my own greatest fear and that of every mother.

Ruth looked at me and repeated, "My baby, my baby."

The woman sitting next to Ruth, with her back to me, turned then and scowled. She looked me up and down and saw not my shock, not my mother's grief, but my pale skin. "What does this have to do with *you*?" she demanded to know. "You leave her alone." And she raised her arm protectively across Ruth's body.

It was as if she had slapped me across the face. But I was numb already, and I didn't fully feel the blow. I looked past that woman, over her arm and into Ruth's eyes.

"Melody, my baby is dead," she said.

"I know darling, I'm sorry," I answered. I couldn't reach Ruth to touch her, so I walked back home.

At the hospital later that week, Michael and Jamal were in the same room, side by side in beds pushed close together. Michael's hands were bandaged. Michael showed me the letters taped to the wall written by the firemen who had tried, as Michael had, to save Amina. "Dear Michael, you are a brave man," one fireman wrote.

Jamal's burns were worse, and his face and arms and hands were coated with gray salve over livid pink. It was hard to look at Jamal, remembering his round pert face from before, his beautiful eyes, his smooth kindergartner's skin.

Jamal, his eyes still beautiful, offered a shy smile for the soft toy otter I brought. He and I played animal lotto, he pointing to the cards and I turning them over. We matched all the baby animals to their mothers.

Ruth lay in the hospital room curled on her side in a chair next to the window, crying as if she would never stop. She seemed in far more danger, somehow, than Jamal or Michael. She could hardly speak. She just looked at me. "Oh, Melody," she said, and laid her head back down.

How could I comfort her, I wondered. I thought about people I had met who worked at a Buddhist hospice, who said that the task was just to be with a suffering person as they were. All I could do was sit beside Ruth and press my hand on her back between her shoulder blades.

When they left the hospital, Ruth and her family moved in with relatives in Oakland. "Ruth said she can't stand to come back to Alma Street," Libby said.

For years my friend Hiram and I had been able to talk honestly across the black-white racial divide. Hiram hadn't gone outside the morning of the fire, but he had heard about it, of course, and he had seen the soot stains that flared black from the windows of the burned apartment.

Sitting in his dimly lit kitchen, I told him the story of the woman who had pushed me away from comforting Ruth. "I know racism isn't about white people's hurt feelings," I said, "but that hurt."

"Well," he said slowly, "for some, color is everything. Maybe especially at a time like that when a person is upset."

"I guess it's a teaching for me," I said, "about how painful it is not to be seen as who you are."

"That happens to *her* every day," Hiram said. He sighed. "Can you imagine how hurt *she* is, for her to treat you that way at that time?"

I nodded sadly. "The way things are going," I said, "I can't imagine what it's going to take to heal it."

CHAPTER EIGHT

Vows

S o, what's Buddhism like?" my son Jonathan asked me, "Contemplation, right?"

"Right," I said. "The idea is to pay attention, live in the moment, really *do* what you're doing. Want to hear a Buddhist joke?"

"Okay."

"You know how I'm always doing more than one thing at a time? Like reading while I'm eating?"

"Yeah?"

"Well, now when I read and eat, I *just* read and eat."

My interest in Buddhism got Stan and Rosemary started too. Stan and I often went to Zen lectures with our Zen friend Lil, and Rosemary attended talks by a Vipassana teacher. Lil said that San Francisco Bay was like a famous lake in a lush valley in China. Buddhist monasteries had been clustered around the lake a thousand years ago, and monks had walked from temple to temple, studying with the renowned teachers. "Only we don't walk," she said. "We drive our cars on freeways."

When the Dalai Lama visited the Bay Area to teach, Rosemary and I decided to go. The Dalai Lama had just been awarded the Nobel Peace Prize, and this was the first time these teachings had been given in the United States. Rosemary and I sat together in a cavernous indoor stadium with five thousand people, but when His Holiness spoke, sitting cross-legged in his robes on a raised platform with dozens of robed monks sitting around him, we felt as if we were alone with him.

His Holiness asked us to "develop a very deep insight into the suffering nature of life in general. If your understanding is not deep enough, you might feel envy for rich people, and not see how all people are caught up in a fruitless cycle of dissatisfaction."

His Holiness spoke in Tibetan, and everything was translated. At one point, he spoke so quickly and intensely in Tibetan, not waiting for the translator, that all of us in the stadium moved to the front of our seats and leaned toward him, inspired. When he stopped, the translator said, "I'm not sure I got all of that," and everyone laughed. It had really been a fervent transmission of emptiness.

At the end of the two days, His Holiness invited everyone to take part in a ceremony that would include taking refuge in Buddhism and taking vows. Rosemary and I looked at each other. We had taken a lot of classes, and we had even gone on a week-long silent retreat together, but we had never taken vows.

"Maybe we should go home now," Rosemary said. I thought so too.

"We're such rookie Buddhists," I said. "I don't think we're supposed to participate in this part."

But then His Holiness invited even the news media people in the stadium to take part, if they wished. "It will be beneficial," he said.

"Well, we're probably at least as Buddhist as those TV cameramen," Rosemary said. We stayed and took refuge in the "three jewels" — the Buddha, the Dharma (teachings), and the Sangha (the community) — and we took the bodhisattva vow to save all beings.

"When you take this vow," His Holiness said, "you are generating the aspiration to save all beings." Rosemary and I thought we could at least generate the aspiration.

Each person in the stadium was given an inch-wide strip of red cloth to tie around our foreheads during part of the ceremony. Before I went to San Quentin the next time, I cut mine in half lengthwise and smuggled one of the thin red strips in to Jarvis, who wove it into his knitted cap. "Now I always have something over my head that's been blessed by the Dalai Lama," he said.

I read some of my notes from the teachings to Jarvis: "Please develop a sense of the unbearableness of the suffering of all sentient beings. Compassion alone is not enough: wisdom is necessary, or one will be idealistic."

"At the end," I told Jarvis, "His Holiness said, 'What I have taught you will only be beneficial if it is complemented by meditation. Sustained effort is necessary.' "

"So, Melody," Jarvis said, "let's keep on trying."

After endless delays, Jarvis's trial started. For a defense investigator, a major trial is like stage-managing an opera, handling the cast, props, and costumes for the production. This trial, with three defendants, lasted months.

Jarvis's legal team did our best, but Jarvis was found guilty. We forged ahead with the sentencing phase trial.

My favorite witness at Jarvis's trial was Joe Hershey, who was a correctional counselor at a youth authority prison where Jarvis had been when he was fifteen and sixteen. I met Hershey for lunch out in Stockton, near the juvenile prison there. He wanted to go to a salad bar, because he was dieting, he said. Hershey was a large African-American man, probably imposing in his uniform, but the day we met, he was in slacks and a jacket. He had very good recall of Jarvis as a youngster.

"I saw something in Jarvis," Hershey said. "I saw him just watching sometimes, you know, studying what was going on."

Hershey had run a special program in which Jarvis had excelled. In fact, when Jarvis was released, Hershey had helped him to find a job in Stockton and a room to live in. Jarvis had told me this was the only time he had tried to live on his own, and he had been just too lonely. He had tried to visit Hershey at the prison, but once kids were released, they could not get back in. Jarvis bought a bus ticket back to Harbor City, met up with an older armed robber there, and the rest was history.

After the official interview, we helped ourselves to the ice cream section of the salad bar where you could make your own sundaes and talked for a while. "How's that special program going now?" I asked.

"Oh, they ended that long ago. Even though we showed that it worked in many cases. They don't want to pay for counseling for kids now, just punishment."

Even though it wasn't popular with the other correctional officers, Hershey came to court for Jarvis, during his sentencing trial, as did his sisters and several of his foster mothers.

It did no good. The jurors sentenced him to die.

After the trial, Jarvis's lawyers made one last motion to the judge to overturn the jury's sentence because of Jarvis's youth, and because he had not been the actual killer. The young man who was convicted of stabbing Sergeant Burchfield to death had been given life in prison without possibility of parole. Our motion asked the judge to sentence Jarvis to the same.

I was in court when the judge announced her decision. I was sitting just a few seats from Sergeant Burchfield's widow. My heart went out to her, raising her children alone, and I wondered how she felt about how the sentences had come out, but she had declined, politely, to speak to me. Once, she and I found ourselves washing our hands in the courthouse ladies' room at the same time, tensely pulling paper towels out of the dispenser, avoiding eye contact in the mirror.

All through the trial, Jarvis had had a soft spot for the judge, a petite white-haired woman old enough to be his grandmother who had seemed to like him. She smiled at him quite a few times during the trial. But in pronouncing her decision, the judge spoke of Jarvis's mother Shorty and her inability to care for her children, saying words to the effect that it would have been better if Shorty had not had them.

Then she confirmed the jury's decision that Jarvis should die.

A few minutes after the sentence was pronounced, I saw Jarvis upstairs in the jail. We picked up the phones, each on our own side of the glass, but we didn't say much.

"She thinks I never should have been born," Jarvis said, his head down. "Maybe that makes it easier for her to kill me."

We sat together until the officers came, and then I joined Rosemary, Stan, and Elyse, who had come for the sentencing, on the sidewalk outside. We stayed until the police car emerged from the courthouse basement to drive Jarvis, surrounded by officers, to death row. He couldn't wave to us because his handcuffs were clipped to his waist chains.

Exhausted from the trial, I stayed home for a week. The only place

I found comfort was close to Jarvis's magnolia tree in my garden. I kept going outside to stand among its shiny, dark green leaves.

I went to a lecture at the Zen center with Lil. The abbot said, "Things are not as they should be. Things are as they are."

After the lecture, during the teatime, I told the abbot about Jarvis and the death sentence.

"Sooner or later, of course," he said, "death will arrive and give all of us a very hard time. Tell your friend that the work we want to be doing is with that part of ourselves that still wants to ask, 'Why me? Why am I dying?' We don't want to get caught in one of the two big traps. We don't want to be saying, 'I'm getting a raw deal,' or, 'I deserve to be hurt.' We should ask ourselves, 'Am I doing what I really want to do? Am I acting with compassion for others?' "

I wrote everything he said down and read it to Jarvis on my next visit to the prison. "I might as well start right now," Jarvis said, "without wasting a moment."

He continued his studies by mail with Chagdud Rinpoche, a Tibetan lama. When one of the lama's students called me to tell me that Chagdud Rinpoche would be coming to San Quentin to perform a vow-taking ceremony for Jarvis, I rushed up to the prison to let him know it would be the next day.

Jarvis's first reaction was fear. "Call them and cancel," he said. "I don't deserve it."

"Listen, Jarvis, if you weren't deserving, no Tibetan lamas would be coming to see you. Just relax," I told him. "It will benefit you."

"I'm not ready."

"I think it's good you're scared," I said. "Anyone would be. It shows you're taking it seriously."

"I'm taking it *very* seriously," he said.

The associate warden had already denied the request for the ceremony to take place inside a locked room, where the lama would have been able to touch Jarvis and use the sacred objects with which the ceremony was normally done. It would have to take place by phone, through a glass window.

On my way out, I asked the friendliest officer who guarded the visiting room if he would please give us the far telephone the next day in order to afford us some privacy. I told him that a Tibetan lama would be coming to the prison. He said he'd seen the movie *The Golden Child.*

"Is Eddie Murphy coming too?" he joked.

I arrived at the prison to find the Rinpoche and his interpreter, a woman named Tsering Everest, waiting on a hard bench outside the door to the visiting entrance. The hallway was jammed with waiting visitors—smoking, talking loudly, babies crying. The Rinpoche, an old man, sat quietly, telling the beads of his rosary with his brown wrinkled fingers, his bright eyes taking in everything. He was quite a sight, in his floor-length burgundy skirt and his gray topknot and frizzled beard. As the noon-hour time for the door to be opened grew closer, the crowd, which had been waiting since early morning, grew more tense. Right in front of the Rinpoche, two young women began a loud dispute over their place in line. They cursed in vulgar street language, while the Rinpoche watched quietly.

With several people listening to him, the Rinpoche told a story of a Chinese prison in Tibet. He said that the Chinese made thousands of Tibetans dig deep holes. The hole was the prison of the person digging it. In the hole they were fed, in the hole they slept, exposed to rain or cold. In the hole they died, and the hole became their grave. Sixty thousand people, the Rinpoche said, were so imprisoned in Tibet.

At last our turn came. When Jarvis appeared on the other side of the scratched and dirty glass, in the noisy hall, the Rinpoche's interpreter picked up the phone on our side of the window. I stood to one side with my notebook, having promised to take notes for Jarvis. He leaned toward the glass, his phone pressed to his ear, a dim light barely illuminating his face from above. His smiling and slightly worried eyes were clearly visible.

"Is your mind clear?" began the Rinpoche. "I ask you to look at things in a very broad way. You'll notice that an angry prisoner is really sad because he is making bad karma. Don't blame others for your difficulties. All that is behind you now. From right now, go forward. Before all beings, make a promise: I won't be angry, I won't hurt anyone with my actions. That's my priority every day, even if it costs my life. In

Altars in the Street

your own words compose your promise and say it before God, Angels, Buddhism, everyone."

Jarvis answered, "From this day forward I will not harm or hurt other people even if it costs my life."

The Rinpoche went on: "The second vow. From this day forward I will try to end suffering of all human beings and other beings." Jarvis repeated the words. Then he asked, "Helping others could cost me my life today or tomorrow in here. Can I qualify my vow by common sense?"

The Rinpoche explained. "We relate to our bodies since babyhood as solid. This is not the whole truth. The teachings change our minds about our bodies. Now it is alive—now it is dead and gone. There is space between the molecules, vast openness, vast emptiness. Emptiness is the basis of everything—in it is wisdom, which doesn't get born or die but is forever true.

"This life is only a dream. Everything is in how I think of it. For example, a prison—you can think it's bad, but a person who lives in a beautiful house may kill himself. Everyone sits somewhere, whether beautiful or miserable. Hell is one's own nightmare—hell is the result of hatred within one.

"The way to practice is to see everyone as pure whether they hurt or help you—even animals, criminals, and guards, see their *perfection*. Hear every sound as perfection, as Tara talking."

Jarvis asked, "What if I break my vows?"

"At the end of every day confess your bad thoughts and actions and recommit yourself," the Rinpoche said. "Every time you do something good, instantly give it all away. Confess every mistake, let it go. It's like swimming, just keep going."

Saying good-bye, bowing to Chagdud Rinpoche, Jarvis looked very happy.

On our way out, we passed an Asian guard walking with some other officers. He came to an abrupt halt and I heard him exclaim, "That's a lama!"

CHAPTER NINE

Quakes

A long dry spell settled over California, punctuated by shocks. I was in my kitchen one morning when I heard the sound of a siren approaching. I looked out the window and saw an ambulance come to a stop in front of Ti's house. I ran out and joined the small crowd gathered on the sidewalk. I went to Ti's open door, but a paramedic waved me away. I paced on her front porch until Ti, looking gray and smaller, her eyes closed, was carried out.

"A heart attack," one of the paramedics said.

Ti survived that attack, but she had to stay in a nursing home. She said it "wasn't too bad," but she missed her garden. A few months later, without ever coming home again, she died.

I missed Ti, and so did her plants. When her nephew put her house on the market I went over and heaved the little Norfolk pine in its pot into my wheelbarrow and rolled it back to my yard and planted it there. It took me a long time to warm up to the new people, a nice white couple who seemed to be gone at work a lot and who never joined our block committee. I liked them, but they weren't gardeners. They took out Ti's vegetables and put in a lawn. Whenever I gardened, I felt as though I were still working alongside Ti.

I was alone in the house when the next big shock after Ti's death came. The Loma Prieta earthquake — in English, the earthquake of the shadowed hills — moved from deep out of the coast range to the south, a strong dark motion that rolled through our house, tossing the books off the shelves and knocking apart one of our two brick chimneys. I stood in the kitchen doorway holding on, while my body swayed with the house and a pot of hot soup on the back burner of the stove sloshed but did not fall. Stan and every one of the kids phoned in the next few minutes to say they were okay, and right after that the phone went dead for the next few hours.

Most people did not go out for a couple of days after the earthquake. Although most chimneys in Lorin were down, our area had done well, with no injuries or fires. On TV we watched the efforts to free people from the collapsed freeways and tried to come to terms with the incredible fact that the Bay Bridge had been broken by the movement of the earth. When I did go out again, to the grocery store, I noticed that everyone I saw looked tired and disturbed.

For Elyse the psychotherapist, it was amazing to see a whole society with symptoms of trauma. "The children at school say they can't sleep, can't stop thinking about the earthquake," she said. "A lot of them don't want to leave home at all."

"That's how we all feel in our neighborhood when there's gunfire," I told her. "Our whole little society is traumatized, and we hardly have time to get over it before it happens again."

We assessed the quake damage to our home. Except for one chimney, our house was fine. Elliott had been laid off from his job as a laborer at the army base, and he and Camille were really struggling on her wage as a teacher's aide. Hoping to help a little bit, we hired Elliott to help Stan and Jonathan climb up onto the roof and remove the chimney, one bucket of bricks at a time, making a neat pile of them in a corner of the garden. Then they put in modern vents for the stove and heater.

We were still nervous from the earthquake when one afternoon, "in broad daylight," as they say, when none of us was home, the inevitable happened. Percy, our mailman, saw that one of our front windows was smashed. He ran to Libby's and phoned the police.

I got home after Stan, and he took me by the shoulders and said, "Melody, we've been burglarized, and some of your things are gone." The full can of beer someone had hurled through the windowpane to break it was still lying on the rug. There were trailing wires where the VCR had been. I raced into the bedroom, saw my dresser drawers open, and my little wooden jewelry box, with my sister Skye's ivory earrings inside it, gone. Skye's earrings had been from Alaska, ivory carved into the shape of feathers. They would not come back, just as Skye would not come back. I cried and cried.

A white officer arrived the next day to take a report. Looking out our smashed front window at the block with its mothers and children out on a sunny afternoon, he all but sneered, "How can you live here?" I knew he wouldn't ask me that if I were black. And probably not if *he* were black. As hurt as I was about the burglary, I knew we weren't the only neighborhood with burglaries.

"Because it's my home," I said. "Where do *you* live?" He lived in a suburb.

"Why do you live here?" I imagined a Martian asking an Earth person. "Your planet's getting too warm and it has a hole in its atmosphere. Why don't you move?"

Meditating, I practiced watching my feather earrings fly away. They would not come back, Skye would not come back, and neither would Ti. I found something in a book Zen teacher Aitken Roshi had written: "When something precious gets stolen/I vow with all beings/to acknowledge that soon I'll release/all things to the king of thieves."

I'd heard of monasteries where an important part of the monks' daily practice was sweeping the temple grounds. Ti had often swept the sidewalk, and I decided to take up the task. The purpose of my sweeping would not be just to clean up, but to try to walk out my gate and meet Alma Street with a fresh outlook each morning, as if for the first time. No need to visit a monastery in Tibet or Japan.

I came to be known in the neighborhood, I think, as the lady who sweeps. Sometimes I felt angry, inwardly scolding the kids who threw down candy wrappers from the corner store, the drinkers who'd left malt-liquor cans and fortified-wine bottles inside brown bags. But usually, the sweeping itself calmed me. I tackled it all in thick orange rubber gloves, wielding my broom and dustpan, dragging my garbage can along with me. I recycled what I could. There were clothes, or shoes, or car parts. Occasionally, I fished a used syringe out of the hedge. A quote from Martin Luther King, Jr., on my refrigerator reminded me of "the inescapable network of mutuality."

"This is *all* sacred," I told myself. "All of it."

If I was feeling fearless I swept right near the feet of whoever was looking out for the cops. The lookout job seemed to be lonely and boring, with very long hours, given to someone low on the drug-dealing totem pole who was addicted and doing it just for some crack.

One cold morning, a woman had that miserable job. She was as thin as a famine victim, and she looked sick. She leaned on the mailbox weakly, watching me work. We said hi to each other. As mad as I was about the loss of my peace and quiet, I knew that all this was so much worse for her than it was for me. For me, it hurt to see her suffering. For her, it *was* suffering.

CHAPTER TEN

Some Way, Somehow, It Has to Stop

I was struggling with the Buddhist vow not to kill at the time of the murder. The Saturday before the murder, Stan and I had heard Mel Weitsman, the abbot of Berkeley Zen Center, lecture on the precept against killing living beings. He said that taking the vow not to kill did not mean that we would never kill another being. Mel, a down-to-earth man in his sixties, admitted to his own problems with garden snails. The vow not to kill, he said, asks us to be more aware of the creatures we do kill.

At the time, the house was being overrun by mice. They were becoming very bold in the kitchen, and I imagined them in there at night, making toast and spreading butter and honey on it. There was an unmistakable clue that they had even come into our bedroom: my meditation cushion sat in the bay window, and the mice had eaten a little bowl of rice I kept there. The rice served to hold incense sticks, but one morning the sticks were all lying on the rug and there was nothing in the bowl but mouse droppings. I figured if they left enough droppings I could just use those to hold up the incense sticks. While I thought about trying not to kill, the mice multiplied.

Meanwhile Lynn, one of Amina's friends, arrived to stay a week. A pretty blond cowgirl, she was visiting from Santa Fe where she worked with horses. She even wore cowboy boots. She was dubious about the neighborhood, I could tell, not used to being someplace where she couldn't walk outside at night. We always felt sort of defensive when guests came from out of town, because the neighborhood seemed so dangerous to them, so we explained that we'd been here many years, and we loved our home and our neighbors. "This used to be a good, quiet, interracial community," I told Lynn. A thriving drug trade among the lovely Victorian homes seemed incongruous to Lynn.

Noticing the mouse problem, Lynn got to work and dispatched the mice on the last day of her visit, cheerfully setting and emptying traps until she killed about a dozen. She joked about how if she skinned them they would make great little gray leather hacky-sacks. I knew it was a cop-out to have someone else kill the mice, but I was also glad to be rid of them. I kept my thoughts about Buddhist precepts to myself. After Lynn left, I was still thinking a lot about what my life would be like if I seriously tried not to kill.

Saturday night Stan sat up late, working at his desk, but I went to bed early and fell asleep reading, with the light on. It was 1:00 A.M. when the first shot woke me instantly. As had become my habit with gunshots, I began to count them with the first one. There was a pause after the first three . . . then four, five, six, seven.

Next I heard a man's voice and footsteps. He was walking, haltingly, as if staggering, coming up the sidewalk, getting closer to my window. He was talking. Over and over he said, "Oh, baby, oh, baby," regretfully, deep sorrow in his voice.

He was shot, I knew, many times, and somehow the feeling in his voice told me he was dying, and knew he was dying. I could hear Stan's voice in the other room, talking to 911 on the phone, telling them to send an ambulance.

The man fell right under my window, just a few feet away. My meditation cushion was at the foot of the bed, with the incense. Then the window glass, covered with lace, then the hedge, and then the sidewalk. And on the sidewalk, someone was dying.

Stan, Amina, and I, each in separate rooms along the side of the house, could hear his moans. The moans had meaning: regret and complete unwillingness. If his moans had been words they would have said, "Oh no, now I'm dying. No, I don't want it. No."

I switched off my reading light and stood up, moving to the window. I was afraid to pull the curtain aside to look out. I stood with my palms together in front of me, in a posture of prayer, and listened to him. The thought came to me: "A human being is dying now." For a brief instant I had the feeling of knowing exactly what to do: just be there, just be there with him.

I stood still, staying with the man as he moaned. His moans turned to harsh, loud breathing, then congested breathing. The breaths rattled in his throat, and the phrase "death rattle" came to my mind. Then his breathing stopped. I knew he had died.

All of this transpired in only one or two minutes. Stan, now off the phone, wanted to go to the man, and he started to unlock the door, but we realized the killer might be outside. Stan is much taller than I am. Together we peeked through a crack at the edge of the curtain, his head above mine. Amina stayed in the hall with Alaska, keeping walls between herself and possible bullets from outside.

We saw a police officer peering around the corner of the house across the street. The officer was frozen in place, holding a shotgun and looking terrified. A half minute later more police cars arrived, and one shone headlights down the sidewalk from the corner, lighting the body. The police approached the body cautiously. We stepped out onto our porch.

When I looked down at the young man, I thought, "He has a mother." I began to cry, seeing his hand outstretched, palm up, helpless and lifeless.

The ambulance was there very quickly, but everyone knew he was already dead. I stood looking down over the porch rail and I thought about some people I'd seen on TV who told about near-death experiences. They'd all said they had looked down on their own bodies. I realized that the young man's spirit might have been in almost the same position I was in, standing on my porch. He might be hovering over the scene below, watching the police and paramedics working over his body.

After the ambulance left, the police stayed for a couple of hours, searching for bullets, for blood spots. We heard an officer call out, "Here's a rock of crack."

Stan and Amina and I sat together on the living room couch, our arms around each other, crying. I remember saying, while I cried, that the bedroom would never be the same again. Stan and I slept in the living room that night, on the sofa bed, because the living room, facing the garden, not the street, felt safer.

I woke up at dawn after only a couple of hours of sleep and immediately I went outside. A chalk outline of the young man's body was on the sidewalk, and a large amount of blood coagulated where his head had been. Three pairs of blood-covered rubber gloves, left by the police technicians, I supposed, were also scattered around. I got out my garden hose. I'd swept here so many times, but never had I cleaned up after a murder. Hosing the sidewalk, I sensed my own state of shock. I jumped when the blood coursed into the gutter and stained a long distance down the street. Suddenly I turned off the water, not sure if I should do this. Maybe the police wanted to work here some more, I thought. Maybe, I thought, this isn't my job, and I'm doing myself some kind of harm. Still, I picked up the bloody gloves with my fingertips and put them into the gutter. I couldn't stand to leave them where people walking by would have to step over them.

I went into the house and stood at my bedroom window as children gathered at the school bus stop, most of them accompanied by their mothers or fathers. Shaking, I thought about them growing up only to be gunned down in the street. I panicked at the idea that the children might see the blood, but none of them seemed to notice.

I still kept school supplies around from my teaching days. I went to the closet and chose a big roll of bright blue butcher paper. I cut a long piece and wrote:

> This morning, October 1, 1990, at about 1:00 A.M., a
> young man was shot here and died. Seven shots were
> fired. A rock of crack was found. Neighbors, write your
> prayers and comments here if you wish.

I put it outside next to the chalk outline and the bloodstain, with a jar of pens, incense, and pots of flowers from my garden.

I wrote: "I will think about his mother, whoever she is. I know she is hurting, and I pray for her. Once more, I will ask our mayor and city council for a drug treatment center."

People gathered and started to write on the blue paper. The first clue to the victim's identity was when a man wrote, "We love you Ian." Later someone wrote,

> Some way some how it have to stop. Look at ourself. We are dying. Let's stop the war. Love to Ian Freedman. God be with you."

It emerged that his name was Ian Freedman, that he was twenty-seven, that his mother had lived for years a few blocks away, that he had gone to Berkeley High and had been in jail or prison. Many people in the neighborhood knew him, or his mother or sisters or brothers. He was the father of an eight-year-old son.

His last name, Freedman, kept coming into my thoughts. I wondered if Ian had an ancestor who took that surname after slavery was abolished, 125 years before.

In the late morning, I decided to call the mayor's office. She had knocked on my door while campaigning a few days before. The mayor was a sincere, well-meaning white woman I could identify with: she was a mother about my age and we both had wavy brown hair. I had followed her down the street, discreetly pointing out the crack houses, talking to her about the need for drug treatment, and also more police. She listened but seemed helpless in the face of the budget cuts she talked about.

I got the mayor's aide on the phone, and I mentioned the bloodstain and the rubber gloves. Half an hour later a fire truck arrived. A firewoman picked up the gloves and hosed the spot. As they drove off she said, "Next time try using hydrogen peroxide, it's good for bloodstains."

"What?" I thought. "Does she think we're in the habit of killing each other and need street-cleaning tips for blood?"

Pearl spent most of the day at the blue paper shrine, shaking her head and pressing her lips tightly together. "I'm almost glad Ti didn't live to see this," she said.

This murder was exactly what we had feared these last five years. Libby and Mrs. Sanders wept as we talked, Potter and Mr. Joe seemed stunned. No one was callous.

Several times tough-looking guys walked up in groups from the

Jackson brothers' crack house down the street. They said little and did not write on the blue paper shrine. Some of them looked sobered, a little scared. All looked grim.

I had never talked to them. When I drove by, they would look at me. I'd look back. We lived in different worlds on the same street. But today, through the opening caused by Ian's death, we talked a little. I told them about how he died, his words, his moans. His blood was there for them to see. I told them I hoped they would not go out and kill someone else because Ian had died.

Rosemary and Jonathan came over when they found out what had happened. At one point, I was giving one of these little speeches for peace while Jonathan was there with me. He looked at me in disbelief, obviously thinking, "What are you doing, Mom, lecturing these scary guys?" But later, he told me what I'd said was fine, because I just let them know I didn't want them to kill or be killed.

That same message was the theme of the writings on the blue paper:

I hope things will change. We black people need to be more together than this. I feel for your parents because I lost my son last year.

Let the violence stop and the healing of this neighborhood begin.

It is time to stop all this madness. We're all in the same gang!

Many people used the paper to write directly to Ian, to speak to him one last time.

Although we all have to go, it hurts to see you go like this. God rest your soul comrade.

Rest in Peace, young man, for this world has little to offer. Bless you and your beloved grieving loved ones. Please God give them strength!

In the afternoon, his mother and sisters came. When I thought of his mother at 1:00 A.M., I never imagined I would see her later that day, but when the family arrived, I realized that of course if your child died, you would go to the place where it happened. I was inside when they came, and their grief was so painful, I did not go out while they were there.

Someone, his sister or girlfriend, broke down completely and wailed, a keening, inconsolable cry that is the expression of primal grief all over the world. I felt the whole neighborhood stop breathing while we listened to the sound of loss.

Ian's mother wrote that she would think of him each and every day. As a mother, I knew that was the truth.

I couldn't go to work the day of Ian's murder. I'd interviewed scores of witnesses to killings, never dreaming I would become a witness myself. To keep busy and comfort myself, I worked in our garden, with the help of Camille's younger son Sam-Sam. He and I would weed and clip, and then go back out to the sidewalk shrine for a while.

I'd known Sam-Sam since he was five years old, when he got big enough to come down the block to play with Alaska. He was taller than me now, and shy. The last couple of years he'd done yard work for me in return for an hourly wage and instruction in how to care for plants. This year, Sam-Sam really needed work because he'd dropped out of school at sixteen.

Sam-Sam said he was used to drug-related murder in a way, because it was everywhere he went—in Los Angeles where his uncle lived, in Oakland where he had friends. But in another way, he said, "I'm not used to it. It scares me, and I hate it. . . . I could have gotten into it," he told me, meaning the crack trade, "but I decided not to." He pointed to the blood. "Because of that."

All day Sam-Sam and I had a running discussion about the killing, drugs, money, and work. Sam-Sam said plenty of people he knew said they wouldn't work for five dollars an hour, when they could make two hundred selling crack, but he didn't want to get killed selling drugs. I told him I'd met lots of youngsters on my job who were in jail for selling drugs or killing someone. I philosophized about how some rich people make money legally, some illegally, like stealing from savings and loans, but that almost nobody was satisfied with what they had. Both the crack dealers and the crooked bankers wanted more.

Sam-Sam replied, "I think it's better to be like you and me."

"What do you mean?" I asked.

"It's better to be satisfied with things like plants and birds," said Sam-Sam. At that moment he seemed wise beyond his years. But what was to become of him? He said he was afraid to go out at night.

All day people came to the blue paper shrine. There were rumors about why the murder happened. Different people said different things: Ian wasn't a dealer, he was a dealer, he was selling bad dope, it was a personal thing. Whatever the truth was, the penalty for getting involved in the drug trade was often death, by bullet or by needle.

Skeeter talked about feeling like crying because drugs hurt people so much. I knew Skeeter was trying to stay in AA. He did cry, right there. And he wrote,

> I cried for the person who got shot, and for his family,
> I pray that God touches their heart in a special way.
> This doesn't have to continue.

Rosemary and I brought out another piece of paper in the late afternoon; the first one was filled. People kept writing:

> One love, Rasta Jah.
> Crack kills, brothers and sisters, stop the violence.

Some of the writing was in the childish script of the young girls on the block, and they signed their pretty names, Somika, LaKeisha, and Aisha. They wrote, "I do not know you, but I love you."

I went inside to sit for a few minutes in my kitchen window, on the other side of the house from the bloody sidewalk. Looking out on my yard, I could see other realities to our neighborhood besides crime. My apricot tree cast its yellow leaves onto the grass. The last of the raspberries and rhubarb were ready to be picked, and the Cecile Brunner rosebush Ti and I had planted, tall now, had finished blooming. The Buddha sat under the fraying Tibetan prayer flags, contemplating a red rock. Up the middle of the block the beautiful old trees in the backyards were subtly fading to their fall colors.

Just before dark, the mayor and the chief of police drove up together in a police car to visit the blue paper shrine. This was my first personal contact with the chief, a tall African-American man. I invited them inside to talk. They took seats on our couch side by side and listened while Stan and I told about the killing.

The chief sat uncomfortably, shifting his weight as if his uniform were too tight. I thought maybe he was girding himself for our anger, expecting Stan and me to demand some kind of police action. But anger wasn't our mood. While we talked, both Stan and I came close to tears. The mayor and the chief were silent, the way people are when men almost cry.

Then the chief told us his mother lived not too far away. He said he cared about this neighborhood, but he didn't have any answers. He too was searching for ideas. Neither the chief nor the mayor gave us glib promises, and I appreciated that.

Stan and I talked to each other, and to our kids: should we try to sell the house and leave? Could we stay in a house where someone had been shot to death right outside?

Amina, who had sought solace for her trauma from some of her friends at San Francisco State, came home upset by the people in her classes who withheld sympathy. She said one woman asked her, "Why do you live there?" as if we could solve the problem by moving away and forgetting it. "Why should we go?" Amina said. "Why shouldn't the drug dealers go instead?"

Rosemary, Jonathan, and Neal were uneasy about our safety, but they said they would be sad to see us leave the home where they grew up. They would support whatever we decided to do.

Money was an issue. Property values were going down, and we weren't sure we could afford another house if we sold this one cheap, as we would have to do. We knew we either had to leave or commit ourselves to working harder to make things better.

I consulted each of my two best friends.

Lil and I met, as usual, in a coffee shop. She folded her tall slender self into a booth opposite me, and we pondered my family's dilemma. Lil's house was only a mile away on a quiet street. She said she couldn't believe we shared the same zip code, our worlds were so different. Lil didn't give me advice, she just listened, frowned, pushed her unruly gray-flecked brown hair out of her eyes, and asked therapist-type questions like, "How would it feel to sell the house?"

"It feels impossible," I answered her. "I can't imagine leaving it."

Elyse the therapist had no trouble giving me advice. "I'm not your therapist, I'm your friend, and I think you should definitely leave as soon as possible," she said flatly when she heard about the murder. In Elyse's mind, I deserved a peaceful home, especially, she said, since my private investigations job was so stressful.

"It's not that I don't think I deserve to move," I said. "It's that so much of my self is a part of my neighborhood. I would really miss my neighbors, and I don't want to leave them behind." We walked a little in silence. "I'm not a quitter," I said.

Our neighbors were unwilling to lose their neighborhood to violence without resisting. Potter came by to pick up the blue paper on his way to the city council meeting a week after the shooting. There he spread it on the floor of the council chamber and told them to do what they could: more cops, more streetlights.

"What more important agenda item could the city council have than the citizens being murdered in the streets?" he asked. But the council members could only express sympathy. Every week there was something more to be cut from their budget, and a homicide like this was hardly even a news item in our local paper.

In the nights that followed the murder I was never once able to wake up without feeling that I had been awakened by Ian Freedman. For me, that was how it had happened. I was asleep, and I was awakened by his death. At least once every night, and again in the morning, I opened my eyes and thought of him, instantly.

Some Buddhists believe that when people die suddenly, with no time to prepare, their spirits have a hard time leaving their bodies. I imagined that some part of Ian was still hovering near my meditation cushion.

I hadn't been able to meditate. I decided to sit down and try to talk to Ian, since he seemed so present in my room. At first, I had no idea what to say. Then I just told him that I had heard him: "I know you weren't ready to die. I heard that you didn't want to go. It's okay. It's okay to go now."

I did this meditation several times. I imagined the neighborhood without houses or apartment buildings, as the sun-browned open meadow which it was before white people or black people came to live here. I imagined myself sitting there, on the grass, and another person, a young man, who was wounded somehow, walking a long way over the meadow to lie down in front of me to die. It would have been natural for him to come close to me to die, to be comforted.

If I subtracted the houses, the asphalt, the cars and guns and sirens, I could stop being afraid. There was only him, leaving this life, and me, with him for one minute at the end. In that vision was the essence of what happened. Knowing that, I was glad I was there.

When I took out the garbage two weeks afterward, two girls were walking to Malcolm X, the nearby elementary school, carrying their books, one toting a violin case. When they got to my driveway they swerved out into the middle of the street and didn't get back on the sidewalk until they were well past the place where Ian Freedman died.

How does a neighborhood's memory of something like this shooting fade, I wondered? Would there come a day when we could walk past the spot and not remember?

In the end, Stan and I decided to stay and keep on trying. We made our decision to stay as a commitment to our neighbors. If we were going to try to keep our home, it wouldn't be a halfway effort. The neighborhood would become my part-time unpaid job, and Stan would work harder at lawyering to take up the financial slack. When we were asked, "How can you live there?" our answer would be, "Wholeheartedly."

Our intention was in tune with something Abbot Mel Weitsman had said in one of his lectures at the Zen center:

"Wherever you are, be there completely."

CHAPTER ELEVEN

Balance

As we struggled that autumn to recover from the shock of Ian Freedman's murder, the world readied for war.

The violence in the Persian Gulf became the backdrop for the war in the streets around us. I made a sign, "No War For Oil," and put it in my window. I wrote letters to Congress and the president asking for peace. I passed out leaflets at the subway station and the federal building with Lil and her Buddhist Peace Fellowship friends. When the group met at our house, I had to tell them to walk each other out to their cars to keep them safe from the guns on our street.

Elyse and I walked in the hills, anxious. "Here I am, trying to teach youngsters to talk out their disputes," she said, "and the president only has 'Kick butt' to say."

Overwhelmed by violence, I went to my Tibetan Buddhist teacher Eric, who tried to help me. "The trick is not to deny painful realities— or to get sunk into negativity. The goal is to bring ourselves into balance. This comes with meditation, with openness. Balance isn't positive or negative; it's a whole different order of experience infused with intelligence."

"Eric, the best I can do right now," I told him, "is to try to know I'm *not* balanced. I have lost my balance. That much I know."

During the hundred days of the war I felt soaked in violence, like the cormorant I saw on TV drowning in oil, gasping for air. I went to a lecture at Green Gulch Zen Center, but I couldn't listen to Abbot Reb Anderson very well. I saw a sign there in the dining room, "Drinking this cup of tea, I stop the war."

During the question period, I said to the abbot: "Right now, those words have no meaning to me. I cannot understand them." The abbot was sitting cross-legged in his black robe. I had last seen him sitting beside the altar of a San Francisco cathedral, representing Buddhists at an interfaith antiwar service. I wanted him to know the answer to my question.

"What does 'Drinking this cup of tea, I end the war' mean to you?" he asked me back.

"I don't know," I said, despairing, and went on, knowing I was saying something absurd. "I tried to prevent the war. I did everything I knew how to do, and I failed completely."

He looked at me, standing up at the back of the room near the door, so tense, so close to tears, I was ready to open it and run out. "You held up your truth. Now go on holding up your truth. You want world peace right now. So don't be optimistic, you might become complacent. You must take care of your aspiration to compassion. Just *want* to make these changes, just take it on, with joy. If it doesn't matter to us how long it takes for world peace, we can have it right now, with complete joy."

I left that day not understanding but somehow breathing a little more easily. At the Tibetan Institute, there had been little mention of the outside world. Through earthquake and war, we continued with our quiet practice, sitting, chanting, visualizing. The prayer wheels turned, the incense burned, all went on as usual. For me, it was too much like the family of my childhood—where we pretended to the outside world everything was fine no matter what. To me, the war overseas and around my home had become the elephant in the meditation hall no one was talking about.

At the Tibetan Institute, I had found two of the Three Treasures the Dalai Lama had talked about: Buddha and Dharma. But the third, Sangha—community—was lacking. I knew I had to practice the teachings with people who were more involved in the world.

After nearly four years of study with Eric Meller, I said good-bye. Eric knew I was leaving to become a member of the Berkeley Zen Center and to practice with the Zen center abbots who had said, during the war, "We can't just sit around."

The last day of February, after the bombing ended, the oil fires still burning, I left for the mountains alone. I walked in the woods close to Yosemite where in July the year before a forest fire had raged downhill to the Merced river, leaping the boulders, moving so fast that firefighters and deer had run ahead of it.

I stopped on the trail feeling that I was breathing for the first time in months. I looked around me at the burned forest on both sides of the trail. As far as I could see were fire-shattered trees, black trunks, bark scorched in charcoal squares the way clay cracks in dry river washes. From the base of every tree tender green stalks and folded leaves pushed up, ready to open. I had no choice but to believe in restoration, a force, like gravity. Here was the evidence, pulling me down to touch those sprouts, thrust up from deep roots into the fire zone.

I was sweeping the sidewalk one day when I saw Ruth's tall form coming toward me, her son Jamal beside her holding her hand. I hadn't seen her since the day I had visited her in the hospital after the fire in her apartment. She stopped in front of me without speaking at first, and then smoothed her blouse down over her stomach to show that she was pregnant.

"I'm expecting," she beamed, "and I'm back." Ruth's family had moved into another apartment on Alma Street. We hugged, and for a minute, we both cried, holding each other, thinking of the fire and little Amina. Jamal's burn scars were still being treated, but he was a beautiful little boy who loved to play outside with the other kids. They were kind to him, and his big brother Dondi was usually by his side.

Since it was the first spring after the murder and the war, and we were going to stay, I decided that what my garden needed was a sacred circle. Camille's son Sam-Sam helped me to dig a round bed twenty feet across. We built a low wall around the circle out of the bricks that had been our quake-ruined chimney. Our project attracted Ruth's boys

Balance

Dondi and Jamal and four or five other little kids who pitched in. The bricks were pale red and sandy, a century old, many of them marked with an enigmatic "P," the initial, I supposed, of the brick maker. We laid a pretty pale red path through the circle. I harvested long canes of black bamboo from Lil's backyard, and Sam-Sam and I lashed them together to form two arched trellises for the ends of the path.

Sam-Sam loved nurseries, and we toured them, driving from one to another in my station wagon, looking for four perfect climbing roses for the trellises. We put lavender and rosemary, oregano and sage in the wheel we had built, and I put our Buddha at its edge. I hung Tibetan prayer flags between the trellises. I started a practice of carrying my cup outside in the mornings and sitting under them.

Pearl and I were at my kitchen table in the window one morning when she peered out at the row of white squares—the prayer flags flapping on their green twine between the rosebushes. They had been there for weeks.

"Honey, can I take those hand towels in for you?" she offered.

I explained about prayer flags sending blessings into the wind in Tibet. Pearl laughed, a little embarrassed. "Well, I know how busy you always are, sugar. I thought you just forgot your wash. Prayer flags! Those are real nice. Ti would have liked them."

CHAPTER TWELVE

The Koans of Alma Street

The mayor formed a task force on Lorin's problems and assigned June Rivers, a young African-American woman with a degree in city planning, to work with us. The committee members' first reaction to her was anger. It was as if we had been telling them about a dangerous intersection for years, and they had waited until a child was killed by a car and then put up a STOP sign. Poor June was given a hard time about why she hadn't shown up sooner.

When everybody calmed down, we found we liked June Rivers. She had attended a national conference on urban drug problems and she brought us a new idea: the CARS program—Citizens Against Rock Sales.

The city would install signs along the sidewalks warning drug buyers that their license numbers were being reported to police. We would be given CARS postcards, and we were supposed to write license numbers down on them when we were certain we had seen a drug transaction involving a car. June would run the license numbers on the police computer and mail the registered owners a letter, telling them that their vehicle was seen in a "known drug area."

"And that's *us*," Mr. Joe said sadly.

We were all gathered at the church on the evening June was to give us the CARS cards when CJ and Nathan suddenly walked in. We all knew they worked for the Jacksons and were here as spies—all except June Rivers, who didn't have a clue.

There were no more seats at the table, so CJ and Nathan pulled folding chairs up behind the group. Quickly, I wrote out a note in big block letters: DON'T TALK ABOUT CARS. The warning note passed around the group slowly, under the table from lap to lap with a lot of furtive nudging. When it reached June, she looked around, confused. I wasn't about to chair the meeting and emerge as the leader in the eyes of the spies. I got up and went over to June and whispered to her to get up and chair. Everybody called out agenda items utterly lacking in law enforcement concerns: how the street trees were growing, announcement of the tutoring program at the school, the problem of litter. It was the shortest meeting we ever had.

After we adjourned and the spies left, we explained to June what had happened. She had gotten the idea that CJ and Nathan were a problem, but when we told her who they were, she looked terrified.

"Are you all right?" I asked her.

"Melody, I was raised in a very protected environment," she told me. "My parents are really worried about me taking this job, and this gives me second thoughts."

The CARS program wasn't going to be a secret, anyway. Everyone would know as soon as the street signs went up. But after CJ's and Nathan's surprise visit to our meeting, the dealers knew most of who was in the block committee. They couldn't say our committee was just the white people; there had been plenty of black faces around the table that night. I was especially worried about Addie and Mr. Joe, who lived right next door to where the main dealing was going on. No one knew what would happen.

It was hard for me to be afraid of CJ or Nathan—I'd known them for years. It was even harder for me to want to see them locked up. They presented our committee with a koan: an almost unsolvable Zen riddle. So many young men were being arrested for nonviolent drug offenses, Mr. Joe called it "the new form of slavery. Black men without jobs," he said, "put back in chains." On the other hand most of us, and Mr. Joe himself, would argue that we had to stop them from terrorizing the old people and the children.

"We've got to stop making excuses for them," Potter Woods said. "Everybody wants to say, 'My son is a victim of the system, but your son is a thug!' "

"Just say no isn't working," Libby said. "They have to have something to say yes to."

We wanted the courts and police to wisely distinguish between nonviolent drug offenders who could be saved and the people who were truly dangerous. But instead of a scalpel the system was using a sledgehammer—long mandatory sentences for possession and sales of drugs.

"The war on drugs is a war on *people*," Saul Schwartz said. Saul always wanted to talk about legalizing drugs.

"Okay, Saul, fine!" Louis the bus driver would cry. "Good idea, let's try it! But it ain't *happening*, man, anytime soon, and probably never, so why *talk* about it?"

The CARS program seemed to offer a middle way. If we could chase the customers away, perhaps we could reduce the amount of dealing and the number of guns on our block.

The CARS signs made everyone laugh. They said: DRUGS — BUYERS AND DEALERS BEWARE. YOUR LICENSE NUMBERS ARE BEING REPORTED TO POLICE. The word "drugs" was in such big print that from a distance the signs looked like ads for the dealers' wares. The buyers pulled up and the dealers waved them a few blocks away where they made their purchases. We noticed that the dealers started wearing one identifiable piece of clothing every day, say, a yellow shirt. The lookouts were obviously saying, "Go around the corner and look for the guys in the yellow shirts, they'll sell to you."

No doubt some buyers were scared off. I could just imagine the reactions of some young people's parents, and some owners of company cars, when they opened those letters. But the volume of dealing didn't decrease.

All of a sudden dozens of cars drove around the neighborhood without license plates, and there were hardly ever any cop cars around to give them tickets. We understood why the dealers didn't retaliate against us; why bother when they could so easily adapt their business to CARS?

We were grateful to June for trying, though. When she left for another job after a year, I filled in one of the CARS cards for her to keep. Where it said, "Describe activity," I wrote: "Unstinting hard work and care for the community. Race: African-American. Sex: Woman. Distinguishing marks: Energy, Love, and Intelligence."

What CARS did yield was the depressing news that the vehicle owners lived all over the place. We found out Lorin was a regional drug market for people from suburbs and cities forty miles away.

Berkeley had district representatives on its city council. Only one of the seven councilors was beholden to us; we couldn't vote for the others, so they didn't have to care about us. Our own city councilwoman was Maudelle Shirek, an African-American woman in her seventies, who came from the old school of Berkeley radical politics. She was a kind and active elder revered in the community.

Maudelle met with our committee rarely, because she always got a fight from our group. All of us wanted more police protection, our black members almost more so than the rest. Potter said, "We are dealing with the legacy of past racism, and today we are still being ignored."

Pearl said, "I want to hire some of these young men to go and stand over there in front of a nice restaurant and see how long they last!"

"I've seen police cars on the north side just sitting, waiting to catch someone running a stop sign!" Libby would say. "We call about drug dealing, and no one comes."

I knew from Elyse that people on her side of town thought they had *too many* police sometimes. She said that when two black junior high boys took a shortcut over a fence and through someone's yard, five police cars responded before the boys got to the end of the block. "It was ridiculous," Elyse said.

Maudelle was worried about police brutality and priorities. She would say, "We don't need more *police* in our community! What we need is good jobs, not police!"

Everyone wanted more jobs, and no one wanted police who would beat people up.

Like Maudelle, I came to the drug war suspicious of police. I had investigated many lawsuits against police for use of excessive force, interviewing emergency room personnel who'd seen injuries inflicted by police. I'd talked to people who'd seen police beat people in jails and on sidewalks and shoot at their backs. Like Maudelle, I wanted the police to be well trained and subject to review. I started out wanting jobs first, police second. Slowly, though, against my will, safety rose to the top of my list.

As Reverend Clara said, "Nothing good can happen unless we end the violence first." Customers would not come to an area with so much crime. Our pharmacy closed, then a black-owned hardware store, and several restaurants. We'd had a branch of a major bank in a lovely old building. It closed, was replaced by a savings and loan that quickly folded, and finally a high-fee check-cashing store came in.

Then there was the riddle of civil liberties. Maudelle said people had the right to stand on the public street without being harassed. Stan and I supported that right, but it was hard when a drug dealer loitered on our corner, leaning on the mailbox, all night long, even in the pouring rain, with no purpose except to sell drugs, and yet police had no probable cause to ask him why he was there. When Stan was awakened by whistles and loud voices, he would flop over in bed and irritably mutter, "I'm going to burn my damned ACLU card."

Maudelle lived on the edge of Lorin, in a small, dead-end cul-de-sac with no traffic at all, in a much safer area of Berkeley. While the drug war changed me, she had a hard time admitting that so many of her African-American constituents were addicted. Whenever she spoke publicly, she talked about white people coming into the neighborhood to buy drugs. There was some of that—with my own eyes I saw white drivers pull up to buy drugs from the Jacksons—but those were perhaps one in ten of the customers I saw.

"I hear African-American politicians and ministers having a hard time talking truthfully about addiction," Reverend Clara said. "Too many of our pastors over the years never mentioned alcoholism hurting families in their churches. And now we pretend drugs are not here, and very often, it is some of the same families affected."

People fought about jobs and treatment versus police, as if they were mutually exclusive. As a Buddhist student, I was learning that whenever I found myself thinking dualistically, as if there were only two opposite choices, I was probably wrong. I wanted to see a Middle Way. Over and over I said: "The police cannot solve our problems for us. And we can't solve our problems without the police."

Sitting in Reverend Clara's office, I talked with her about our mutual struggle to mix compassion with responsibility. "Jesus fed the hungry, but he also chased the money changers from the temple," she said. "These drug dealers out here are causing crack babies, making people sick. I understand young men need jobs, they need education. But I ask them to find another way. And I want them away from in front of my church."

"On many Buddhist altars," I said, "there are two images, one for compassion and one for wisdom. The wise one holds a sword, and uses it to make distinctions—like the cut between a crack baby and a drug dealer."

Reverend Clara liked the phrase "tough love": "It's still love," she said, "but it's tough."

The city came up with some new ammunition for the War On Drugs. The police department acquired a sort of tank. It was a full-sized passenger bus painted black and white so that it looked like a big whale of a police car. They called it ORCA, short for Operational Response and Communication Auxiliary—perfect for a war. They gave us a tour. Inside, it had a conference table, a row of radios and phones, a microwave, and a refrigerator. You couldn't *see* the cops inside the blackened windows, but they could see you.

At a press conference, the mayor and the chief announced they were going to use ORCA to "make life miserable" for the dealers by parking it at "hot spots." I don't know if the dealers' lives were more miserable or not, but ORCA did repel them. When ORCA was on Alma Street, the Jackson brothers and their employees were nearby, usually right near the door of a seedy liquor store.

"Now *that* is where they belong," I told Libby. "If we can't get rid of them, why don't we set a goal of getting them out of Wallace's building? They can sell next to the liquor store."

"That makes sense," Libby said. "Buy your alcohol and your crack at the same convenient location."

People all over Lorin and West Berkeley wanted ORCA to come chase *their* drug dealers away. The trouble was, ORCAs are expensive, and Berkeley had only one. Within hours after ORCA pulled away, the drug dealers reappeared.

The odd thing about ORCA was not knowing exactly how to act around it. If I happened to see an officer at ORCA who had been to one of our committee meetings, it was tempting to wave, or say hi, but in this war, that wasn't always safe. I just couldn't maintain an even level of paranoia. Sometimes I carefully ignored the cops, afraid to even look their way. Other times, if the street was quiet, I felt more bold and knocked on ORCA's door to talk, even offer them a plate of home-baked cookies.

At night, like a big space station, ORCA blinked and hummed while its satellite ships, the police cars, came and went. When it parked on the corner in front of our house, which was often, we felt kind of ridiculous lying in bed a few feet from it, as if we had decided to sleep in the parking lot of a police station. We didn't sleep soundly, but at least we knew there wouldn't be gunfire that night.

If ORCA was out front when our friends from other parts of town came over, they were speechless with amazement when we opened the door. "We asked them to come just for *you*," we would tell them. "We wanted you to feel safe."

Much better than ORCA, the city sent us a woman. Mahalia Peters was someone new at the police department: a community services worker. She was a social worker by training and experience, versed in mental health skills. When Mahalia introduced herself by saying that she was with the police department, I almost laughed out loud with delight and disbelief.

Here was a woman who looked every inch a shaman, the kind of woman I imagined would be an important leader in a traditional African village. Mahalia was large and beautiful and wore her long African print dresses and her beaded, braided hair and heavy necklaces as if she were born to them. She had the equanimity of a person who had done a great deal of spiritual work in her life already and was ready to do more. In meetings, she seemed able to take people's intense feelings into herself and say them back in a way that took the danger out of them. She listened, and then she would say, "I hear a lot of anger," or "I hear the fear in this."

At every meeting, she would write a list of things we wanted her to tell the police. She always called back with an answer, even if it wasn't what we wanted to hear. Mahalia came to Lorin often, usually in the afternoons when people were out on the sidewalks, and she walked, talking to everyone, knocking on doors, going into apartments to speak to people.

Mahalia's efforts with the police began to change things. Sergeant Terry Ross began to work with us regularly. Sergeant Terry, in his thirties, was a soft-spoken man who had grown up in Oakland. When he said he had become a police officer to help the community, I believed him. There was a new drug task force, he said, and it had decided to go after the Jackson brothers, but Sergeant Terry couldn't tell us what they were going to do.

Within two months, the Jacksons were both arrested! As soon as we got the news, I went down to the courthouse and read the search warrant affidavit. It told me that officers had secreted themselves in a position where they could videotape the Jacksons dealing drugs. They had then followed them to the subway as they commuted home after "work" on Alma Street. The cops had then obtained a warrant for the Jacksons' apartment miles away in Oakland, and when they searched, they arrested them with a scary arsenal of guns and ammunition, including an automatic assault rifle.

I phoned our committee; we needed to move fast. I wrote two letters: one to the police to thank them, and one to the judge who would hear the Jacksons' bail motion, asking her to make staying off Alma Street a condition of their bail.

"Those guns," I wrote, "were meant to be used on Alma Street where children live, and where there have been numerous shootings." Then I called the DA and told him we wanted him to follow through with opposing bail and to argue for the stay-away order if it was granted. Our committee signed the letter, but I mailed copies with our names omitted, because I knew it would end up in the Jacksons' court files where their lawyers could read it. Mahalia said she would confirm to the judge that we had all signed.

It worked. The judge let the Jacksons out of jail, but she ordered them to stay away. We saw them nearby in their cars, collecting their money from their employees, but they couldn't loiter on Alma Street openly. Quickly we threatened Wallace, the Jacksons' landlord, with a lawsuit if he did not evict the Jacksons' friends while they were away. We were surprised when he agreed to do it—we supposed he was fed up with the whole thing himself.

The evictions took weeks. The drug people in that building hung on, not paying rent, even after the utilities were turned off, until the day the sheriff carried their last poor belongings out onto the sidewalk. The Jacksons went to prison, and the young men who inherited their business did indeed go around the corner to the liquor store to sell, just where Libby and I had planned for them to be. They had been in that driveway next door to the Josephs robbing all of us of our sleep for five long years.

Wallace sold the building to an extended family of people newly arrived from Mexico who filled all four units. In no time, there was a nice fence and a garden, new paint and plaster. Addie and Mr. Joe were grateful. "It's so nice and peaceful," Addie said. "I can go out to my garden again."

I felt exhausted but elated. At least we had succeeded with one building on our list.

"It's great," Libby said. "But you know, at work I see people all the time like those addicts who got evicted from Wallace's building. Now they're out on the street somewhere. I wish our strategy to save our neighborhood didn't make more people homeless." All I could do was shake my head and puzzle over another unsolvable riddle: the koan of drug houses and homelessness.

Lorin seemed completely isolated from the rest of Berkeley, a world apart. Yet when the Zen center's computer was stolen in a burglary, the police found it in a drug house they raided just a block from us.

Nature had no boundaries between hills and flatlands, rich and poor. In the dry autumn of 1991 a rare hot wind from the east turned a brushfire in the Berkeley hills into a firestorm that killed more than twenty people and burned nearly five thousand homes. Stan and I walked east that night through the smoke-filled town until we reached the police lines, and we stood with a crowd in a parking lot watching orange flames sweep like a flow of lava over the trees and houses. It was terrible to think of the lost lives of people and animals, the books and paintings, Buddhas, pianos, violins—so much beauty being consumed up there.

Right after the fire, a red-tailed hawk came to my garden for the first time, a refugee from the burned hills. I heard his cry and looked up and saw him poised regally on the very top of a fir tree that normally belonged to the doves. They built their twig nests on its branches, lining them with Alaska's soft white fur.

The red-tail upset our ecosystem. He surveyed the garden from his high perch and then streaked its length, swooping low over the brick circle of herbs. The doves cowered on the ground under shrubs and the finches retreated deep into the bushes where they clung, screaming their heads off in terror.

Altars in the Street

CHAPTER THIRTEEN

How Will It Ever End?

I was working at my computer one afternoon when I glanced out the window and saw a gaggle of well-dressed white people, most of them holding clipboards and pens, stepping along the sidewalk close together, looking around in every direction, conferring with each other and making notes. I stepped out on my porch.

"Are you people studying our neighborhood?" I wanted to know.

"Well—yes," a nice-looking woman in a wool skirt and blazer admitted. They weren't eager to answer my questions, but they had no reason to lie, either. It turned out they were from a San Francisco city planning firm hired as consultants to make plans for our area.

In our committee, we couldn't believe we had tried so hard to get city hall to listen and then they had spent money to hire outsiders to take a look at us without talking to us.

Berkeley has an extensive sister city program. "Maybe Lorin should secede," I told our committee, "and apply to become a sister city. Then they could send us aid—maybe open a drug clinic."

When the mayor issued her plan for the drug war, the result of the city planners' study, we had to admit it was our wish list: drug treatment, activities and jobs for teens, economic development of our business streets. It couldn't have been better if we had written it ourselves. At the meeting in her office, however, she said they hadn't found funding for it yet. We could see she was trying, though.

She sent us some fresh help from the city staff. At our next committee meeting, Shyaam Shabaka introduced himself. "I'm here to work with the young people," he said, "to see if I can help them stay out of trouble."

Shyaam, a slim and fit brown-skinned man about my age, already knew some of the people at our meeting, because he had worked for the city for a long time. Shyaam had a master's degree in public health from UC Berkeley and years of experience working with families. When we talked, we found we had a lot of the same memories of the civil rights movement in the Bay Area. We had even both been at the same demonstrations to integrate hotel and restaurant staffs in 1966.

With some donated tickets and a city van, Shyaam started his work with the children of Alma Street by taking them to a football game. Since I knew most of the kids, I volunteered to get the adults' permission. The neediest kids had parents on drugs, and it didn't work to drop off a form to be signed. I had to catch those parents in the mood to open the door and have them sign right there. After repeated visits to some places, I managed to get permission for all the kids who wanted to go.

When the day came, Shyaam pulled the van up to the barricade where a dozen kids were waiting.

"Are we going to play football, Melody?" Jamal asked me.

"No, we're *watching* it," Dondi answered, lifting him up into the van. "You'll see."

After that trip, Shyaam and his staff took the kids camping and fishing and to parks. Amina went along to a black history exhibit at the Oakland Museum. "Shyaam is great," she said. "He's really good with the kids."

Our committee made its own plans for Alma Street. We decided to join the city tree planting program. "They don't deal drugs on nice-looking, landscaped streets," Libby said. "Besides, it's free." Men from the public works department came and cut squares in the sidewalk for us, reaming out holes with a machine that looked like a big screw. On planting day, we invited the mayor. She showed up in a sweatshirt and jeans and helped the kids plant the trees. I made tags for the trees, a poem on each one, and the kids gave each tree a name. "Hi, my name's Greenie. I'm special, lovely, new and neat, just like the kids on Alma

Street." If we made the trees seem more like people, I thought, maybe the kids would let them live.

Amina took photos. There was one of Jamal grinning next to Dondi pointing to the sign on a sapling named Kermit. Smiling behind the children were Shyaam and the mayor and our city councilwoman Maudelle with her white Afro hairdo, their arms linked. Behind them, tall and looking happy, was Ruth, holding Libby's little girl Aurora on one hip and her own new baby boy on the other. Leaning in from the side of the photo was Libby with a madcap expression and dirt on her chin.

But in spite of all our efforts, when night fell on Alma Street, the outlaws took over, and we stayed inside.

The users woke up in the late afternoon and gathered on the sidewalk, drinking. Then, after work, there was a rush hour of drug buyers who came in cars from outside the neighborhood. Dealing continued all night, the addicts walking to get their drugs, lookouts whistling a warning if a cop car was about to drive by.

The big drug delivery was brought in sometime in the wee hours, when only a few police were on duty in the whole city. Sometimes, unable to sleep, I would see it happen. A dozen lookouts, mostly skeletal addicts, would come out, one on every corner. Then a rental car or a van would pull cautiously into view and stop just for a minute while someone ran out of a crack house and a quick exchange took place.

As dawn broke, the addicts began to drift away as homeless people rumbled past with their shopping carts, taking loads of recyclables to sell. By 7:30, a happy interracial group of children and mothers, some holding babies, had gathered catty-corner from our house waiting for the school bus to take the little kids out of Lorin under Berkeley's racial integration plan. Around school bus time, the people with jobs started to leave for work. But as the sound of the lookout whistles became more common, the sound of car engines starting up in the morning to carry people to work diminished.

At 8:00 A.M. the Arab store opened, and housewives and the unemployed passed by and gathered at the mailbox in front of Mr. Howard's closed store to talk. Around that time I went out to sweep almost every morning.

How Will It Ever End?

If I was working on my computer at home, in midafternoon I would hear the school bus pull up and the voices of the returning children. By that time, the brown-bag drinkers were back outside, and the night shift got started all over again. Right around dark, the law-abiding people disappeared inside again.

Our paranoia rose and fell like the ocean tides. It was impossible to get a firm grasp on how frightened to feel. We talked about it at our meetings. In this war, the disputed territory went block by block. People just two or three blocks away sometimes told me, "Things aren't bad here at all, but I've heard terrible things about Alma Street."

We read in the papers that a man who was standing in his kitchen was killed by a stray bullet. I heard of a woman who went into her bedroom to dress. A shot rang out outside, and later the woman's sister found her dead—that one shot had hit her in the head. None of us could ever quite believe something like that would happen to us. Still, people put their children to sleep in the rear of their dwellings, away from the street, if they could.

Our committee's lawsuit against the owners of the Green Gables apartment building had been dragging on. The building still harbored crack users and still went unrepaired. At last the court date arrived. I was out of town, working. Libby and Potter led our committee's presentation. To our surprise, we won: we split a total judgment of $30,000 among nineteen plaintiffs. We each got handy little checks from the landlord's insurance company after we paid our lawyer Dave, one of our members, for his trouble.

We didn't want our photos in the paper, but pictures of the posters Libby had made to show the judge appeared in the news. She had taped syringes found in the Green Gables parking garage onto poster board and photos of the drug people loitering there. Some of the truly brave residents of the Green Gables had testified against the landlord, as plaintiffs, and they got money too.

The Green Gables drug dealers seemed to exist in a world different from ours. They didn't read court transcripts, and they didn't read newspapers either. There was no retaliation against us for the suit.

The settlement caused the owner to sell the Green Gables, and two ambitious contractors in their thirties bought it: Peter, who was black, and Max, who was white. Peter moved in to manage the building. They put in a fence, lights, and a lawn, and painted the building yellow—we couldn't even call it Green Gables anymore. We had proved that a good landlord can make a building safe. We had a victory, and credibility.

The trouble was, by that time the crack trade was so well established on Alma Street that the Green Gables dealers emptied themselves out onto the sidewalks and kept right on selling. The women involved with them moved to other nearby apartments and kept right on providing safe haven to the dealers.

One drug group got into a building across from Potter Woods. "They're like cockroaches," Potter said bitterly at a meeting, making me wince. I wouldn't have called people cockroaches myself. "You can spray over here," Potter said, "but they'll just run over there."

"This is my last meeting," Potter suddenly said.

There was silence. "I've got me a gun, and I'm telling them: If they stand in front of my house, I will kill them. Period. Other than that, I don't care what they do. You're still my neighbors, and I give you my blessing. But no more meetings for me." And Potter got up and walked out the church door. We sat quietly.

Then Pearl, in a low voice, said, "How will it ever end?" She looked so small on her folding chair, and the lines in her face looked deep.

"Someday, this is going to be over," I said more bravely than I felt. "This *will* end. We'll be saying, 'Remember the crack time, how it was back then?' and we'll shake our heads and laugh a little sadly. But it'll be over."

"That's like saying television will end," Louis the bus driver said. "It's been invented—there's no going back."

"It'll end because people like ourselves will see that it ruins our lives and brain-damages our babies," Shyaam said. "The young people will refuse to touch it. Black people, who have overcome being stolen from Africa, and slavery, and segregation, are not going to be destroyed by a drug."

"That's what I think," Libby said. "Is our consumer culture so strong that whole peoples and their histories can be destroyed by guns, alcohol, and cocaine?

"Look at tobacco," she went on. "That's hopeful—now people don't want smoking in planes and restaurants—that's education. Education works."

Stan hadn't bought a gun, but he also had told me he didn't want to come to any more meetings. He felt as if the losing battle for Alma Street was dominating his life. "It's hard enough to live in the neighborhood without struggling about it all the time," he said. "When I have free time, I want to spend it *away* from here, doing positive things." Libby's husband, Jim, felt the same way. We were becoming a committee of women, except for Mr. Joe, Louis the bus driver, and Saul Schwartz.

I sat on Libby's lumpy couch watching Aurora roar around the living room with her little plastic shopping cart full of toys. "It's not as if Stan and Jim aren't right," Libby said. "Potter was exactly right. He said the crack houses would just move, and they did. We can't sustain the energy we put into the Green Gables suit if all we get for it is a little money."

"The dealers can adapt to anything we do," I said. "After all, they're businessmen—they design new marketing schemes all the time."

"Yeah, well, we're adapting to *them*," Libby said. "Look at us! We drive our cars on new routes to get home, because of all the barricades. We've imprisoned ourselves with all these burglar alarms and car alarms and locks and bars on our windows."

"Libby, have you ever thought about the fact that no one ever takes a burglar alarm *out* again?" I asked her.

"Oh, yeah, like the day would come when we'd say, Hallelujah, the war's over, we can get rid of all the alarms now!" she said.

"*I* want to get rid of the alar-um," Aurora said.

"I know you do, sweetie," Libby said, pulling Aurora onto her lap. "Melody, my new motto is, Just keep breathing and don't buy a gun."

CHAPTER FOURTEEN

Hello, My Anger

I think my best-ever day in American race relations was the sunny Saturday when Stan and I went to greet Nelson Mandela, free at last and coming to Oakland, and it seemed as if the whole world was going with us. Stan and I held hands and gave ourselves up to being pressed along by the people of every shade of skin surging into the baseball stadium as if we were one joyful organism, shuffling along on our thousands of feet.

We had dreamed, but never really believed, that apartheid would end within our lifetime, and that the achievement of one-person, one-vote would be largely a nonviolent change. "It's like with the end of the cold war," Stan said. "We can have all kinds of ideas or fears about how things are going to happen, but really, we can't predict what human beings will do."

I tried to hold on to my memories of our great day together with Nelson Mandela when I saw the TV tape of the Los Angeles police beating Rodney King. A few days after the beating I heard one African-American kid on Alma Street say to another, "I'm going to Rodney Fucking King your butt!" and Jarvis said he'd heard that new threat too, at the prison. "Now *that's* internalized oppression!" Jarvis said.

I hadn't seen Reverend Clara for a long time, but she didn't come to all our committee meetings, and I assumed she was working hard on her dissertation. I left some messages on her home answering machine, but I didn't get a call.

Finally she phoned late in the summer of 1991 to tell me that her son Frankie, the handsome young man in the military uniform in the pictures on the wall of her study, had died.

"Oh, Clara," I said, "I'm so sorry."

"He was in the war in the gulf," she said.

"And he was killed?" I asked.

"No, he lived through all that. It was after the war, on his way home. He was in Virginia," she said.

"Oh, I'm so sorry. What happened to him?" I asked.

"He was shot, no one knows why. It was just a random bullet while he was riding in a car. There was no reason. No one was caught."

"Was this in the papers?" I asked her. "I read about a young man killed right after the war."

"Just a small article," she said in a small voice. "Frankie was one of several Gulf War soldiers killed in America. There wasn't much news about it."

Reverend Clara took more time off, and then resumed her ministry. She was thinner, and tired looking, and in our talks in her study, she sometimes seemed angry.

"I blame black people," she said. "We have to take responsibility for ourselves. We have to *raise* our sons, teach them to protect life, not to take it."

"You're right," I said.

"And I don't agree with the white liberals in my congregation," she said, eyeing me sternly, "who want to talk about people as victims all the time, and excuse their behavior."

"Clara, I don't want to make excuses for anybody. People should not be doing wrong. I am trying to understand *why* they are doing it."

The Vietnamese monk Thich Nhat Hanh sat cross-legged on the stage at Berkeley High School, looking out at the packed auditorium, and said that he had been so angry when the bombing started in the Gulf War that he had decided on the spot not to come to America. He added that the beating of Rodney King, soon after the war, also made him want to stay at his home in France.

I was glad to hear that Thich Nhat Hanh sometimes got hopping mad like me—and irrational—since, after all, most of us hoping to hear his teachings wanted nonviolence. The Pentagon and the LAPD probably wouldn't mind if he hadn't come.

"At least my anger is in good company," I thought. "He's not saying not to *get* angry. He's telling us what to do with it."

I was up in the balcony of the theater, and from there Thich Nhat Hanh looked like a tiny Buddha statue placed on a Persian rug far below.

"Make friends with our anger," he said. "Say, 'Hello, my little anger. You are my friend. I'll take good care of you.' Breathing in, I say hello to my anger. Breathing out, I embrace it."

Thich Nhat Hanh said we all have positive seeds of love, peace, and joy in us, and we can water those. We also have seeds of anger, despair, hatred, violence, and fear in us, he said. The more these negative seeds are watered, the stronger they will become in our minds.

"Television, with its violent images," Thich Nhat Hanh said, "can water our negative seeds every day."

A year later, home alone in the morning, I turned on the TV to watch Los Angeles burn after the Rodney King police trial verdict. "Hello, my little despair," I thought. I was sitting on our living room couch, the warm spring sunshine revealing a fuzzy web of Alaska's long white dog hair on our threadbare rug. It was an ordinary day, and I could have been vacuuming, or gardening, but America was coming apart.

When I'd heard the verdict on the radio, I'd pulled my car over and beat my hands on the steering wheel in frustration. Pam said, "I was sitting at my desk when I heard the verdict and I wanted to get up and throw my chair through the window. Melody, very bad things are going to come of this."

Over and over the screen replayed the helicopter camera film of three young black men pulling Reginald Denny out of his truck and beating him.

"They're acting out the video of the police beating Rodney King," I thought. "They're doing what we've all seen on TV dozens of times."

Suddenly shots rang out very close, right outside on the corner. I dropped to my hands and knees onto the rug and crawled fast to the phone in the hall.

"Who is shooting?" the dispatcher asked me.

"I don't know," I gasped, starting to cry.

"Can you look outside and see anyone?" she persisted.

"No! No I can't!" I sobbed into the phone. "I'm too scared to look out! Just send the police!"

As soon as I hung up, the phone rang again, and it was Stan, at his law office. "Stay inside," he said.

"I am! I'm not moving."

He'd called to tell me that a big march of high school students was on the freeway blocking the traffic and coming toward his office building. He said in case the building burned he was going to put his computer in his car and drive home on the streets, not the freeway.

I stayed on the floor in the hall until after I heard cars pull up and voices outside talking. After a while, I could hear Skeeter's laugh, and Pearl's querulous tone. I looked out. There were two police cars and a little knot of neighbors.

I went out and joined them. Pearl and Skeeter were shaking their heads and complaining, saying, "It's terrible," and, "It's stupid."

"It was just some guy shooting at another dude," said Skeeter. "If they get mad, they shoot, that's how they do."

"You mean this isn't the beginning of the end of the world after all?" I said, wiping my damp cheeks with the flat of my hand. "I just about had a heart attack."

Skeeter looked at me closely. "Are you okay?" he asked. "Did you get scared it's going to be a riot here?"

"Well, yes, it crosses a person's mind," I answered. What had crossed my mind, I had to admit to myself, was a split second of fear that someone black would attack me because I was white—a very American fear that white Americans, like white South Africans, are heir to, even though almost all the violence is black on black, or white on black.

"Nope," Skeeter said. "Just some little old dope thing. I don't think any riot's going to happen up here, though who knows why not."

No one was hit, and both the shooter and the target had run off. The police never found anybody to arrest. Skeeter trundled off up the street stepping heavily on his small feet that always seemed too delicate for his round body. Pearl and I stood around talking and then headed back inside.

"If we're not having a riot right here," she said, "we might as well go on inside and watch the one on television. I think it's pitiful."

When the march that passed by Stan's office building reached downtown, they held a peaceful rally, led by religious leaders of all faiths. We were surprised to learn later that Rosemary and her girlfriends had joined a march down the freeway in the opposite direction and had sat down and blocked the Bay Bridge.

"It was one of the most wonderful demonstrations I've ever been to," Rosemary said. "All races mixed together, and completely peaceful." Afterward a few stragglers had set fire to a police car, and that was featured on the news.

Lil was desperately worried about her son who was living in Los Angeles. She couldn't reach him by phone for a day. When she did, he said he had been out at peaceful interracial demonstrations. "He said the peaceful events weren't reported," Lil said.

Elyse told me that the students at the junior high poured out of the classrooms when they heard of the verdict. The teachers had invited them into the auditorium and helped them to make protest posters and then allowed them to march to the Berkeley police station where our African-American chief of police made a speech to them.

"He was great," Elyse said. "He talked to them about police brutality and about how Berkeley has a police review board. He was critical of the verdict," Elyse said.

"You were helping the kids say hello to their anger," I told her.

The news report about Los Angeles that stayed with me longest was about a black-owned, black-run social service center that was burned to the ground by black people. I saw an interview with the people who had run the place. Standing among the ruins, they said they had been there twenty years, working to provide food, classes, job training for the neighborhood. We could have used a center like that for Lorin, I thought.

"It's suicide," Pam said. "It's just like one black man killing another. You're killing yourself, you're killing your hope."

CHAPTER FIFTEEN

Bypassing the Heart

Melody, I have to tell you some bad news," Libby said on the phone. "I'm pretty sure Ruth is on crack."

"Ruth? How can she be? I haven't seen Ruth for ages. What makes you think so?"

Libby said Ruth's husband hadn't been working. They had been fighting, and he had left her. Libby knew Ruth had been drinking. Then Libby had seen Ruth down by the liquor store where crack was sold too many times in a row.

It was days before I saw Ruth myself, strolling up the street with her baby boy on her hip and a bottle in a sack, looking loose and slightly disheveled.

"Maybe she's not on crack," I thought. "She doesn't look good, but she's not thin." Ruth stopped by my hedge and peered through the leaves at me.

"Hi, Melody," she said.

"How are you, Ruth? I'm worried you're having a hard time."

"I am, honey. I just can't keep it together right now, you know. But I'll get it together, you know I will."

"I'll pray for you, Ruth, every day," I told her, by which I meant that when I meditated, I would think of her with loving kindness.

I decided to talk to Libby about Ruth. She was an expert on substance abuse; she worked as a counselor and drama therapist at a halfway house for drug addicts in the next county.

"What does it really take to get off crack?" I asked her.

"It's medically tricky," Libby said. "Most crack addicts need anti-depressants at least, and therapy, and support starting a new life. The withdrawal can be easy at first, but about two or three weeks into it, the craving gets incredibly intense. And for a long time, if they see anyone doing it, the craving is extreme."

"That's why people start again when they come back to Alma Street from jail," I said.

"The biggest pull on them to start again is the pain of getting sober and seeing what they've done to their lives," she said. "They don't own anything anymore, the kids have been taken away—they can go into a major depression. It can seem like there's nothing left to stay sober for."

"But some people say they just kick it on their own. How do they do that?"

"A lot of those people are talking about an *episode* with drugs—a one-time, under-stress type of thing," she said, "like during a divorce."

"Why don't they stay hooked?"

"Something pulls them back—like a job, or an important relationship. Some chronic addicts can beat it by joining AA, or NA, but there has to be something pulling on them—some strong motive like keeping custody of their kids. Even that might not work if they're too depressed to try. Recovery is a lot of work, and most people have to try two times—or four times—to get these programs to work." She paused. "How's your sister doing?"

"Better," I was glad to say.

Naomi had been fighting her own drug war. She'd been divorced from her cocaine and alcohol-using husband and started a relationship with a man she met in AA. "She says no one but another recovering addict can really understand what she's going through," I told Libby.

Things were better now between me and Naomi; she drank, but she wasn't always drunk. Sometimes we could talk about it, and that made all the difference. One day at a time, I was getting my sister back.

"What about supporting Ruth? Isn't the way to help the kids to help the mother?"

"Well, we can, but she might not go into treatment, or she might not stay. These programs are set up all wrong, with waiting lists. What crack addicts need is a place to go on demand, on the day they decide they need help, before they change their minds and get loaded again. If they don't get help, this is really a progressive condition—you don't just go along as a crack addict—it gets worse and worse until something happens, and it's usually something bad."

"What's the deal with smoking crack? Why is it more addictive than snorting it or taking speed in a pill?"

"It goes straight from the lungs to the brain in six seconds flat. It bypasses the heart."

CHAPTER SIXTEEN

Cells for Seven-Year-Olds

The last thing I wanted to be was one of George Bush's Thousand Points of Light. Why should I volunteer *my* time in an underfunded school while he spent *his* time cutting the education budget?

But Amina wanted me to. She had moved to San Francisco to be closer to the state university where she was majoring in American Studies.

"Sweetheart, I hope somebody hires you to study America," I told her.

Amina's plan was, she would take the subway to Alma Street twice a week. She and I would each tutor one pupil at our neighborhood school, Malcolm X, where there was a new after-school program. Afterward, she would come home for dinner. This way, she would get teaching experience and two free meals a week. "And get to see you, of course," she added as a bonus.

There were about forty adults at the orientation session in the school library, gathered from three sources. A third were employees of Kaiser Corporation, which had released them, with pay, for four hours a week to tutor. Another group were college students like Amina, the majority of them young people of color. As they were introduced, almost every one of the students said he or she had come from a neighborhood like this one and wanted to help other kids like themselves. Most of these angels said they were working at part-time jobs as well.

I didn't have to say anything, since Amina went first, and introduced me. "And that's my mom," she said, pointing at me. I was part of the group of volunteers from the community, most of us women, many retired.

Our pupils were randomly assigned. Two little boys, African-American fourth-graders, were entrusted to Amina and me. We met their beleaguered teacher, Mrs. Chambers, a soft-spoken, motherly African-American woman who lived with her husband in the hills north of the university.

Amina had Gideon, or rather, he had her. It was obvious, looking at the two of them putting their heads together at a desk, that this was a love-at-first-sight match. Gideon was a beautiful child with an infectious smile whose bright eyes had a wise-beyond-his-years expression. He was a favorite with Mrs. Chambers because, she said, he was such a smart boy, but he was failing the fourth grade, mostly because he had trouble paying attention. He needed individual help, and the one he got it from was Amina.

My pupil Jeron was less of a class star, a shy, lanky boy almost my height. Jeron was so soft-spoken I had to bend close to hear his voice. Reading was pain for him. The first day, assessing his skills, I realized he was reading haltingly at the second-grade level. "How does a kid fall two full years behind when he's only been in school for four?" I wondered to Amina.

I suggested to Jeron that we both draw pictures of our families to get acquainted. Jeron drew himself, his sister, who was across the room with her own tutor, and two adults: "My grandmother," he said, placing a careful finger on each figure, "and my grandfather."

"You don't live with your mom or dad, Jeron?" I ventured. He didn't look at me, and with downcast eyes, shook his head no.

Amina's new friend Gideon lived in an apartment right on Alma Street, with an aunt and several cousins. He told Amina his father stayed there too, but he made no mention of his mother.

We wondered: Prison? Dead? On the streets on drugs? But we didn't ask. Their closed faces told us that somehow these children's parents had disappeared in the drug war.

Jeron spoke a thick dialect of southern-accented Black English. He understood perfectly what I called "television English" as spoken by me and Amina and his teacher. But he didn't speak it. I could understand him, but I overheard a lot of the corporate tutors saying, "What?" to their pupils at first.

I had lived in the neighborhood and worked in the prisons around black people who spoke southern dialects and other dialects for all these many years, but I had not learned how to speak like that myself. Nobody expected me to, and a lot of people would have been offended if I had tried to imitate the way they talked. Yet Jeron would quickly need to master *our* way of talking and also learn to write it if he were to do well in school.

The longer I worked with Jeron, the more I admired him. At nine, he had a firm belief that school was good for him and an innocent hope for himself that I prayed would never be defeated. He never missed a day of tutoring, though I sometimes did because of my job. On those days Jeron joined Gideon and Amina.

To practice reading, Jeron and I moved to a battered couch in a corner of the room. I brought the few second-grade level library books I could find on sports, Jeron's love. But anyone could see that they were big, flat, babyish books, and he was ashamed to be seen with them. So I brought the sports section of the newspaper, and after we enjoyed that, we conspired to hide our books behind it.

Jeron's frustration slid him so low that he sank until his wiggly spine was on the couch cushion, his chin was on his chest, and I was awkwardly holding the book up on his stomach. "Oh-oh, Jeron, you're horizontal again," I'd say, and he'd groan and dig his elbows into the couch to hunch himself upright and start again. He didn't make an excuse to leave the room as some kids did. He kept trying, "renewing his intention," as we said at the Zen center. As the abbot said to do with meditation, Jeron "just showed up," put his restless self on the couch, and learned to read.

There got to be a warm and cozy feeling in that library, all of us working among the shelves of books, sitting at tables or on the carpet. Within the sea of violence in the neighborhood around it, Malcolm X

School was an island of safety. Jeron and I relaxed together, him droning on, me running my finger along under the words, my mind wandering ten years ahead to his possible future.

By the time these children turned seventeen, I knew, thousands more cells would be ready in California, and I only hoped Jeron could manage to stay out of one. If he spent years of his life in one of the new prisons, it would seem as if everything had gone according to plan.

One day in the Malcolm X library, looking around at the pairs of adults and kids working together, Jeron said, "I wish this was real school."

He's absolutely right, I thought. A ratio closer to one-to-one than Mrs. Chambers's thirty-two-to-one would be more like education.

The tutoring program provided a snack: crackers, apples, and juice. Jeron ate his snack or left it, like most of the other kids. But Gideon always drank his juice and put his fruit or cookies into his jacket pocket. Amina always gave him hers too, and he pocketed that food too. I tried offering him mine, and it went into his pocket. We got the impression there wasn't going to be any dinner at home.

The tutors were supposed to walk the kids home through the dangerous neighborhood—that was part of the program. Since Jeron's grandfather picked him up every day in a big sedan, I walked with Gideon and Amina to Alma Street.

Gideon, unlike Jeron, was completely bilingual: he could call out to people he knew in heavily accented slang and then turn his head and speak in TV English to Amina and me. He wasn't smarter than Jeron, but he was gifted with linguistic ability.

Amina tried to introduce herself at the apartment where Gideon was living. His aunt turned out to be a skinny young woman with bloodshot eyes named Angela who poked her head out of the door of the gloomy ground-floor apartment briefly, said hello vaguely to Amina, and didn't smile. Gideon waved good-bye and disappeared inside.

It didn't take much to find out that Gideon was living in a bad situation. My old-man friend Hiram lived right across the street. As soon as I mentioned Gideon, he said, "Oh, Angela's nephew—that's a crack house."

Gideon's Aunt Angela had two kids of her own: Terrel, thirteen, and DeShawn, five. Angela's tough-looking boyfriend whose name was

Askari lived with her too, and *his* eleven-year-old son made four children, all boys, living in the one-bedroom apartment with three adults: Angela and her boyfriend Askari and Angela's brother, who was Gideon's dad. Everybody called Amina's pupil "little Gideon," and his dad "big Gideon."

"See, now, this is why I didn't want to get started on this," I harangued Amina as we cooked our dinner. "I agree to give three hours a week, and I end up worrying day and night about a whole houseful of hungry kids."

I washed lettuce furiously. Above my sink, lost in my splashing, was a quote I had framed from a famous Zen chef: "May I awaken to what this task offers."

Amina, at the table, glanced my way and kept on neatly cutting vegetables. Her reputation as the calm person in the family has been secure since the minute she was born, took a look around, and yawned.

I raved on, tearing handfuls of lettuce as if I were ripping up an old sheet to make bandages. "It's like I put one toe into the water, and I wind up sucked down into a seething whirlpool."

Amina cut a carrot in two lengthwise. "Well, we wouldn't want *that*, would we?" she said drily.

Mrs. Chambers had no idea what Gideon's home was like, and it wasn't our job to tell her. He came to school reasonably well dressed—up to the standard of the neighborhood. Gideon never talked about life in Angela's apartment, but he talked about his grandmother all the time, and someday he wanted to go back to Atlanta to see her. He had lived with his grandmother until his father had brought him to California from Georgia, and she regularly mailed boxes of clothing to him and his cousins. When Amina took a picture of Gideon, he brought his grandmother's address to school in his childish printing. Amina helped him write a letter to his grandmother to go with the photo.

Gideon started coming over to our house. He would ring the bell and when I opened it, there he was with his dazzling smile; behind him, with his fingers in his mouth, would be shy DeShawn, Gideon's five-year-old cousin and sidekick. "Is Amina home?" they would say in unison. She hardly ever was, but if I wasn't too busy, I would let them in to play and eat. They joined the crew that played in our garden that year.

On our weekly dog walk in the hills, Elyse mentioned Gideon's cousin Terrel out of the blue: "One of your neighbor kids came up in a meeting this week," she said. "The counselor from the other junior high said that a boy named Terrel from Alma Street was being suspended for bringing a knife to school."

Sure enough, I saw Terrel out in the street all day every day during school hours. I phoned Shyaam: "What is the deal, Shyaam, with kids suspended from school? Isn't there anything for them to do but hang out around the drug dealers?"

Shyaam said he would come over and talk to Terrel. Somehow, he found an informal foster home for Terrel with an openhearted white couple he knew, and Angela agreed to the plan.

I marveled at how resourceful Shyaam was. He had all sorts of contacts and ways of trying to keep kids out of trouble and out of the court system.

My relationship with Angela improved. I went to see her regularly to get her to sign permission slips for the kids to go on outings with Shyaam. When I did that, I would linger in the doorway of her tiny, dark apartment, and we would talk. It was easy to see in her face that she loved her kids, even if I couldn't see it most of the time in her actions. She always thanked me sincerely for helping the kids, and she was pretty open about her problems.

"I've got to get away from all this mess," she said. "I came up here from Atlanta to get away from crack."

"Where could you go?" I asked her.

"I don't know, maybe Oakland."

"Well, there's crack in Oakland too, Angela," I told her.

"I know," she said, sounding hopeless.

From the distance of San Quentin, Jarvis loved to hear about the tutoring project and the lives of the children on Alma Street. Once Jarvis heard that Gideon was living in a drug house, he identified with him completely. Gideon, Jarvis was sure, was threatened by all the adults around him not to tell anything about his home life.

"That's how it was for me," Jarvis said. "If you have drug parents, they don't care what you do, as long as you don't bring any police around."

"You know, Jarvis," I told him, "maybe *inside* his apartment Gideon's childhood is like yours was, but *outside*, the level of violence makes it nothing like when you grew up in the seventies. I don't think either you or I can imagine what it's like to be born right into a war. Gideon has never known anything else."

It was certainly true that as much as Gideon loved Amina, he did not open up to her about his life at home. Whenever she was home, Amina invited Gideon and DeShawn into the house and brought puzzles and games up from the basement for them, and did extra reading practice with Gideon, finishing off with a snack. Summer or winter, the children always wanted exactly what they had eaten the first time they had come over: cinnamon toast and hot chocolate.

Five-year-old DeShawn would accuse me if I changed anything: "You moved this!" he would say disapprovingly. He wanted to count on every chair and vase being in the same place when he came back. He would stand on my grandson Benji's step stool at the cutting board in the kitchen and carefully spread butter, then brown sugar, right out to the edge of his toast, and then solemnly sprinkle on the cinnamon.

Occasionally I would see Gideon's father, "big Gideon," coming or going from Angela's. He was a tall, thin man with a patchy goatee.

One day Skeeter was huffing and puffing, helping me in the garden, when he told me that big Gideon was gone. There was a warrant out for his arrest for burglary. He had broken into a house only a block away, Skeeter said, and the police had found fingerprints that identified him. Big Gideon had disappeared, leaving little Gideon behind in Angela's care.

At school, Gideon said nothing about it. He still smiled, but he looked worried when his face was at rest.

"He's not going to say *nothing*," Jarvis told me later. "He knows not to tell. He'd rather not *eat* than tell."

Angela's boyfriend Askari was a menacing presence on Alma Street. He walked around like a gunslinging cowboy and hardly ever spoke. If he answered the door when I went to Angela's to say something to her about the kids, he simply turned away, without saying one word to me.

Pam and I had had several clients in prison with the chosen Swahili name Askari. I asked Pam, "Do you remember what Askari means?"

She was in one of her mischievous moods, and she made her voice deep and serious. "It's Swahili for 'He Who Goes to the Joint!' " she intoned, and then she dissolved into giggles.

"Pam!" I said, shocked at her.

"I'm just trying to keep my sense of humor here!" she cried. "Okay, okay, it means 'soldier.' "

Everyone on Alma Street knew Askari hit Angela. One afternoon I was in my garden when Angela was walking by with a bruised face, and I heard Louis the bus driver yell at Askari, "Hey, Pancake Batter!"

"Fuck you, motherfucker," Askari yelled back.

"Yeah, and in your face!" Louis replied, not skipping a beat. "Your name's Pancake 'til you quit your battering!"

In the spring of our tutoring year, the children in Mrs. Chambers' class were selling candy to raise money for the kind of educational field trip that had been free when I was a schoolchild, and even when I was a teacher. The class was going to a historical state park to spend two nights, and each child had to raise fifty dollars for the bus, meals, and park fees. Gideon had to sell fifty candy bars door-to-door to go. We bought candy—the whole block committee bought candy—and Gideon told Amina one afternoon that he had sold all fifty of his.

The next morning early, before school, Gideon arrived at my door in tears, shaking with fear. I had never seen him cry before. His story came out in sobs. While he slept the money had been stolen from the pocket of his jacket which he had put under his head. Gideon and I both knew that a member of his household had taken the money and that it was now irretrievably spent on alcohol and drugs. But we didn't say that.

He managed to explain that he was frightened because he thought he owed Mrs. Chambers fifty dollars. "I don't care about the trip no more," he kept saying. "I don't even care about the trip."

There comes a time in my long interviews with all my death row clients when each of them, talking about his childhood, says something like, "After that, I just didn't care anymore."

I looked at Gideon standing shaking in my front hall, and I thought, This could be that day for him.

I took Gideon by the hand, walked him to school, and explained to Mrs. Chambers that the money was gone. It was Gideon who, to my surprise, told her that it was taken away from him at home. She told him not to worry, that her church members had loaned her the money to buy the candy. He didn't have to pay it back.

"But how can his money be taken from his own house at night?" she asked me privately. I just shrugged. I knew that anything told to teachers that sounded like child abuse had to be reported by them to Children's Protective Services.

Elyse often told me of her agonies over the fate of children whose abusive homes were reported to her. "I'm legally required to call," she often told me, "but so many times I don't want to."

"My husband and I have enough to donate the money for Gideon to go on the trip," I told Mrs. Chambers. "Would that be okay?"

It would.

Amina decided to loan Gideon her own sleeping bag and an eating kit. I went over to the school on the morning of the field trip to help Mrs. Chambers put name tags on piles of kids' belongings, so I was there in the roomful of excited kids to see Gideon beam with pride when Amina showed up with his equipment and helped him to pack it into the backpack she loaned him too.

"What do you think, Elyse," I asked her on our next dog walk. "Will Gideon remember the trauma of having the candy money stolen, or the joy of the overnight trip?"

"He'll probably remember the trauma," Elyse said, "and have some lasting shame attached to it. I don't know about the field trip, but I bet he'll remember Amina and feeling loved by her. And that might make the difference."

"Amina adores that little boy," I said. "Elyse, why is it a secret that the key to happiness is helping other people?"

Jarvis didn't want the kids to be put into foster care as he had been as a child. He thought it was better for Gideon to stay on Alma Street around his cousins and Mrs. Chambers and Amina, and I agreed with him, but I was worried.

But Skeeter, who lived in the apartment upstairs from Angela, finally tried on his own to have the kids taken away. Skeeter saw Mahalia making her rounds on Alma Street and told her that DeShawn, five, and

Gideon, nine, were being left alone at night. I had seen that myself. Sometimes if DeShawn was at my house, he would ask me to walk him home. When we got there, sometimes no one was home, and little De-Shawn would say, "Maybe she's on Sacramento," meaning the street where Angela could be buying crack or alcohol.

Skeeter had told Mahalia that he could smell the crack Angela and her friends were smoking coming up through the floorboards of his apartment, and then he could hear the kids up almost all night, because they were getting high too, from the fumes. He also told Mahalia that the kids were hungry and he was sick of giving them bread and butter and cereal and milk to eat from his own refrigerator.

That did it. Mahalia called Children's Protective Services. Some police arrived, with Mahalia and another social worker. No adults were in the house, but thirteen-year-old Terrel was at home when they came, and no drugs were found, so the kids were left. Mahalia explained to me later that a thirteen-year-old in the house counts as enough supervision.

Skeeter had already threatened Angela to her face to call CPS on her, so she knew he was the one who did it. I was over at Hiram's across the street when we heard them yelling and watched out Hiram's open kitchen door: Skeeter was upstairs on his balcony yelling at Angela, who stood down in the driveway yelling back.

"You keep out of my business, Skeeter, I know you called the police on me."

"Damn right I called, and I'll call some more too, if you leave them kids again, and let 'em go hungry."

"You mess with my kids, that's death row," she yelled. "That's death row, Skeeter!"

"What's she mean by that?" I asked Hiram.

"She means, she doesn't care if she has to kill him and go to death row to keep him out of her business," Hiram said.

"Wait a minute," I said. "You're telling me that if a person says 'death row,' they're saying they're willing to go there if that's what it takes?"

When I told that to Jarvis, he couldn't believe it.

"*Wow*," he said. "Now *there's* something I've never heard before. So much for deterrence!"

I didn't know about DeShawn's birthday until I saw him on the sidewalk as I was climbing my front steps, tired out from work. "Melody, I'm six!" he said.

After supper, I rummaged around our basement until I found six things: four little plastic toys, a magnet, and a little flashlight on a key chain. I found DeShawn in front of his building and handed him the box. I helped him spell out the writing on top: "6 things for a nice boy who is 6." He ripped it open. "Thanks!" he threw over his shoulder as he tore up the street to show the other kids.

"So, DeShawn," I asked him a week later. "What else did you get for your birthday?"

"Nothing," he said, not sounding sad. "Just my six from you, Melody."

I was sorry I'd asked. I kept thinking, no cake?

The school year came to a close, and at the pizza party in the school basement, the teachers pronounced the tutoring program a success. Both Gideon and Jeron had made a lot of progress, and Amina took a photo of Jeron with me, both of us smiling proudly.

That summer, Mahalia and Reverend Clara and I planned for a special meeting to be held at the church. There had been some crimes at the university, and in response, antistress meetings had been held for students.

"Why couldn't we have an antistress meeting?" I asked Mahalia.

"NO POLICE!" our bright blue leaflet said: "Just neighbors who would like some time together to express our frustration, fear, anger, whatever, at the harm done to our lives by drugs, addiction, stress and violence in our families."

The meeting was underway, about twenty people sitting in a circle venting their feelings to Reverend Clara and Mahalia, when I looked up amazed to see Angela slipping into the room. We could hand out all the leaflets we wanted, but addicts never came to any of our meetings.

Angela made eye contact with me and I wedged another folding chair between mine and Mahalia's and gestured Angela into it. She ate a little bit while Mahalia and I exchanged an amazed glance over her head. I listened as the people poured out their feelings and fears, but I was most aware of Angela's thigh pressed against mine, and her arm against my arm. She sat leaning into me as if for warmth for an hour. I didn't move a muscle, and I could have sworn we synchronized our breathing.

Suddenly I felt her stiffen. I looked around and saw her boyfriend Askari standing in the doorway, staring a stony command into Angela's eyes. She rose like a robot and walked out the door.

One rainy day Skeeter appeared at my door out of breath. "Melody, can you come and see Angela? She's been beat up by some drug dealers."

I was working hard around that time, and I'd been saying no a lot lately. I wanted to say no now.

"Does she want me to come?" I asked him.

"Yeah, she told me to come and get you."

As I was getting my raincoat and umbrella, I realized I could have just said, "Call Mahalia." Walking up the street I felt like a meddler and I thought, I'm going to have to remember to ask the abbot what the difference is between a wanna-be bodhisattva and a neighborhood busybody. On the other hand, I knew Skeeter didn't have a phone and neither did Angela.

It was a school day, but the door was opened by Askari's eleven-year-old son. I crouched down beside the mattress in the front room where Angela was lying, her mouth bloody and her eyes swollen almost shut. The only other thing in the room was a TV set with a broken vertical hold. The boy sat on the mattress with his back to Angela and me and stared at the flipping TV.

"They beat me up, Melody," she whispered.

"Where are you hurt?"

"The worst is my foot," she said. I drew the blanket back. One of her feet looked as if it had been crushed by a boot or a blow.

"Will you let me call Mahalia for you?" I asked. "I think she can come and take you to the hospital."

There was a long pause. Then Angela said, "Okay," with a sigh.

I opened the refrigerator. Nothing. I went home and called Mahalia, who said she would come right away. "Mahalia, I don't know what we would do without you," I said.

"I don't know what we would do without *you*," she said.

I was late to work, but the emptiness inside Angela's refrigerator was gnawing at me. The little boy had seen me open its door and look inside. Yet taking food there seemed like some kind of condescension. Looking around my homey big house with its old-fashioned pantry full of food, I felt like a rich lady in a manor house about to send some leftovers to the people out back in the shacks. I felt angry at being in this position, angry at everything that conspired to put that child where he was.

The last time I had heard the abbot lecture, he had spoken on giving, and I remembered what he'd said: "Every human being is the result of tremendous virtue. When we are giving, we should give to the virtue in each one." Somehow, that made it easier to put a can of soup and some tea bags, a carton of milk and a loaf of bread in a bag.

I handed the bag to the little boy when he opened the door. I saw Mahalia drive up as I was pulling away, and I drove along examining myself, not wanting to feel like a good person or a bad person, wanting to release myself from both sanctimony and guilt.

"It's just half an hour and some food," I thought. "No big deal."

Two days later, I was walking past Angela's on my way to the school when I saw the door to her apartment was wide open. I walked over and peered in. There was nothing inside to show that Angela and the children had ever lived on Alma Street, nothing at all but some trash.

When Stan went out to our driveway that same day he found an old metal box spring thrown onto the trunk of his car, leaving deep scratches in the finish. I wondered if Angela's boyfriend, or even Angela herself, had thrown that rusty old thing as a last gesture of anger as they left.

I'd never know for sure. All I knew was, it was hard to have so much more than some of my neighbors. I had everything: a home, a family, all the food we could eat, two cars, even car insurance for the scratches. And now I had an old bedspring too.

CHAPTER SEVENTEEN

Why?

I was drawn to my upstairs bedroom window by shouting in the street. The shouter was a middle-aged black man in shabby pants, and he strode, fast, right down the middle of the street. Storming across the intersection, the man beat the air with his fists, and shouted into the sky. "Somalia!" he cried. "Somalia!"

This was when airlifts of food to the Horn of Africa were all over the nightly news. "What do you mean?" I wondered. "Why there? Why feed them but not you?"

Then he walked up to the fledgling street tree under my window, grabbed its skinny trunk with both his hands, yanked it over sideways, and cracked it in half on his knee. He threw the tree's leafy top onto the sidewalk, and stomped off, cursing. I pressed my palms to the glass as he disappeared up the sidewalk.

Our young street trees were having a hard time. Idle kids swung on them like playground poles and peeled off strips of bark with their nervous little fingers. One of the saplings our block committee had planted in front of my house had fallen victim to a car, and now the other one had been murdered by the man mad about Somalia.

Discouraged, I let the holes in the cement choke with crabgrass. In the center of each square, a pathetic stick of dead trunk stuck up.

Mahalia's office was in the basement of the police station. To visit her, I had to be buzzed in through a locked door and walk down a busy hall lit by fluorescent lights past officers, their heavy gun belts hung with keys, cuffs, and billy clubs clanking as they let me pass.

Mahalia's space was the size of a closet, crowded with a desk, two chairs, and a constantly ringing phone. The ground-level window let in hardly any light. She had decorated the walls with inspirational messages and photos of Sophia, her lovely teenaged daughter.

Mahalia herself, in her African print dresses, her deep, patient voice on the phone, looked like nobody who could have anything to do with a police station. "I've come to see the secret priestess in the basement!" I told her, knocking on the frame of her door. She laughed, and said, "I can't believe I work here myself; most of them don't know what to do with me." The truth was, all the officers who really got the point of community-involved policing gravitated to Mahalia as soon as she got the job.

"Maybe you don't run the place, but for me, you're its anchor," I told her. "If I didn't come in here to find you, I wouldn't come in here at all."

Mahalia and I phoned each other so often I knew her work number by heart. But when I dialed it after our vacation, a woman I didn't know answered.

"She isn't in," she said.

I knew Mahalia had been on vacation too. "We're going camping," she had said, pausing in our front doorway. "My family loves the outdoors." We had chatted for a few minutes longer, talking of mountains and rivers.

"When would be a good time to call back?" I asked the woman.

She hesitated. "Are you a friend?"

"Yes," I said, alarmed. "Is something wrong?"

"Mahalia won't be working for a long time. A few days ago, on their vacation, her daughter was drowned."

It was a long time before I found out what had happened. All I knew was that Mahalia had only one child, the almost-grown daughter she talked about so often, and now she was lost. I didn't know the story of Sophia's death, or of what was happening to Mahalia.

Why? was my feeling. Why Mahalia?

The news traveled around the neighborhood. Camille said, "There are some things that we can't understand how God can let them happen."

"Naw, naw, Melody, it can't be true," Hiram said when I told him that Mahalia's daughter would have a funeral the next day. "She showed me her daughter's picture," he said. "She was so proud of that girl."

Mahalia was someone Hiram and I both had counted on to be stronger than us.

"I don't want to be selfish, Melody," Hiram said, "but I'm afraid she might not come back." I felt exactly the same way, selfish, but not ready to go on without Mahalia. Hiram wanted to go to the funeral, to show Mahalia that we loved her.

When we pulled up in front of a big church in Oakland, the sidewalk in front was crowded with groups of teary-eyed high school students holding each other. We found seats near the back.

Reverend Clara started the service, and then, from the back of the church, Mahalia emerged, dressed all in white, in a flowing African robe. She walked, holding a white urn against her body—Sophia's ashes. Mahalia's arms cradled the urn exactly as a woman sometimes holds her pregnant womb. In the bravest act I had ever seen, she bore her daughter's remains down the aisle before her as if to say, "Here is my child." Walking as if she were a bride, Mahalia married herself to Sophia's death, embracing it fully.

During the service, Mahalia poured out her love to Sophia's friends and to her teachers, and all of us who had not known Sophia learned about her that day, as person after person came to stand beside Reverend Clara and speak about Sophia and her wonderful mother.

Sophia had been a track star, they said, one of the best young women athletes in the state, she had played and danced and made everyone laugh, and most of all, she had shared her special relationship with her mother.

"I was having trouble with my mother," one girl said. "I didn't know how to talk to her, but I went to see Mahalia and Sophia, and they showed me how."

Having had such a child, Mahalia could never be childless, I thought, looking at her.

"But I'm afraid the harder part is ahead," I told Hiram, going home in the car. "In all the months and years when Sophia isn't there."

I was surprised to hear Mahalia's voice on my answering machine a few days later, saying, "I looked out there and saw you and Hiram, and it meant so much to me, that people from Alma Street were there."

I didn't hear from her again during her leave of absence. I sent her a note, telling her how Sophia's picture from the service was on our home altar next to our figure of Buddha. I often picked the picture up to look at the vivacious brown-skinned girl, dressed up for a party and smiling into the camera. It seemed impossible that this young woman sparkling with excitement was gone. I tried to make myself believe it, repeating a Buddhist phrase, ". . . things arise . . . things dissolve . . ."

New life was arising in our family. Amina announced that she was going to have a baby. She and her boyfriend were, as he put it, "on a collision course with adulthood."

"How can our little baby sister Amina-pie become a mother?" her siblings wanted to know.

I teased Amina, "Bring me your old report cards. I want to see what grade you got in social living class. Weren't you *listening?*" But after all, she was twenty-one, quite a bit older than I had been, and I knew she would be a good mother.

When Mahalia came back to work, we talked in her cramped basement room. "Do you want me to tell you about Sophia?" she asked me. "It's hard to hear, but if people don't know, then I'm alone with it."

"I'm ready to hear," I said.

The four of them—Mahalia, her husband and his young son, and Sophia—had been playing in shallow rapids in a northern California river, jumping into the foamy current, floating down, and scrambling out onto the hot, sandy banks. Sophia's foot had caught between rocks, and she could not get her head above the water. Mahalia and her husband had tried to save her—had tried to blow air into her mouth under the swift current. People had come, rangers had come, Sophia's body had been freed from the rocks, not breathing, and hours had passed before the rangers had given up trying to make her breathe.

Mahalia described how two of the rangers had been women, a

white woman and a Latina woman, she said, both of them mothers, and how, at the end, the two of them and Mahalia had stayed on the beach for a long time, holding each other, crying together.

"I hadn't wanted to leave them," Mahalia said. "I stayed with them as long as I could.

"I know you're a Buddhist," Mahalia said when she finished, "and Buddhists believe in trying to accept things, but I don't know if I ever can."

"I'm not that kind of Buddhist," I said. And then I was confused. What kind of Buddhist was I? "My Buddhism is something about trying to stay open to living," I said. "Mahalia, you're better at that than anyone I know."

She and I often ended up in the same meetings, and sometimes she sat without talking, Mahalia diminished, as if she were barely there. Mahalia had to live by mourning openly. Too many people counseled her to "put it behind her," to "get on with her life."

"I never realized before," she said, "how death-denying is the same thing as life-denying. I just can't tell you how many people want me to get over this."

"Keep on doing what you need to," I told her. "You're teaching all of us, the way you always do."

When Amina's baby Liam was born, my second grandson, I told Mahalia about it on the phone. She kept asking me questions and getting me to describe how our whole big family had gathered at the hospital around Amina, and how Liam's father and Rosemary and I and Liam's paternal grandmother had all been in the room when Liam was born, how for the birth I had put the same cloth under Amina's back that she had been born on, and how the nurses had liked that so much, and how Liam had raised one tiny fist in the air like a champion as he emerged, and then peed a foot-tall stream straight up into the air.

"Such a male entry into the world for a fine big boy," I crowed to Mahalia.

"Mahalia, how is it for you to hear all this?" I finally asked her, aware that her heart must be aching, no grandchildren coming anytime for her.

"If you don't tell me about it, Melody," she said, "then I've lost something more."

The day came when Mahalia handed me an invitation. She wanted me to come to see the healing work she had done in a doll-making class. Mahalia said she had worked for nearly a year to make a doll as a memorial to Sophia.

There were dozens of dolls in the exhibit, many of them life-sized, each with head, hands, and feet formed of porcelain clay. The dolls were dressed and placed in settings evoking the meaning of each doll in the life of the doll maker. Some were portraits made by mourners.

I saw an altar made by a woman whose young husband, a mountaineer, had been killed by lightning in the mountains. On the altar were photos of him with her and their young children, and the doll was the widow herself. A gentle-looking woman with long hair held a translucent, bolt-shaped shard of glass, and she gazed at it, a look of wonder and longing on her face that said something like, How could fire take him?

And then we came to the water that took Sophia. Mahalia had made a life-sized image of Sophia, dressed in robes of red and purple African cloth, seated beside a small stream Mahalia had placed at her feet. One strong brown foot reached out beneath the gown, and over it, water flowed. The girl beside the stream was at peace, except that her face seemed to ask a question.

CHAPTER EIGHTEEN

Marcus

Twice, the police did sting-type arrests on Alma Street. Once they sent a black plainclothes officer from another city to buy crack, making one arrest. Another night, the police took over the dealing themselves. Plainclothes cops sold pieces of baking soda to anyone who wanted to buy. When the buyers walked around the corner, other police arrested them. The baking soda buyers were released the next morning with misdemeanor tickets.

The bad news, Mahalia told our committee, was that the soda-selling police had had dozens of customers, a steady stream. A few had driven up in cars, but most were on foot and lived within four blocks. We now had proof that the level of addiction in the surrounding community was even higher than we had suspected. It made sense, though, based on the people we knew ourselves who were drinking too much and using crack.

After Camille's husband Elliott was laid off from his job as a laborer at the army base, he started walking to the Arab store several times a day. Each time he passed our house on his way back, he was holding a brown sack with a bottle in it.

There was a whole new plague of alcohol adding to our crack problems. More and more shelf space in the little corner markets was used up by forty-ounce malt liquors and ales advertised to black people by rappers and athletes.

"I really notice the difference with these 'forties,' " I told Shyaam. "More people are drinking and people are drunker."

"No wonder," he said. "I read that *one* forty-ounce can of malt liquor has almost as much alcohol as a whole six-pack of beer. I really resent these companies using slogans like 'king of the pack'—that's a gang term."

"If you flood people with cheap strong alcohol you turn them into famous drunks," I said. "That's what happened to the Irish and the Native Americans—my ancestors. I always say my family's in AA: Alcohol and Abandonment."

The first time I saw Elliott loitering near the drug dealers, I could hardly believe it. He still said hello to me on the street, but he didn't look into my face.

"I'm so fed up, Melody," Camille told me. "I'm trying to pay for everything by myself, and he's spending everything I have." Camille had come to our meetings at first, but now that Elliott was on crack, she was too embarrassed to be a part of the group. "Things are getting so hard," she said. "If I could have it the way I want it, I would have a whole different world for my kids to grow up in than the way this one is right now."

There was no more night on Alma Street. We had demanded, and gotten, so many streetlights, and people had installed spotlights on their houses, until a dim electric daytime lasted until dawn. At first, the dealers moved farther into the shadows. Later, as we lost ground, they stood brazenly under the lights, the better to see to make their sales.

In the wee hours, the squeal of tires, the gunning of an engine, headlights raking the ceiling of our room—any or all of these brought us instantly awake. We did not speak but waited, hardly breathing, for gunfire.

And when shots came, in a heartbeat, without even crying out, Stan and I scrambled over the edge of the bed, me following him onto the floor on his side, away from the window. When the shots ended, one of us crawled to the phone, pulled it to the floor by its cord, and dialed 911.

On a warm September night, shots came. We looked outside after we dialed 911 and saw a man lying on the sidewalk across the street next to the mailbox. This time, it was different. The man screamed, and kept on screaming, yelling, "Help me."

We were afraid to go out. A split second after the shots, we'd heard a car roar away. In the brief eternity before the ambulance arrived, two neighbors braver than we—the white man who fixed the little kids' bicycles, and the black man who worked for the railroad—cautiously approached the screaming man. They knelt helplessly over him. It seemed as if they didn't know what to do for him.

A short, plump woman in a housecoat emerged from the darkness farther down the block and knelt down beside him, then stood up and paced the sidewalk, frantically looking around and crying. "That must be his mother," I said to Stan. At last the ambulance came and took him away.

The next morning, after a nearly sleepless night, I went out to ask what had happened. People said the victim had been Marcus, a young man who had been in the same high school class as Amina. He lived with his mother Carolina in the next block, and he was going to junior college. I told Pearl that Stan and I had dialed 911 within seconds of the shots. She said as far as she knew, Marcus was still alive.

Days later, Carolina, the mother we had seen in her housecoat, introduced herself at our door. She was about my age and height, with a youthful-looking face the color of dark honey and a pleasing round body.

"You and your husband saved Marcus's life," she said. "You saved him, and I will always thank God for what you did."

"All we did was dial 911," I protested. "Anybody would do that."

"No, they wouldn't," she insisted. "I'll always be grateful to you."

Marcus was paralyzed below his chest. Carolina spent her days with him at the hospital. "He's very bad," she said. "I can hardly stand to see him sometimes."

After that, if Carolina and I caught sight of each other from a block away, we'd walk toward each other until we could talk. She dressed in colorful outfits like a fashion-conscious hippie—maybe red tights with a red and black polka-dotted miniskirt, a beaded sweater with a red scarf around her neck, gold earrings dangling, her hair in braids wrapped up in twists over her ears like a French peasant girl.

Her vivacious personality sometimes pushed her sadness aside.

Carolina touched people easily while she talked, quick to offer a hug. She would smile, showing her gold-filled teeth, and talk up a storm. Other times, though, she cried about Marcus and asked for a hug.

An article in the paper about gunshot victims with spinal injuries quoted Marcus, who admitted he had been standing on our corner selling drugs the night he was shot. Another young black man had driven up to him, he said, and had simply shot him and taken the crack.

"What kind of person would do a thing like that?" Carolina asked me.

"It's so hard to understand," I said.

But Pam and I had met plenty of young men who would do just such a thing, and who had. Pam regarded such crimes as quasi-suicidal acts. "What else can it mean," Pam asked me, "to shoot a gun at someone so much like yourself?"

"These youngsters are like *that*," Pam was fond of saying, "because we are like *this*. Cause and effect. The cause of violence is violence."

No one was surprised when our neighbor Camille's husband, Elliott, was arrested for possession of crack for sale. But he was very surprised when I had him brought out of his cell to the visiting phones at San Quentin.

"What are *you* doing here, Melody?" he asked.

"I work here sometimes. I'm visiting today on death row and I thought I'd find out how you're doing."

"I have to stay eight months, and I'm spending it in my cell as much as I can. I'm scared all the time," he said. "This is a terrible place."

"It's especially tense in here right now because the first execution is supposed to happen soon," I replied.

I gave Elliott some writing paper and promised to send him some stamps.

"Keep yourself safe, Elliott," I told him.

"Pray for me, Melody," he asked, saying good-bye.

The best word to describe Robert Alton Harris was *ordinary*—a white man with unremarkable features, brown hair, medium weight, medium height. When I looked over at him, hunched over in the visiting cell next to mine, talking seriously with his face close to his attorney's, I found it impossible to believe that he would be dead in a week.

When that night came, I was with Stan and Lil and Rosemary at San Quentin's gate with hundreds of others, while inside on death row Jarvis and the rest maintained silence.

A woman prison chaplain led us in prayer for the soul of Robert Harris and for his victims, two young men, and for the officers who were carrying out the execution. She prayed also for the legal workers. "This is not about your having failed," she said. "This is about having the faith to keep on doing your very best every day."

When, not long after, the head gardener at the Zen center lectured, she talked about what is to be learned from gingko trees. I'd always liked their fan-shaped leaves, bright gold in the fall, but I hadn't known they were ancient, evolved thousands of years ago. They exist nowhere in the wild, the gardener said, but were fostered by monks in gardens in China and Japan. Somehow, gingkos have adapted so that they thrive in cities, in polluted air. They reminded me of the kids on Alma Street, so full of life in spite of everything.

The day after the lecture, I went to the nursery, ready to try planting trees again in the empty holes in the sidewalk in front of our house. I chose two gingkos, and dedicated one to Ian Freedman, the other to Marcus in his wheelchair. I built fortified cages for them of four strong metal posts and thick wire mesh. Trees in jail, I thought. To weed them, I had to kneel on the sidewalk and reach in, trying not to scratch my wrist on the wire. Kneeling there, I accepted on faith that the little trees would do their best to grow according to their own plan, and as they did so, they came to express my faith that every person wants a better life.

CHAPTER NINETEEN

Whither Thou Goest

Stan and I had been a couple, "partners" we said, for nearly twenty years, without benefit of matrimony. We sometimes needed time together away from Alma Street. We divided the John Muir Trail that rides along the spine of the Sierra Nevada into sections we could hike on short vacations. After a few days walking in the mountains we always camped near some remote unmarked hot springs on the east side of the Sierra. The place is a high, flat desert valley enclosed on the east by worn-down volcanoes. The wall of the Sierra rises to the west. Stan and I lay flat out in a pool of hot alkaline water together. I let my arms float out and I imagined one of the little gingkos in front of our house growing upright from my left palm. Out of my right palm, an ancient bristlecone pine of the White Mountains. This is how the trees live on the earth, as out of one body, I thought. They are not separate. The roots of the city tree and the summit tree pass through my heart and tangle.

In the morning, I walked a quarter mile west, then turned back toward Stan. A mirage floated between us. Shiny, it mirrored him, then disappeared as I came back. He was hunkered down on his oversize feet, long boots planted in the white chalky dust, hat-matted gray hair around his bald spot, the ends blowing in the breeze.

In jeans and holey T-shirt, he was ministering to the Coleman stove. He'd set it in the dirt and opened its green wings, and he had the pump in pieces, screwing some interior part onto another with a tool on his knife, the pieces very small in his long fingers between his feet. He was absorbed.

For many years I've come upon this man fixing things and watched him. He learned all this, he once told me, by staying close to his grandfather and his father while they worked. All the men of that family chew on their tongues when using their hands, as he was doing now, as if his tongue and his hands together felt how the pieces fit.

"If it's not one thing, it's another," he said, good-natured. "I have to fix this thing before I can make coffee, but I'd like to have a cup before I fix it."

"Wherever we live, I want to live there with you," I said.

"Well, thank you, ma'am." He smiled at me.

On our twentieth anniversary, at the Autumnal Equinox, our abbot Mel Weitsman married us in a Buddhist ceremony, outside, overlooking a meadow in the Berkeley hills. Lil, wearing her long Buddhist robe, assisted Mel Weitsman by ringing the bells for the ceremony. We were surrounded by our big family: all of our former spouses and their partners and children were there. Stan's former mother-in-law helped his mother serve the huge chocolate wedding cake Naomi and I had baked. Friends came from all of the overlapping circles of our lives. Elyse was my maid of honor, and Libby, holding a glass of champagne aloft, toasted us by saying, "Jim and I couldn't survive on Alma Street without Melody and Stan."

CHAPTER TWENTY

Day of the Dead

We were proud that our block of Alma Street had two students enrolled at San Francisco State: Mary, an African-American young woman who lived with her parents at the other end of the block was a year ahead of Amina. I heard from some of the teenagers that Mary was going to have a party at a nearby restaurant to celebrate her graduation.

The day after the party, Skeeter came by with the bad news. A young man named Reece, who lived around the corner from us, had left the party and walked to the store to buy some extra soft drinks. When he came out, he was shot to death in a drive-by on the sidewalk.

The next Sunday I saw dozens of people in their best clothes spilling out of Reece's parents' house and into their front yard. Crying-eyed people kept walking past our house to their parked cars. There was a sad feeling in the neighborhood.

At our block meeting, Sergeant Terry was discouraged. "Even when something great happens, like this young woman's graduation, it turns into something bad."

From my bedroom window, I could have drawn a map of our drug war losses. On the far corner, Reece's parents. Across the street from Reece's was the home of the couple whose son was killed in Oakland. Opposite my driveway was the apartment where Rosemary's schoolmate CJ had grown up. CJ was in prison, serving twenty-three years to life because after he got addicted, someone had been shot when he and some other people had robbed a gas station. Under my window Ian Freedman had died, and on the corner was the spot where Marcus had been shot and paralyzed. Ours wasn't even a long block. "Maybe there are wars with a higher percentage of losses to families," I told Shyaam, "but not many."

I wanted to turn myself into an artist like Mahalia. I imagined myself making sculptures, life-sized human forms, neutral, perhaps ghostly light gray, in color. I wanted to place them outside, each of the three dead bodies lying on the sidewalks, and a figure of Marcus in his wheelchair, and also I wanted to weld a cell, four sides and a top made of bars, with CJ's ghostly figure inside, holding on, looking out at Alma Street, so that Alma could look in at him.

In my vision, also, there always was an Ohlone man, stopped in his stride, his hand raised in surprise, as if he had walked from two hundred years ago into this scene. My fantasy sidewalk exhibit appeared before my mind's eye so many times, I began to feel frustrated that I was not a sculptor, able to shape what I needed to bring to light.

Sitting in Reverend Clara's study, I asked her how we could show people what was going on. Talking together, we decided to have a march for peace around the neighborhood.

We knew there were a lot of fatalities in this war, but we had never counted them. I called the police department. It took only a few minutes on the phone for a homicide detective to give me the names of sixteen people who had been murdered in our small police beat—the blocks surrounding my house and the church. Sixteen people in five years. Fifteen men, one woman. "We can't expect young men to protect life if we don't honor theirs," Reverend Clara said.

Reverend Clara called politicians and I called the press. She also phoned other ministers in the neighborhood, but most did not return her calls. She had expected that they might not want to work with her, she said, since they were all men.

"Some of them will tell me to my face that they do not like to see a woman in the pulpit," she said, shaking her head.

I wrote a letter to our abbot, Mel Weitsman, asking him to sponsor the march, and I was excited when Reverend Clara said he had phoned her and offered to come, saying that since the Zen center was only a few blocks away, he wanted to be involved.

We composed a leaflet: "Our purpose is to acknowledge the killings, honor the victims, and rededicate ourselves to ending violence." We listed the names of the sixteen victims and the dates they were killed. I put on my running shoes and went on one of my urban hikes, stapling leaflets to telephone poles and asking merchants to post them in their windows.

I took one to the house on Alma Street everybody called the Blues Band House because a whole group of African-American musicians lived there. I gave one to Suleiman, the bandleader, who promised to come.

When I gave the leaflet to young guys hanging out on the corners, they were obviously moved. "I knew him," a young man would say, pointing to a name, or, "I remember him."

When I knocked on Camille's door, Elliott answered. "I got an early release," he said.

"Well, welcome home," I told him.

"I don't want to go back," he said. "Never."

"There's a new social worker at the church named Herb who runs an AA group, Elliott. You might want to check that out."

"Thanks, Melody," he said, and took my leaflet.

The night before the march, we had a poster-making party at Libby's house. Carolina came, and a bunch of kids. We made a sign for each victim. One read: "Near this place Ian Freedman lost his life to violence on October 1, 1990. He is remembered."

We also made two large butcher-paper banners, and the kids colored in the letters: SOUTH BERKELEY'S MARCH FOR PEACE — REMEMBERING THE VICTIMS OF VIOLENCE. And A LIFE REMEMBERED IS ONE STEP TOWARD PEACE.

We didn't know if many people would show up to march, but Reverend Clara said it wouldn't matter if we were the only ones; the important thing was to begin healing our neighborhood.

On a cloudy November Sunday afternoon Stan and I found a ragtag group of about twenty-five people gathered on the steps of the church. We were a diverse group, different ages, different colors.

Day of the Dead

Reverend Clara spoke. "We are small in number but more powerful than any military power," she said, "because love is the stronger force." I believed her when she said it. Because we were so few, just taking the first step felt powerful.

Abbot Mel Weitsman was the only other clergyperson there. He was wearing ordinary clothes, and around his neck was his rakusu, a small biblike square of stitched fabric representing Buddha's robes. Mel asked us to be silent for a moment and then he talked about compassion for both the murdered and the murderers.

Reverend Clara asked people to wear the signs we'd made for each victim. I wore Ian Freedman's name around my neck. Herb, our new community mental health worker, wore a name. He had just started a support group at Reverend Clara's church for alcoholics and one for grandmothers raising grandchildren alone. Lil found a parking place and joined us just in time to claim the only female victim's name, and she picked out a sign to carry too, saying, "A mother walking against guns." Even the reporters who came from local newspapers took signs.

I had made a map, with a star for each murder site. The first two were in the same block as the church. We hung the signs honoring those victims on a tree. After that, we tried to find trees for all the names. We found trees for all except the names of two men murdered in a liquor store parking lot where there was only a telephone pole, so we used that.

The majority of killings were clustered near drug-dealing "hot spots," and those were mostly near where alcohol was sold. Reverend Clara said it was the first time she had ever led prayers at liquor stores.

At each murder site, the children left a bouquet of wildflowers, and a red rose, placing the flowers respectfully, like tending a real altar, not a sidewalk-surrounded tree. Reverend Clara led us in prayer each time. "Thank you God," she said, "for the life of Joseph Wilson, and we lift up our prayers also for the soul of whoever has taken his life."

Pearl told how Mrs. Sanders's grandson Ed had been killed over a minor argument. If it hadn't been for a gun and too much alcohol, the two men would have laughed about it the next day. But one was dead and the other in prison.

When we got to our house, first we had to shush our dog Alaska, who wanted to bark at the march, and then Stan talked about how Ian

Freedman's mother had come to grieve in front of our house. "We will have to learn to open our hearts and value life, every life," Stan told the marchers. I hung Ian's sign on the wire cage protecting the little gingko tree dedicated to him.

Mel Weitsman trundled the wheelbarrow that held the flowers. I told him there must be a Zen story about the monk pushing the wheelbarrow. He said, "This *is* that Zen story," and together we made it up: *The monk pushed a wheelbarrow for peace. He didn't make peace, and he didn't NOT make peace. He just pushed.*

Most of us were on foot, but some had wheels. Libby pulled Aurora along in a red wagon, holding a sign she had composed herself the night before: "Put the guns in the garbage!" Pearl drove along slowly in her car, getting out at every stop. And there was a guy none of us knew who came on a bicycle in a big eagle-feather headdress with a black doll and a white doll in his back pocket.

Carolina pushed her grandson Raven in a stroller, stopping often to cry. Raven, born full of drugs, was in Carolina's care because his mother, Carolina's daughter Sheila, was addicted to crack. Raven was the same age as Amina's baby Liam, but much smaller, and sometimes he seemed listless in his stroller. Marcus had recovered enough to join a group called Youth Alive! — wheelchair-using young people who had been disabled by guns. They spoke to teens, urging them to stay away from drugs, and Carolina was very proud of him. When the march reached the corner where Marcus was gunned down, Carolina spoke about the night he was shot. "He was going to college," she said, leaning on the handles of Raven's stroller and crying. She left out the part about Marcus's having been selling drugs that night. I supposed that in front of so many people, she just couldn't say it.

When we reached the block where victims number ten, eleven, twelve, thirteen had died we hung all four names in a circle around a tree, and Reverend Clara prayed for them. Then Reverend Clara's own young daughter reached up and whispered something to her. Embarrassed, Reverend Clara told the marchers, "My daughter wants to know why we don't pray for her brother."

So we all prayed for Reverend Clara's son Frankie, senselessly killed like all the rest. I cried for Frankie, and for the sixteen others, but mostly because I felt overwhelmed by Reverend Clara. I marveled that she, whose son was killed, could pray, not only for sixteen murder victims unknown to her, but also for sixteen unknown murderers.

Two city councilwomen from the nicer side of town walked the whole route with us, and when they left they said they'd learned a lot. They had tears in their eyes.

Back at the church, we found Suleiman and the Blues Band waiting for us on the steps. Their soloist Tina sang the blues in a red velveteen dress, the sound pouring out of her matching red-lipsticked mouth, and our pious mood broke. We even danced on the sidewalk in front of the church a little, even though it was starting to rain, and everybody laughed when Reverend Clara told the band she expected to see them all in church the next Sunday.

For days afterward, I saw people pausing to read the fading signs on the trees. The ink was runny from the light rain, but you could still read the words.

I met with Reverend Clara in her office, decorated for Christmas, to sum it all up. Our march had been in all the papers. A color photo of Dolly from the Zen center and Herb our social worker hanging the name of a murder victim on a tree had even been on the front page of the *Oakland Tribune*.

Reverend Clara's only regret was that so few members of her church had marched. "I don't know how to get my parishioners involved in this community. Most of them don't seem to understand the problems."

"That's true of many Buddhists too," I said. I told Reverend Clara about a conversation I had had at a meditation retreat. I was sitting with an attractive white woman during a break, sipping tea. The woman asked me about my life, and I told her about our problems with guns and drugs.

"Why do you live there?" she had asked. I talked about my good neighbors, and our interracial committee.

"But if, as you say, your neighbors are good people, couldn't you all move away somewhere together?" she asked. "Why couldn't you all buy land in the country, and move there?"

"There was a long pause," I told Reverend Clara, "while I pictured the whole neighborhood, say, right up against Yellowstone. I didn't know where to begin, so I just thanked her for her suggestion."

Reverend Clara laughed, and then she sighed. "We have a lot of education to do," she said.

A few days later, the newspaper published a letter from a mother who wrote: "The story about people going around their neighborhood honoring the young men and women that were murdered made me realize that I had never visited the site where my son was found. He died of a drug overdose at a housing project three years ago. He was found out in the street, without his shoes on, dead. I would drive by and look the other way. My pain was too great to stop and look around.

"However, as a result of this article, I called a friend and she and I went there. We met several women who showed us a mural on a building there with the names of people who have been killed, but my son's name wasn't on it. Now it will be added, and my friend and I are purchasing a bench for the courtyard there."

Reverend Clara had said, "People have to imagine something for it to come true." We had imagined our little march, and it had happened. I could even imagine our neighborhood at peace. After all, I thought, every war stops sometime.

CHAPTER TWENTY-ONE

Edna White's Garage Burns

After our peace march, our block committee was so famous, Mahalia cited us as an example of a well-organized neighborhood.

She brought some leaflets to our meeting about a rally to support an Oakland woman named Edna White who was attacked for trying to get some drug dealers off her street.

Pam and I were out working that day, and we decided to drive over to the rally. We found a sound truck parked in a narrow street in front of a house with a charred garage and boarded-up windows. There were balloons tied to the truck, and the members of a high school band were milling around it in their yellow and red uniforms getting ready to play. A few hundred people were eating hot dogs and listening to speeches.

Edna White herself was a tall black woman, middle-aged, who looked as if she had a lot of determination. When she spoke she bravely pointed up the street toward a run-down apartment house and told the crowd that was the crack house she wanted closed. She said her garage had been set on fire after she had written letters to the owners signed with her own name.

Pam and I stayed long enough to hear the mayor of Oakland speak and to see him give Mrs. White a hug.

"I never want a rally like this for me," I told Pam.

"What happens to her after everybody leaves?" Pam asked. "What about tonight, after dark? You can't have police here every minute."

"The way to organize is to always stay together with a big group," I said. "Don't ever strike out on your own like Edna White did."

Mahalia was still working on getting the police to become partners with the community. Berkeley's top police went to a conference on community policing where they won an award for the ORCA mobile police station.

Louis the bus driver thought a cop should be just like the person who delivers the mail. "It should be the same person for years in the same small area," he said, "and they should walk every block every day and know every name that belongs in every house, who's moving in, who's moving out, who's on welfare, who owns the home, who's renting, all the kids, which dogs bite, everything."

"I don't think they're going to go that far," said Mahalia.

"I like that cops-as-postal-people idea," Saul said. "Maybe it would work, if the police delivered the checks and didn't wear guns."

The first change we noticed in the police was that they rode around on bicycles, and the ORCA acquired a bike rack that made it look like a space-age whale with training wheels. The police rode right up on the sidewalk and got into conversations they wouldn't have in their cars. The drug lookouts still whistled when they saw them coming, but now at least little kids got to know the cops better.

We continued, though, to have trouble with our beat cops changing all the time, and our first steps with community policing got off on the wrong foot. At our first meeting after the conference, none of the officers was free to attend except an old-timer of a white-man cop who was the soul of cynicism. He tipped back in his chair and delivered a kind of stream-of-consciousness speech that left most of our committee speechless.

"None of our men want to work down here in this corridor," he proclaimed. "Every watch, all the men groan when this beat comes up, and we draw straws to see who has to work it. This corridor has always been the worst area of town, and there's nothing the police can do.

"There's no point in arresting drug dealers anyway," he carried on. "The war on drugs is a joke — it just pushes them from one place to another, and the judges always let them go anyway. I don't see why you people live here."

Nobody said much until after the officer left.

"Well, at least he told the truth about how they feel about us," Pearl said.

"I hate *corridor!*" I said. "They never call nice streets that. It's like we're the bad kids in class and we have to go out in the *corridor.*"

"Did you notice how he talked as if they'd never hired a female police officer yet?" Libby pointed out.

"That officer was a disaster," I told Sergeant Terry on the phone. "I don't want community-involved policing if I have to get involved with *him.*"

"Melody, it was a mix-up," he said. "He would have been my absolute last choice for someone to attend a community meeting. I'm sorry. We'll do better next time."

Libby and I decided to write down our suggestions for community policing, and we mailed Sergeant Terry a letter:

HOW THE POLICE CAN EMPOWER AND ORGANIZE A NEIGHBORHOOD

Be truthful with crime facts and statistics. Remember that the neighbors themselves know their own situation better than you do.

Police officers are really in the same boat as the neighbors: None of us can stop drug sales or use, or violence. The neighbors have to live with it, day and night, and the officers have to work with it, day and night. But we can act right here, right now, to improve things, together. Other neighborhoods have improved, and we can too.

Advise neighbors to stick together, and never to endanger themselves by confronting dealers or resorting to vigilantism. This is what they will do if they don't trust the police.

If you are feeling discouraged and overwhelmed, ask for support. No one who is demoralized should feel they have to go to work everyday without getting help, from fellow officers, from the neighbors in the community, from mental health care if needed. Empower yourself first.

Notice the good kids, the good families, the positive

things going on. If you have to work in a neighborhood that scares you and depresses you, find people there you admire and get to know them. The community meetings are a great place to start.

Sergeant Terry called me back. "Guess what, Melody? The captain liked your letter so much, he's reading it out loud to every watch."

"I can't believe it," I told him. "I never thought the police would be listening to anything I had to say. Do you remember I work for the defense?"

"I know, I know," he said, laughing.

On a cold morning in January, Carolina told me she was going to the jail to help her daughter Sheila get out on her own recognizance. "But I don't really want to," Carolina said. "As soon as she gets out, she'll be back on crack. Maybe jail will do her some good."

I shrugged.

Carolina answered herself. "I doubt it."

"I wish she could go straight from the jail to drug treatment," I said.

"That's what she needs, no ifs, ands, or buts, for a whole year. That would be the only thing for her," Carolina said, "but there's no place. We're not saying anything I don't know already." And she added, "Sheila's pregnant."

My heart sank, thinking of Raven, only eighteen months old.

"Where's Raven today?" I asked.

"With his other grandmother," Carolina said.

"Carolina, if Sheila is pregnant again, that means she's having un-protected sex, and she's going to get HIV," I said in a rush of anxiety.

"I know, I know," Carolina said, backing away from me, waving and swatting her hands frantically, as if warding off an invisible swarm of bees.

"I'm sorry," I said. "I know you know."

"Melody, if *you* only knew," she said, her eyes suddenly full of tears, but she walked away before I could ask her what she meant. Later, it dawned on me that perhaps Sheila was already HIV-positive, or even Carolina herself, and I felt sick at heart.

Sergeant Terry invited me to a conference of community leaders to talk about the war on crime recently announced by President Clinton. Our congresspeople would be there to hear what we wanted them to tell the new administration in Washington.

I went out looking for Carolina and found her at the Blues Band House, sitting on the steps visiting. She was wearing yellow denim overalls over a white and red striped T-shirt. Her earrings were wooden parrots, red, yellow, green, and blue.

"You look terrific today," I said.

"Put together," she replied. "My color-coordinated look."

I showed her the conference leaflet. "Carolina, I wish you would come with me to this meeting, and get up and talk."

"Oh, no, I couldn't do that," she said.

"You could tell them better than anyone what the price of the drug war is, because you've paid it," I urged her. "You speak so well, and I know they never hear from a mother like you. I wish you would come with me."

"I don't feel too well," she said. "I don't think I could do that, but thanks for inviting me."

"Okay, I understand," I said. "I'll do my best to tell them about Marcus and the Youth Alive! group myself."

"Listen, I'll *try* to come," she said. "It's Tuesday? If I can, I'll come over to your house on Tuesday morning."

Carolina didn't show up, so I drove by myself to the auditorium in downtown Richmond. The mayors and police chiefs of four cities were there, school and court people, city officials, and dozens of officers. Sergeant Terry Ross was the first person I saw when I came into the auditorium, and he came over to give me a hug. Looking at all the uniforms and guns, I thought, Uh-oh, some of these guys are the *real* police, not the Berkeley police!

When we divided ourselves into working groups, all of us interested in youth issues went into one room, and the police went off to meet by themselves. The most passionate people in our meeting had come with their teacher from a high school for kids who were on juvenile probation.

"I mean, things are really bad," one young man pleaded. "I mean, there's babies with nothing to eat!"

A young woman who looked really scared said she feared being attacked by other kids who might be drunk. "They sell malt liquor to kids," she said. "I could buy a forty right now, right by our school."

We emerged from our session with a wish list: mentors, after-school activities, jobs for teens, more sports, close down liquor outlets that sell to kids, start some teen centers. A young man who had been vocal in our group called out our list to the moderator, who wrote it on a blackboard.

Sergeant Terry was the officer who reported from the police group. They wanted to see mentors for youth, after-school programs, jobs for teens, teen centers, crack down on sales of alcohol to youths, gun control, and sports programs!

I was speechless with surprise. My idea of a police wish list was helicopters, drug-sniffing dogs, maybe new search and seizure laws.

Sergeant Terry explained: "We are tired of seeing an endless stream of young people entering the drug trade. Our figures show that about 10 percent of seventeen-year-olds commit much of the violent crime. You might think, okay, we can lock that many up. The trouble is, next year there's another 10 percent. Who knows where it will end? We want alternatives for kids."

Here is a news story, I thought, that will never be reported.

CHAPTER TWENTY-TWO

Elders

One of Mr. Howard's tenants was an elderly lady who had brought up two children. They were grown and on their own, but when both of them became addicted to crack, they moved back in with her. Mr. Howard didn't want to evict the lady, but he couldn't figure out a way to keep her children away. When they took their mother's coats and lamps and other small items to the nearby flea market to try to sell them, Mr. Howard called the police, and Sergeant Terry retrieved most of the things.

Finally, members of the lady's church came and took her away to a senior home. Mr. Howard boarded up the windows and changed the locks so that her children could not get back in.

Mr. Howard said he used to hire local kids to do yard work, but now, he said, "I have to admit, if they ring my doorbell, I tell them to get off my property. You can't trust them anymore. They haven't been raised."

Mahalia called the old peoples' problems "elder abuse," and she tried to help. She tried with Royal Alioto, one of the old men who liked to visit in front of Mr. Howard's closed store. Royal was a dark-skinned, wrinkled old black man who some time in American history had acquired an Italian last name. He was the son of an even older black man who owned a building with six apartments in it that we could see from our living room window. Royal was a drinker, rarely without a brown bag in his hand, and he made a meager living by hauling loads in his tilting, smoking truck with high wooden sides—the kind people try to steer clear of on a freeway. Royal parked it in his father's driveway and lived in one of his apartments.

The tenants there were quiet people, and we hardly ever saw them. In ten years the only one I spoke to besides Royal was a middle-aged nurse, a cousin of Royal's, whom I saw sometimes coming home from work in her uniform. But then Royal's father passed away, leaving no will, and Royal inherited the place.

The nurse moved out, and Royal, whose management skills were nil, rented all the units to people involved with drugs. All day long a group of brown-bag drinkers partied on the front lawn, which grew knee-high. All night, cars and motorcycles pulled up and roared away.

Royal claimed he wanted the addicts to leave, but he couldn't make them go. "I don't know these peoples, Melody," he told me.

Royal's place appeared on our agenda at every block committee meeting. It was no good sending letters to Royal; he drank so much, everything he attempted was ineffectual.

Royal came to me one day and said that some people were taking the property away from him. He showed me foreclosure papers from a mortgage company. I saw that Royal had signed up for a high-interest mortgage with astronomical fees. He had gotten a few thousand dollars cash, which he had already spent, and had made no mortgage payments. I called Mahalia.

She took Royal to see a legal aid lawyer, but at our block meeting, Mahalia reported that the attorney had said Royal had no recourse. I decided to research the lenders. At the courthouse and the library I read all about the Continental Mortgage Company. I found out Continental consisted of just two men, and they were being sued for turning elderly widows out of their homes with nowhere to go. They specialized in offering loans to poor black people like Royal in neighborhoods like Lorin all over the Bay Area. "They should be called Catfish Mortgage," I told Mahalia. "Kings of the bottom feeders."

Royal's mortgage papers had been drawn up by a woman lawyer with offices high in a fancy building in San Francisco. She had charged huge fees, which she paid to herself out of Royal's loan before she gave him the leftover cash.

I had to write a threatening letter before she finally took one of my many calls. She told me she was no longer on the case.

"In other words, you took your money and ran," I said. I should have reported her to the State Bar Association, but how could I find time? No one can right every wrong, I told myself.

Before we knew it, Royal's property was sold cheap on the courthouse steps to Continental Mortgage company—there were no other bidders. On our agenda, we changed the name of the property from Royal's house to the Continental house. It was a raging crack house, squatted by an ever-changing crew of at least two dozen people, and making our lives miserable day and night. The apartments were full of moldy mattresses and trash, and we were afraid of fire. Letters and calls to Continental proved useless. Louis the bus driver and his wife, Manuela, got the worst of it, living right next door.

Berkeley's city manager forced Continental to come to a meeting by levying a series of code violation fines on them, and I attended, along with Mahalia and Sergeant Steve, and the building codes people. One of Continental's two owners came: a sandy-haired man with a blow-dried haircut in his early thirties. His blue eyes had a morally blank "what do you plan to do about it?" look as he stared boldly at his roomful of adversaries. With an innocent air he declared, "I don't know who from our firm negotiated this loan," as if Continental had hundreds of operatives.

"You *don't know*," I said coldly, "which one of the two of you gave a loan to an elderly alcoholic without a job, with no means of support, no hope of making the payments?"

He had the grace to look momentarily embarrassed. Under pressure from the city employees in the room, he made all sorts of promises to evict squatters and fence and board up the building. In return, the city people agreed to waive the fines.

"I had a few questions about his upbringing, and I wanted to demand that he bring his mother along to the next meeting," I told Manuela.

"Yeah," she said, "we could ask her how he turned out so greedy and immoral."

She and I couldn't understand how Continental stood to make money from Royal's place, except that they had gotten it cheaper than the land was worth. Apparently they planned to allow it to decay until it would have to be torn down, and meanwhile we would have to live with it.

Louis and Manuela, Stan and I agreed that we should sue them for destroying our peace. But we were too overwhelmed by the day-to-day stresses of living in Lorin and by our own work and family lives. "There's just a limit to my energy," Manuela said, and I agreed.

Continental did evict Royal, and he moved a few doors down into the Blues Band House and parked his horrendous truck on the street, accumulating parking tickets. Louis reported at our meeting: "Our mailman Percy told me he's delivering envelopes from Continental Mortgage all over the neighborhood. Not just their ads—I'm talking about payment coupons! Lots of people have signed up for those loans."

Stan and I got a call from Hiram one night after ten o'clock, usually far too late for Hiram to be up. He sounded scared. "Could you guys come right over here? I'm having trouble."

We hurried down the block. Hiram's door was wide open, and he was sitting in the kitchen in his wheelchair. The room was dim, lit by light coming from a lamp in the bedroom.

Stan stepped inside, and as he did so, Mrs. Burley's rather menacing looking grandson Wilber appeared from behind the kitchen door. "Hello, Wilber," Stan said steadily. Wilber said hi in a low voice and brushed past me and disappeared into the night.

"He came back again," Hiram said, all excited.

Hiram explained that earlier, he had opened the door to Wilber and some woman—Hiram didn't know her—and they had both pushed their way into his apartment. "They took my money from my wallet and my pain medicine out of the drawer by my bed," Hiram said. Hiram had phoned us from the bedroom as soon as they had left, but before he could get to the kitchen door to lock it, while we were on our way over, Wilber had come back. Hiram didn't know why.

"You scared him," Hiram said. "You ran him off." As he talked, he slowly calmed down.

"Do you want us to call the police?" Stan asked him.

"No," Hiram said. "I'm afraid to do that. No, no, no. He'll hurt me somehow later on. Don't call them."

We were reluctant to agree to that, but it had to be Hiram's decision. Then Hiram said this was the second time Wilber had robbed him; the first time, he'd been outside in his wheelchair and Wilber had taken Hiram's money from his shirt pocket.

"But why did you open the door to him?" I asked.

"I shouldn't have, but he said he just wanted to talk to me."

I looked at Hiram, disheveled in a pajama top and a pair of pants cut open at the cuffs to make room for his swollen feet. We've got to get him out of here, I thought.

Mahalia agreed. She made calls all over town looking for a wheelchair-accessible apartment, but they were scarce. Meanwhile, she set up a checking account for Hiram, with his disability checks automatically deposited to it. Stan put a new light over Hiram's door, so he could see who was outside by looking out the bedroom window.

I was at the church one day when I noticed a new leaflet on the bulletin board. It said, "Apartment for rent, welfare okay, disabled only." When no one was looking, I took it down and put it in my pocket. I couldn't imagine anyone more in need than Hiram.

The place turned out to be light and clean and quiet. Mahalia helped out with the paperwork, and Hiram's social worker made all the arrangements. The young man who delivered food from Meals-on-Wheels to Hiram volunteered his truck to help him move. In the dark on a winter evening, we finished putting Hiram's few belongings into the truck. I followed it with Hiram in my station wagon.

"Kiss Alma Street good-bye, Hiram," I said.

"I'm outta here," he said, "and I'm not looking back."

Libby and Rosemary and I fixed up Hiram's new place with hand-me-downs as if we were playing house. To him, the best part was the shower. Hiram's old apartment had only had a bathtub he couldn't use, and he'd had to wash himself at the sink. Rosemary had an extra shower curtain, and I gave Hiram the plastic shower seat I'd used when I'd torn my Achilles tendon.

"You guys threw me a lifeline," Hiram told Stan, "and I grabbed it."

Hiram hadn't told anyone where he was going. He didn't want Wilber finding him and coming around his new apartment.

Hiram's new place was a haven for me too. I stopped by often to visit and get some peace and quiet. "Come on in, Miss Type A Personality," Hiram would say. "Make yourself a cup of tea and sit down."

"Think about it Hiram," I said, sitting on his couch. "Ohlone people lived where Lorin is now for thousands of years, unbroken. It's only been a hundred and seventy-five years since they lost this place, and no one has been here long at all after that. There's been the Spanish, then Japanese people farmed it, and they both had it taken away. Now the black people are losing Lorin too."

"Right now," Hiram said, "everything black people acquired for fifty years is being taken from them wholesale. Just transferred out of their hands so fast they don't know what's hitting them."

At the prison, Jarvis followed the progress of the whole Continental fiasco and Hiram's flight from Alma Street.

"Sometimes I get so mad, I can't even meditate," I told him. He had a suggestion. His Tibetan teacher Chagdud Rinpoche told him that if he practiced bowing, he could cultivate an attitude of surrender toward the things he could not change. Jarvis and I made a pact to do prostrations together, me at home, and him in his cell. He had just enough room to stretch his body down in a full-length bow on the floor next to his bunk.

We both bowed down and got up until our leg muscles were sore.

"It does help," I reported to him. "When I'm lying flat out on the floor I think, 'I give up,' and for an instant I do surrender. The trouble is, I come up fighting, still wanting to do battle with what isn't fair."

CHAPTER TWENTY-THREE

Right Speech

I was in my garden pulling crabgrass out from under my hedge when I heard Carletta's shrill voice suddenly rise above the voices of the other people drinking forties on the lawn of Continental Mortgage's squatter house across the street.

"A-*POL*-ogize!" she screeched. "A-*POL*-ogize right now!"

I peeked between the bushes. Carletta's two-year-old son Troy was blubbering and pulling away from her as she tugged and jerked him by the hand to face old Royal sitting on the grass, drunk out of his mind.

"You tell Royal you're sorry for what you said, right now!" Royal, leaning back on the grass on his elbows, cradling his forty in one hand, didn't look as if he needed an apology from a baby.

"He's two," I thought. "Two is never having to say you're sorry."

Carletta didn't want to have to put down her malt liquor, so she managed to switch Troy's tiny hand to her left hand, squeezing it into her grip along with the can, freeing up her right arm, which she swung back and then down, sending his diapered bottom, his little legs, and tiny shoes swinging forward with the blow. Troy's blubbering turned abruptly into a scream, and then a prolonged wail.

Old Mrs. Burley's drug-dealer nephew Wilber Gates was in the drinking group too, and he called out helpfully to Carletta, "Make him shut up!"

I dropped back down on my hands and knees, breathing hard, sending huffs of air out my nose in gusts, and I saw myself race out of my garden gate and across the street and grab Carletta. She was about my size, and I imagined myself taking her by surprise and seizing her by her small shoulders and shaking her, the whole time yelling, "Apologize! Apologize, Carletta!" until in my daydream she gave in and went down on her knees and said to Troy, "I'm sorry."

But I just pulled and pulled on crabgrass, hearing my own mother's voice out of control. She had done it to me exactly like Carletta, starting out with yelling, swiftly followed by a slap or a kick or worse, and she was full of hypocrisy too. I wasn't allowed to say "bad" words, even though when she flew into rages and berated me, she would call me a "shit-assed little bastard," and a "piss-ass brat." Once when I was five, I had tried out telling my mother to "shut up," and she had washed my mouth out with soap.

After I learned to meditate, I could hear her voice running like a tape in my mind sometimes, and I wrote down a list of the phrases I could recall from her angry language. Some were enigmatic admonishments like, "You've got another think coming!" and, "I'm telling you in no uncertain terms!" that must have come down to her from my great-grandmother and grandmother to land on my tongue-lashed ears.

What are uncertain terms? I would wonder.

All I knew when she yelled words I couldn't understand was that she was dangerously angry. But looking at my list, I saw that a lot of my mother's profanity was twisted out of her Christian fundamentalist girlhood: I'll knock you to High Heaven! I'll knock you to Kingdom Come! You're going to pay Holy Hell! How can heaven and the Kingdom of God be places to which a child is knocked? How can hell be holy?

One of the phrases on my mother's language list was, "I'm going to beat the living daylights out of you." Looking at those words, I didn't like the beating, but I liked the idea of "living daylights."

Are they enlightenment? I wondered. Are the living daylights the human spirit? If so, they can't be beaten out. The living daylights can dim, but they can never be extinguished. I thought about times I'd yelled at my kids, and I couldn't remember myself apologizing to them.

Right Speech

I'd started out as a young single mother knowing that I didn't want to talk to my own children the way my mother had talked to me, but it had taken me years to learn a better way.

I'd had a roommate who had helped me by threatening to move out if I didn't stop yelling at my kids. When she'd said that, I was standing tensely at the stove in our crowded apartment heating beans and flipping tortillas with my fingers on the griddle, getting ready to feed Rosemary, who was perched at the kitchen table. Rosemary sassed me—I couldn't remember what she'd said—and I not only yelled at her, I threw a taco across the kitchen in her general direction. My roommate walked in just in time to see the beans and lettuce scatter under the legs of Rosemary's chair as she burst into tears.

"Don't ever do something like that again," my roommate said, "or I'm leaving."

"I didn't mean to hit her with it," I'd said defensively. I hadn't "meant" anything. That taco flew out of my hand as mindlessly as the stack of cold tortillas sat next to my frying pan. At least I hadn't thrown the pan, as my mother might have done. Trying to change myself, I used to wonder, is it possible that this is going to stop with me?

Still weeding and trying to remember, I thought I'd probably apologized to my roommate, but I couldn't remember telling Rosemary I was sorry. It's not too late, I thought. She's only thirty.

Gradually my breathing returned to normal as I filled my wheelbarrow with weeds, and Troy's crying subsided too. I wheeled the barrow to my compost heap and emptied it, and then, pulling my gloves off, I walked out my garden gate, and strolled, as if I had nothing better to do, over to the group on the lawn.

Royal and Carletta looked up with their smeary malt-liquor smiles, and Wilber gave me a stare. "How are you all today?" I said, with a geeky fake smile. "It's such a pretty day."

And everyone answered, "Uh-huh," and, "Sure is," except Wilber, who was giving me one of those prison yard stares, and I was ignoring him.

"I think I'll walk up to the flea market," I fibbed, and blathered on for a while, and then I said what I had thought of to say when, in my garden, I had finally composed my mind: "Carletta, I think this little boy Troy of yours must be one of the most beautiful children anywhere around here."

We both stood regarding him, such a short person, such a busy person, climbing up onto the curb and down, and indeed he was a pretty child.

"Yes, he is," she said proudly, and smiled.

CHAPTER TWENTY-FOUR

The Garden of Our Dreams

Whenever Shyaam and I sat around my kitchen table and I told him stories about my investigations job, he shook his head about all the terrible things my clients had done.

"All it takes for a trip to death row is two seconds and a gun," I told him.

"Plenty of kids have that," Shyaam said.

"One capital trial can cost two hundred thousand dollars," I said. "With money like that we could ask ten young drug dealers, 'What were your original dreams?' I'm tired of doing last aid, Shyaam, I want to do something that will show people that kids are not just a problem."

"What if we started a gardening project in South Berkeley?" he suggested. He said that if we suggested boating or camping, the kids would boat or camp. "They want to do *anything* but stand out here doing nothing."

I didn't hesitate. It seemed so good and simple: take kids plus dirt, add water, grow food. Of course, it wasn't that easy.

We only had two things: a group of about ten youths fourteen to seventeen years old, and a chance to pay them the minimum wage. We found out that if we got our garden going, it could become a job site under the Federal Youth Job Training Program started in Lyndon Johnson days, after the Watts riots of 1965, that provided summer jobs for low-income high school kids. Although the program's funding had diminished every year, a few hundred of Berkeley's lowest-income teens still got summer jobs, mostly at the university or with the school district, doing office work or maintenance.

Shyaam wanted to do something the kids could be proud of; something that could eventually do without federal funding. He had worked with a horticulture project in Mali, West Africa, and he had a vision of "restoring people," he said, "to the lost agricultural heritage that's rightfully theirs." African-American families had lived on the land only one or two generations before, but they had lost that connection when they left the South. Agriculture had a negative image with some in the black community because of slavery and sharecropping, Shyaam said, but he and I both knew elderly black people with gardens in their backyards, like Addie Josephs, who could show the kids their love for growing food.

We had our eyes on a vacant lot for our garden. It had a billboard on it that usually advertised alcohol on one side and tobacco on the other, showing smiling black people drinking and smoking. Someone dumped an old mattress among the weeds that the little kids used as a trampoline. There were often night card games on the lot, and twenty-four hours a day, drugs could be bought along the sidewalk. Whenever Shyaam and I looked at that billboard, we pictured vines growing on it and, hanging from its frame, baskets of produce for sale.

Bob Bradford, an African-American man active in the crime-watch committee on that block, owned the lot. He offered us the use of the ground around the billboard for the price of the county taxes. In order to start a garden there, we needed that money and a fence, and we soon found out we would need nonprofit status, a legal lease agreement, and liability insurance. I checked out library books on grant writing and got started.

We decided to act like a garden project even if we didn't have a garden. Shyaam and I got more and more excited about what we wanted to do. Every time I saw the kids on Alma Street, they would ask me, "Melody, when are we going to start our garden?"

We decided to go ahead and clean up the billboard lot, and one Saturday a dozen people harvested four truckloads of debris. It seemed as if the broken glass would never end, but the littlest children seemed to have an inexhaustible fascination with carefully picking it up.

I hauled my round black barbecue over there, and Shyaam cooked hot dogs for everybody while the big kids gave the little kids rides in my wheelbarrow. It felt scary, though, to be out there, flying in the faces of the drug dealers who considered that lot their turf. They crossed the street and hung around in front of a liquor store. "Those guys will be back over here as soon as we leave," Shyaam said.

Turf, I thought, is like a lawn: you mow it, fertilize it, and spray it with weed killer, but you can't eat it. Turf is not a garden.

Shyaam thought that if we occupied the lot and made it beautiful with plants and people, the dealers would move away from it. He pointed out that they didn't hang around the child care center or the gospel music store on the next block. Shyaam nailed a sign up on the frame of the billboard: FUTURE HOME OF COMMUNITY GARDEN.

The only thing I saved out of the trash we raked up was a broken yellow plastic sign: CAUTION, CHILDREN, with the figure of a running child snapped in two. I put the bright yellow sign in my kitchen window as a shrine to broken children everywhere. Its glow made me think of the yellow robes of Buddhist monks. I'd read of a monk in Thailand who ordained rain forest trees, draping them in saffron yellow robes to try to save them from being cut down.

"Maybe I can find someone to ordain the neighbor kids as trees," I told Stan. "Then maybe people would sit down around them to protect them from being hurt."

Gardening for us at first was mostly meetings, with an attorney who donated the lease agreement we needed, and with the board of a non-profit organization to convince them to adopt our project. We wrote our grant applications under their auspices, but then, without warning, that organization folded, leaving us to start looking for sponsorship all over again.

Meanwhile, Shyaam took the youths on trips to organic farms and gardens, and I went along whenever I could. Ruth's son Dondi and Angela's son Terrel were often with us. They were living in foster homes outside Lorin, but Shyaam stayed in close touch with them. Sometimes I asked Terrel about his little brother DeShawn and his cousin Gideon, Amina's former pupil. "They're in East Oakland. They're okay," was all he ever said.

At the university agro-ecology farm in Santa Cruz we met students from all over the world learning how to restore land and grow food using little water. Nearby, we toured a garden where homeless people grew a large amount of food and served a big pot of soup every day.

At a special farm where rare vegetables and fruit trees were culti-vated, the master gardener, a redheaded, bearded man named Doug, started the visit by having us join hands under a big oak tree and intro-duce ourselves. Our group comprised six youths, each of whom said, "I live on Alma Street in Berkeley." The adults were Shyaam and our bus driver, a motherly black woman named Carima, three adult volun-teers — an older black man, a grandma with two little grandchildren with her, and me — and a special West African guest, a man in a flowing out-fit from the horticulture project in Mali that Berkeley sponsored.

It was midsummer, and we walked along grassy paths between mounded beds closely planted with intermingled greens, herbs, and flowers. Doug showed us how the soil, built up over twenty years, was so loose and fertile that we could easily plunge our hands into the warm dirt up to our wrists. It was hard for me to imagine how we would grow anything in the glass-laced, hardened soil of the billboard lot, but I wanted to try. Doug talked about how strong roots are, able to push their way around rocks and under cement, and he recommended plants we could cultivate to loosen our soil.

Doug showed the youths how to plant lettuce. I took photos of them patting seedlings into the earth like tender young fathers putting babies to bed.

"I've never seen these kids' faces so relaxed," our bus driver Carima told me, watching them reaching up into trees to pick a kind of peach none of us had ever seen — a blood peach, bright red on the inside, and very sweet. We all had red juice running down our chins.

At the top of the sloping garden was a small lawn surrounded by stones and planted in low-lying camomile in bloom. We took turns lying down on it and smelling the cloud of pineapplish scent that rose from the plants when our bodies crushed them slightly. The little kids rubbed the camomile with their palms and sniffed their hands.

Nearby I saw what looked like a cage under a tree. "What is this?" I asked Doug.

"That's a humane trap," he said. "Raccoons get in over the deer fence, and we catch them and take them far away. We like them, but we can't let them ruin the garden."

I stood there looking at that trap and wishing there were a simple and humane solution to the problem of gun toters ruining life on Alma Street.

Doug gave the kids pitchforks and showed them how to dig potatoes. I took photos of the kids turning over forkfuls of soil full of potatoes clinging to thin roots. They had never seen potato plants before.

The farm had a big kitchen where the kids washed and cut up the potatoes. They decided to make french fries, a familiar food. The potato varieties were red, yellow, white, and purple, a rainbow of french fries. We made a salad of a dozen kinds of greens, decorated with edible flowers. Shyaam had brought along a big white cake with coconut frosting that one of the grandmothers had contributed for our trip. Doug and the other gardeners, who usually eschewed sugar, had big pieces and said they hadn't eaten anything like that delicious cake for a long time.

Doug told me he wanted to have more "at-risk" teenagers come to the garden. I explained that the kids liked to be called "youth." They cringed whenever they were called "poor" or "low-income," and they thought the word "teenagers" was dumb. They hated euphemisms like "inner city" and "at-risk."

"They *are* at risk, though," I told Doug. "Everybody thinks it means they might get killed or put in prison, but they're even more likely to get depressed or overanxious or to give up."

We ended the day lying around with full bellies under the big oak tree, talking in the shade. The grown-ups spun out their mutual visions of a world where organic food would grow on every spare plot of city land.

When it was time to leave, the kids performed their special goodbye Shyaam had taught them: each one thanked our hosts and said what he had liked best about the visit, and then, with a funny bow from the waist, passed the limelight to the next youth around the circle. Blood peaches and multicolored french fries were the two most popular memories. The first teenager quipped, "I don't really *eat* salad, but thank you very much anyway." The others repeated that line, and we all ended up laughing.

Shyaam and I both were glad the kids had met Doug the gardener; he had a simple life, drove an old car, and was passionate about preserving the earth for future generations.

Very late in the summer, Doug phoned and said, "Yours is the nicest group of youths we ever had visit." He invited us back to meet a documentary film crew.

When we returned, the apples were ripe, and many had fallen to the ground. While the moviemakers filmed, we filled a wheelbarrow with rare varieties of apples, red, gold, striped, green, orange. While the rest of us harvested squash and cabbages, Dondi reduced a whole wheelbarrow full of apples to rich, cloudy juice, using an electric juicer.

"How do you think I could get a job at a place like this?" Dondi asked Doug.

"Learn to be a grower," Doug answered. "There's going to be a need for a lot of organic farmers."

Doug and the seed-saving garden were supported by a foundation; we had applied to the same one, and several others, but hadn't gotten a grant. So far, our garden existed only in our dreams. So when Doug asked me at lunchtime, "How is your project going?" I was reluctant to tell him that the fact was, we had lost our land.

On a sunny day, four guys in a car had driven by the billboard lot and shot three people right there on the corner. Shyaam arrived on the scene just after the cops did. Shyaam, who didn't want to look, saw one man's body lying bloody on the sidewalk in the noontime sun, an officer trying to resuscitate him, but he died.

Shyaam said, "We need a garden, but we also need to feel safe." We realized we couldn't use the billboard lot.

It was hard to describe our conditions to someone like Doug. In the setting of his garden, Alma Street seemed hard to believe. "This is in Berkeley?" he asked me.

The movie crew followed the kids around the garden interviewing them, and they kept saying, "We don't have our own garden yet, but we're going to."

The Garden of Our Dreams

On the way home in the van, Dondi mentioned that he had gone to a store near his foster home. "I saw they don't even *have* the kind of malt liquor they sell at home!" He sounded outraged. One of the kids asked Dondi, "So when are we coming to visit your foster home?"

"Never," Dondi said. He was smiling, but there was an uncomfortable silence, because we knew that the group of boys from Alma Street probably wouldn't be welcome where Dondi was living. Unless they were with Shyaam, they hardly ever left the block. Shyaam said they were afraid of having some kind of trouble, either with other kids, or with police or adults who didn't know them.

Between trips, they so profoundly had nothing to do, that when somebody threw an old sofa out of an apartment building up the block from our house, the kids slouched on that couch and hung over the back of it for months as if it were a life raft.

"At least," I told Stan, "we don't have to worry about our couch potatoes watching too much TV." Many of the sets that once were in their apartments had long since been stolen or sold for dope.

We never did find land for a garden that first summer. School finally started, the rains came and soaked the couch, and city workers hauled its sodden mass away.

If it occurred to either Shyaam or me to give up, we didn't say so to each other. Other urban greeners, such as Cathy Sneed, a San Francisco jail deputy who taught inmates and parolees how to grow vegetables, were our inspiration. After reading an article about her garden, I said to Shyaam, "Maybe the youths could just skip the going-to-jail part and go straight to growing food."

Our grant applications were in passionate prose: "In the countryside, small farmers are dispossessed, rural communities decimated, the knowledge and love of caring for land, almost vanished," I wrote.

"In the cities," Shyaam wrote, "whole populations are malnourished by their alienation from the land and nature's cycles, dependent on fossil fuels to bring expensive food grown far away. There is no large grocery store and no source of affordable, unpoisoned produce."

One section Shyaam wrote said: "The majority of African-American youth in this community has lost faith in the system and has developed a fatalistic and hopeless attitude. Our youth need to connect themselves to nature, heal and renew their community, and acquire skills with which they can provide for their families."

We said we wanted "S.E.E.D.": Sustainable, Ecological Economic Development. While our visions grew in the air, we had nothing on the ground.

Just when I felt most discouraged, I went to hear Joanna Macy, a Buddhist teacher. She showed a photo of monks she had visited in Tibet who had the task of rebuilding after the Chinese government had destroyed their ancient monastery. They had worked for years, and when they had nearly finished, Chinese soldiers again destroyed everything they had built. Joanna Macy showed a photo of the head monk. She had asked him how he could keep going. He told her that if they simply did the work of placing one brick upon another, someday the monastery would be standing again.

When we got a copy of the documentary the youths had starred in at the seed-saving garden, we organized a showing on a rainy winter day at Reverend Clara's church. There were the wheelbarrow full of apples again and Shyaam and the youths harvesting squash. The film was about genetic depletion in food crops all over the earth. There had once been a hundred kinds of broccoli, but now there were two; thousands of kinds of corn were disappearing, replaced by a few hybrids.

I felt nervous watching the film with the kids, its vision was so pessimistic. Shyaam often talked about how the kids said they saw no future for themselves. I wondered how much of their despair came from knowing, even at some subconscious level, that environmental disasters loomed even larger than the gun war around us. They looked glum watching the film. As a grandmother, I wanted to be able to say, "This isn't something you have to worry about, because the adults are taking care of it." But the film showed a decrease in funding for solutions like Doug's seed-saving garden.

Shyaam and I worked all during the rainy winter. By the time the kids got out of school the next summer, we were ready. Shyaam found a fenced rent-free garden at a city-owned senior center across town. It felt safe there, like a secret garden, no drug dealers anywhere around. We were disappointed to have to move to another neighborhood, but there were no open spaces available in Lorin, and we wanted to get started. At first, the seniors weren't so sure about teenagers coming around, but Shyaam and I promised to be responsible for the kids, and we said if it didn't work out, they could evict us anytime.

It turned out to be a perfect match: the kids, so hungry for love and attention from adults, and the seniors, eager to teach what they knew about the hobby they loved. Flora, a black lady who walked with a cane, approached the youths with authority and affection, even though she was shorter than most of them. She told us she had raised goats in Berkeley as a girl, and she taught a class for us on traditional African-American crops, like a squash grown in the South called "kush," an African word. Watching the kids with Flora, I realized that the way you learn to do something like gardening is by putting your body up close to the body of someone who knows how to do it, and doing it with them.

Mrs. Tillman, who was from South Carolina, told the youths how African slaves from Sierra Leone had known how to grow a kind of rice and had taught the whites how to do it in the wetlands of the Carolinas. Shyaam had the group study George Washington Carver's agricultural work.

We advertised in the South Berkeley neighborhood newsletter for volunteers, and Alfred, a black man in his sixties who lived alone, was the only person who phoned me. Moving stiffly on his bad leg, Alfred started all of our first seedlings in cut-open milk cartons on the porch of his tiny apartment. Early every morning, he rode the bus to the garden. Alfred didn't care much for the kids. He related most to plants and bugs. "You think you're climbing Everest, don't you?" he would address a line of ants on a hill of corn.

"Come on now, come on, get your feet on in here," he would admonish a tomato plant as he guided its roots expertly into the ground.

Of the half dozen grant applications we'd made to foundations and corporations, we'd gotten only one: $5,000 from a federally funded substance abuse prevention program. We used the money for our insurance premium and some equipment. An upscale catalog company gave us tools. We won a rototiller in a national community gardens contest.

Alfred and I careered all over town together in my station wagon, picking up donations and making purchases. He insisted on telling me how to drive until I finally told him, "Alfred, I've been driving a car since

I was fifteen, I know what I'm doing." He subsided about my driving, but he carried on a nonstop monologue complaining about the depredations of modern agriculture, global warming, and acid rain, and he hardly needed an "uh-huh" from me to keep on talking. In between his ecological harangue, Alfred would make confidential comments to an invisible passenger: "Can't *believe* she's still in second gear," he would say under his breath. "Can't *stand* to hear an engine lugging." Alfred commandeered all the broken bags of soil at discount nurseries and pressured the store managers into donating them. Three times that first summer we filled my car until it had to be driven back to the garden at twenty miles an hour, low to the ground. My car acquired the nickname, "the dirt car."

We had crude rules, made up by the youths themselves, posted on the garden fence: "No throwing tools," and "No profanity." A lot of dirt clods, bad language, and a few tools flew the first weeks before we made the sign. "Hey!" Shyaam would call out. "Hey! We don't act that way here!"

He gave his dispute resolution class and talked about how to say you're sorry. There was so much to learn: not just gardening, but how to show up, be on time, work and keep working, and in some cases, how to talk to adults with respect.

I reminded myself that adolescence is the push-pull time when responsibility is learned. Even so, more than once I thought about the bumper sticker that reads, "Hire a teenager while he still knows everything."

Half the summer, we pondered our project's name. Shyaam and I knew the kids should name it. One of the youths suggested B-Town Greens. "B-Town" was Berkeley's graffiti tag, and I liked that name, but the kids came up with dozens of other suggestions. In the end, they chose the best one, Strong Roots, and the slogan, "Gardening for Survival."

We were all surprised by how much food we grew: corn, tomatoes, peas, beans, greens. Every few days, the youths filled a plastic tub with their produce and carried it inside the senior center where they offered it to the old people, who thanked them, patted them, and beamed approval upon them while the kids grinned until I thought their faces must be aching. Watching them, I thought that what a person really wants to do in life is to find a thing that needs doing, and do it well.

The Alma Street kids were joined by others from our neighborhood who also qualified for the federal summer jobs program. Not everyone stuck with the program. Some had too many problems a job just couldn't solve, and they dropped out, replaced by other youths from the neighborhood. Dondi and Terrel usually came to work in the garden, commuting by bike from their foster homes.

One day near the end of the summer, I was driving sixteen-year-old Teresa, one of the few girls to join Strong Roots, to pick up her baby daughter. I asked Teresa if she wanted to come back next year.

"No," she said. "I don't really like it. The work is too hard." My shoulders slumped a little as I drove, until she added, "Next year, I'm going to see if I can work in a lab or a pharmacy, because I think that's what I'd like to do." I was certain that Teresa, who'd never cashed a paycheck before Strong Roots, couldn't have aspired to such a job unless she'd had her first one.

Each of the youths earned about $1,000 during the whole summer. Most of them asked Shyaam to keep their money for them. That way no one at home would take it. Shyaam took them to a discount mall where they turned some of their money into school clothes.

CHAPTER TWENTY-FIVE

I Shall Not Be Moved

I pushed my grandbaby Liam in his high chair close to the kitchen window to watch the birds at the feeder. "Buh," he said, "Buh"—and pointed a chubby finger.

The birds, waiting for a turn at the window feeder, flew fast onto the tip ends of the apricot tree's lanky branches and clung there for dear life as the branches bounced and swayed wildly from the impact of their tiny bodies.

"See, Liam," I instructed him. "Birds just want to have fun." When there was a vacant perch, the "buhs" swooped to the feeder. Often two at once fluttered and squawked, squabbling over a place in line. The birds provided perfect perpetual motion for a baby's entertainment.

"I don't want to live with different birds," I told Liam. "I don't want to live with strange trees I don't even know."

Liam didn't understand me. "Mama," he commented, and waved "bye-bye."

"Your mama is coming to pick you up soon," I told him.

When I tried to think of where we could move, I simply could not picture all of us somewhere among trees who would be strangers. Why should I lose my home, I thought, because the country is going to hell and my neighborhood with it?

Keeping Liam at the edge of my peripheral vision, I idly scanned the business section of the paper. I always look at the financial pages because that's where so much crime news is reported, about billion-dollar scams and stock market scandals that end up closing down workplaces and forcing thousands of other families to go looking for strange places to live.

Who *are* these happy bond traders I see in the news photos, I wondered, jubilant over higher unemployment figures? Why should *I* go, just because the government is making sure *they* stay happy? Where do *their* mothers live?

I won't leave. I refuse. It sounds good in French: *"Je refuse!"* I refuse to join the refugee lines of white flight out of the city.

"It will take all races to make a better world," Nelson Mandela says in the paper. We should be coming together now, not flying apart.

Turning the newspaper pages, I took strength from the people in the former Yugoslavia who refused to choose sides. I imagined myself a woman whose mother was a Moslem and whose father was a Serb and who was married to a Croat. There were interviews with such people, who stayed on in Sarajevo, determined to remain true to the tolerant culture they had known in more civilized times.

The bored baby, tired of the "buhs," turned his attention to the pile of cereal bits I dumped onto his high-chair tray. I scooted him over toward the stove so that I'd have him within arm's reach while I heated his tofu and broccoli.

I don't want to live with different people, I thought, let alone strange trees. I can't find a place to live where I know nearly everyone I can see when I look out my window.

I don't want to live where white people are grouped up together. The unawarely racist things they sometimes say, unchallenged, would drive me wild. Moving out of Lorin's isolation into the isolation of white America wouldn't make me more connected; it would only disconnect me from the life I've known.

As I pushed bits of tofu and broccoli temptingly around on Liam's tray, my spirit resisted the prospect of giving up. I'm not a quitter, I thought, and neither am I trying to become a hero or a martyr.

We'd had an all-women's retreat at our Zen center. Our teacher was Maylie Scott, one of our women priests. She said that behind the noise of the dramas we are living, we could hear the sound of our confident inner voices, if we calmed ourselves and listened. "Our Buddha nature is a kind of quiet joy," she said. I wrote, "The quiet joy of confidence" on a piece of turquoise-colored paper and put it on my refrigerator. Every time I read it, I took a deep breath.

I wiped the sated baby's face and hands while he struggled and deposited him on the floor with some cooking pots. I sat down with him and we stacked and banged together. The noisy joy of a grandmother, I thought.

When Amina arrived, she said, "The neighborhood is really nice right now." She was right. A sunny afternoon in the neighborhood is all any urban person could want: children playing, making happy sounds, people out visiting on the sidewalks, cheerful music playing somewhere, all at peace.

I stood in the front doorway as she left and watched her show off her baby to a young man she went to high school with and his girlfriend.

Standing there, I told myself, Give up wanting results. Go day by day, doing what good you can. After all, does the Dalai Lama feel like giving up because the Chinese are still occupying Tibet? The Dalai Lama isn't attached to results. Learn from him. Accept that the neighborhood is getting worse. It doesn't have to get better for me to stay.

CHAPTER TWENTY-SIX

Look

I hardly noticed myself shifting from trying to make the drug people go away to trying to take care of them—at least the few I knew.

On any day when I came home, Ruth was likely to be outside, acting out her full-blown crack psychosis in the street. She would "go off," as we said, wailing, screaming, or rolling around, breaking bottles, or hitting people. Most such episodes ended with the police coming. They would stand around, notebooks out, trying to figure out what was going on, confused by several overwrought people trying to tell their stories at once.

Sometimes Mahalia would come, or someone else from mental health. If they thought Ruth was "a danger to herself or others," they would capture her and drive her away for forty-eight hours of observation, where she would come to her senses enough to be let out again. If Ruth broke the law, such as smashing a window, she would go to the jail for a couple of nights, and then come back.

Frequently she missed court hearings she was supposed to show up for, warrants were issued, and then she would get bail again. She never did anything criminal enough to be sent to a prison.

"All of this fruitless back-and-forth costs so much," Mahalia said. "Ten times what long-term residential care would cost."

We were stuck with Ruth, she was one of ours, and we dealt with her as a medieval village coped with its madwoman. Most people just watched apprehensively out the windows or crossed the street when they saw her coming. People were kind enough to Ruth, but some screamed at her and hit her back. Some offered her a beer. The teenagers, friends of her son Dondi, avoided Ruth, but they were never cruel to her.

My computer listed half a dozen files about Ruth: letters I wrote to judges asking them to sentence her to treatment, letters to treatment facilities trying to get her in. More than once Shyaam coaxed Ruth to go with him to the county's only emergency residential treatment place, where she could have stayed for two weeks, but she didn't have to stay and she came right back, sometimes within two hours. She was simply too far gone to make any self-preserving moves.

Once, the youth van drove around the corner bringing Shyaam and the teenagers, including Ruth's son Dondi, back from a field trip. Louis the bus driver had gone along on the trip with his son, and he told me how it happened.

"We pull up, and oh, shit, there's Ruth down on the ground in the middle of the street and two cops are over her, wrestling around trying to get cuffs on her. Nobody in the van says a word. Dondi looked like, 'Scotty beam me up *now.*' He didn't know where to look. He just jumped out of the van and ran off around the corner. What a shame, seeing your mother like that, in front of all the other kids."

I told Mahalia about how that field trip ended and she said, "That story is a perfect example of how futile it is to provide something for children without meeting the whole family's needs."

Ruth knew I was writing letters about her. I asked her sometimes, "Do you want me to write to the judge for you?" and she would say yes.

"Help, me, Melody, you have to help me."

Once she screamed at me from half a block away, "I love you Melody. You're the only white person I ever loved."

This was a dubious honor because on other days she felt betrayed by me and my letters, and she was equally likely to yell, "I hate you, Melody! I hate Shyaam and Mahalia too!"

After a while, I didn't write any more letters; there was no place to send them. If the old-style mental hospitals had still been open, Ruth would have been in one, drugged or tied to a bed or undergoing shock treatments to her already burning brain. As it was, she was loose on the open ward of our street.

At night, Ruth roamed outside, prey for the predators. Sometimes her deep voice out there would wake me. "Ruth," my dreaming mind would say, and then I would be awake with a sinking heart, listening to hear her voice again. Unable to go back to sleep, I wrapped myself in a blanket and sat on the couch looking out at the night sky yellow from the sulphurous streetlights reflected against the low-lying clouds, waiting to see if I could catch a glimpse of Ruth passing by in the night.

For long periods, Ruth was childless; the children were with relatives or in foster care, and Ruth cried the loss of her children up and down the street. Sometimes she came over to me on the sidewalk and talked about her dead baby.

"My baby Amina's in heaven, Melody," she would say, big tears rolling down her strong-jawed face. She would start out hugging me and end up hanging on me with her full weight. She was so much taller than me, holding her up hurt the small of my back, and I would have to press her upright again. I would put my hand on her chest and push saying, "Let me rub your heart."

I was doing that one morning and she was standing very still with her eyes closed letting me, when she suddenly opened her eyes and looked into mine and said, in her old voice, her normal voice, "I feel like my chest has been cut open and my heart is burning on fire."

Another time, I met her on the sidewalk just about suppertime. "How are you doing, Ruth?" I asked her, but she didn't answer, and she seemed so far away, her eyes unfocused and wandering, she didn't seem to see me. The setting sun on her face lit her coppery skin and hair. She was looking past me over my shoulder when I saw an expression of wonder move softly into her eyes.

"Look!" she whispered, and took my arm and turned me so that I could see that the sky was on fire in the west with a rose and gold autumn sunset.

CHAPTER TWENTY-SEVEN

Community Service

Black History month was green, the February rains turning the meadows in the hills the soft color of new green rising under last year's gray-yellow grass. Lorin's celebration was to be a cultural evening at the senior center. To my surprise, Shyaam phoned to tell me that the Black History month committee at the youth center had chosen me to receive an award for outstanding community service. I was so pleased, I hardly knew what to say. I told Stan, "This is the nicest honor I've ever had in my life."

"It's great to see your work being recognized," Stan said.

"You deserve the award too," I told him. "You've worked hard to donate me to the neighborhood."

"I haven't minded," he said, "but we can't keep doing this forever."

The night of the event, the hall was full of neighbors and city staff people. The Strong Roots youths were all gathered around one table, and a display of photos of our gardens and field trips was on the wall. Most of our block committee was there, along with Mahalia, Sergeant Terry, our social worker Herb, and many others from the city staff.

A troupe of little girls in bright African-print costumes performed a dance, and a drill team of boys showed off their moves. The postmaster of Berkeley, an African-American man, gave an inspirational speech recounting the history of the civil rights movement and Dr. King.

Shyaam was master of ceremonies, and as he called our names, the six honorees, all of us women, all African American except me, came up to be presented. Each of us was given a clock inscribed with our names and the words "Outstanding Service to the Community." I had never felt so proud.

Shyaam's speech was not about the past. He spoke about the struggle to create sustainable employment. He talked, as he often did, about hope.

CHAPTER TWENTY-EIGHT

Gun Control

When I heard, two months later, that two of our youths, Angela's son Terrel, fifteen, and Ruth's son Dondi, seventeen, had been caught on a bus with a loaded gun, I felt as if I had been kicked in the stomach. The last I had seen them, the Saturday before, they had been bent over placing tiny lettuces in rows in the dirt, being teased because their fashionably droopy jeans had to be hiked up constantly for fear of falling off.

Dondi and Terrel were among the most even-tempered and good-humored youths in our group, and I couldn't picture them with a gun. These two were not the kids Shyaam and I had been most worried about. In fact, we were especially proud of them. Living in foster homes, they had been going to the low-achievers' half-day high school like the rest of the youths in the garden group but had wanted to return to Berkeley High and try to graduate. Shyaam had gotten them back in, and they were making it there.

Now Terrel was in juvenile hall, because he had had the gun in his possession. Dondi hadn't actually been armed, so the police had let him go.

I tried to figure out what to do about Terrel. Maybe he should stay in juvenile hall, I thought. He'd never been in trouble before, and this would teach him a lesson. I imagined myself a passenger on that bus, and my mind went wild, wondering if the kids had used the gun somehow, somewhere. I wanted to talk to Shyaam, but he was in South Africa for several weeks, serving as an election monitor.

I felt furious that kids who don't have enough money to go to a movie or buy new clothes and are often hungry can still get a gun. "In America," I told Stan bitterly, "a gun's the one thing you can always get."

Camille's husband Elliott came over to tell us that Terrel and Dondi had taken a gun with them when they went to Terrel's mother Angela's apartment. They had wanted to visit Terrel's little brother DeShawn and his cousin Gideon. At the apartment the youths found Terrel's mother Angela, her boyfriend Askari, and their friends all smoking crack. Terrel, furious that they were using drugs with the children there, had pulled the gun on all of the adults and ordered them to get out of the apartment. One rumor said that Terrel had put the gun up to Angela's head. Another said he intended to shoot Askari but never fired the gun. Everyone knew Askari beat Angela, and some said he used to beat Terrel too. The adults did leave, and the boys started back home on the bus, heading for Terrel's foster home. One of the ousted adults called the police about the gun, and Terrel was arrested as he got off the bus.

Staying in Berkeley and in touch with Shyaam was one of many good choices Terrel made: stay in school, stay away from Angela, don't use drugs, work in the garden. Now, with the gun, Terrel had made a bad choice.

"We better stay out of this one," Stan and I told each other over breakfast, thinking of Askari, Angela's thuggy boyfriend. "We shouldn't get involved." But our resolutions sounded weak to me. We both knew that following through is everything with kids who've been let down a thousand times. The other garden kids kept saying it might not have happened if Shyaam had been around.

Every night I woke up and thought of Terrel in juvenile hall. I'd been in there to see young clients. In the lockup wing where they keep violent or suicidal kids, the cells have thick doors, not bars. There's a tiny window in each door, and walking down the hall you see two young eyes and a nose pressed to many of the windows. In the ceilings of these cells there are video cameras, and the kids are watched on screens from a central monitoring station. I've seen the kids on the TV screens, lying on bunks, or sitting hunched in the corners of those cells.

Maybe Terrel's in the dormitory, I hoped. But I wasn't sure, with a serious charge like having a loaded gun on a bus. Or he could be in the lockup if he were feeling suicidal.

All week I found myself making the phone calls I'd resolved not to make on Terrel's behalf: the juvenile public defender's office, the juvenile probation office, the local teen counseling project. I wished I could dial 811 for a social worker like 911 for police. I also wished we could hire about a thousand more mentors like Shyaam.

I had no official standing, and sometimes I felt like a busybody. On the phone, embarrassed, I explained I was just a volunteer who knew Terrel from a garden project. But when I told Terrel's circumstances to people I phoned, they listened.

Terrel's foster parents, who at first understandably refused to take him back, agreed to try again if he was released. Terrel's attorney, a tired-sounding young white man whose first lawyering job was as a juvenile public defender, told me Terrel would have a hearing in a few days. He said that for the judge even to consider releasing Terrel to go back to school and his foster family, his mother, Angela, had to go to court for him and sign the papers. Otherwise, he would remain in juvenile hall another thirty days, meaning he could not complete the school year, and then he would go to a group home.

But none of us knew where Angela lived, and of course crack addicts don't have phones. Either she'll find out and show up or she won't, I thought, and resolved once more to stay out of this one.

On a sunny afternoon that week, Stan and I went to hear the Dalai Lama speak in Berkeley's Greek Theater. At the end of his talk His Holiness said that if his message of compassion was relevant to us, we should please try to make an effort to make the world a better place. Please increase our efforts.

When I got home from hearing the Dalai Lama I walked over to Dondi's cousin's house, a place not much better than one of Angela's apartments because so many people were crowded into it living together. I knocked, and the door was opened two inches by a woman I didn't know who wanted to know what I wanted. Hoping that by chance

Dondi would be inside listening, I said loudly that I needed to know where Angela lived in order to give her a ride to court in the morning for Terrel.

In a second Dondi was on the porch saying he knew where Angela lived but not the address. He could take me there. I had to look up to talk to Dondi, a long-limbed high school senior with a good sense of humor who changed his hairdo almost every day, a sign of his rapid identity shifts at seventeen. Today he had braids. "I want to go to court too," he said. I told Dondi to be at my door at 8:00 A.M. because Terrel's hearing was at nine. Shyaam and I were always working to improve what we called the kids' "show-up skills," which were poor; their good intentions were easily defeated by distraction or depression. Now the effort would have to be made by Dondi.

That night I dreamed about Shyaam. He was in a sunny garden full of flowers, walking toward me, smiling, and I was so happy to see him, because now that he was here, everything would be all right. They say every figure in a dream is an aspect of the dreamer. I met the protector part of myself, I thought when I woke up in the morning—a black man who is a protector.

I was packing breakfast for Dondi when he showed up right on time, his hair brushed out in an Afro.

"How mad is Angela at you?" I asked as we pulled away from the curb, trying to assess our danger.

"Mad, I guess," Dondi said. "Everybody else is." He confessed right away that the gun had actually been his, obtained from "somebody older."

"*Why?*" I asked him (biting my tongue on the useless "you know better").

"Because I was scared." He hung his head. Was someone gunning for him? No. He was just scared.

"What about your foster home?" I asked him. He told me he had left there because another kid had threatened him. He was about to turn eighteen, and his social worker had said she wouldn't find him another place.

He'd been hanging around his cousin's place, but she kicked Dondi out at night, because too many people were already staying there. The last few nights, he'd gone to Sam-Sam's house, and Camille let him sleep on the couch.

His mother, he didn't have to tell me, couldn't help him. Ruth had gotten out of jail again just a few weeks ago and had been roaming the streets. Dondi said he hadn't seen her for the past two days, and he'd been worried sick about her. He got the gun, he said, because he was afraid of being killed, randomly, by some stranger, "just for nothing."

I told him that in his shoes I would be scared too, and very lonely. I gave him my gun speech. I told him I'd investigated cases where people unwittingly supplied the weapon for their own deaths. This seemed to impress him. I went on. I loved his mom, I said, I knew her when she was well. But he couldn't have a gun around his mom the way she was. She might kill herself or one of the little kids. He couldn't have a gun around people who might be loaded on drugs. He was in more danger with a gun than without it.

We listed the people Dondi could call when he was scared (Shyaam, Mahalia, me, Camille). "Survivors are the ones who call for help," I told him.

I pointed out that none of the youths in the garden group had been shot at. I thought about, but didn't mention, Reece. I wasn't sure Dondi knew Reece, the twenty-one-year-old who'd been shot to death a few blocks away at a barbecue take-out place last June—apparently "for nothing." No one had been arrested for Reece's murder.

Dondi was very smart, the one who wrote our notes on the board at garden meetings, with no spelling errors, and he was six weeks from high school graduation. One of his big problems getting to school, he revealed, was having nowhere to wash his clothes and no money for the laundromat.

We pulled up in front of the dingy apartment building that Dondi pointed to. When Askari answered the door, I said, "Remember me? I'm Shyaam's assistant," cloaking myself in his protection, as if I were on an official mission, not just meddling in Angela's business. Askari let us into a dark room with a filthy floor and absolutely nothing but a bare table and two chairs. Angela said she'd been told about the hearing, and she wanted to come, but she needed a ride. "That's why I've come," I told her. I perched on one of the chairs, waiting for her to get ready while

Askari stood stony faced in a corner, his arms crossed over his chest. My heart sank thinking of Gideon and DeShawn coming home to this place every day.

In the car, to her credit, Angela gave Dondi a mild tongue-lashing about the gun, but mainly she was mad that someone had called the cops. I kept my mouth shut but said a silent thanks to whoever had called because I was so glad the police had that gun now.

In the juvenile court waiting room, full of dejected kids and defeated or exasperated adults, we all met up. Terrel's foster parents brought along their three kids, two black daughters and a white son. It looked like a happy family. The dad, in a suit and tie, had taken the morning off work.

To my surprise, Angela's mother from Georgia was there. She had been contacted by Terrel's foster parents and was in Oakland, staying in a motel. Gideon and DeShawn had told Amina and me of their grandmother's powers of love. She told me she could not, alas, take them and Terrel to live with her. I didn't know her circumstances in Georgia, and I didn't ask. But she lived up to her reputation. I was sure she had never met Dondi before, but with the uncontested authority such a grandmother has, she started right in on Dondi with her own antigun speech, which beat mine in emphasizing self-discipline and personal responsibility. Dondi, the picture of apologetic respect, stood smiling sheepishly down at this short, round lady as she told him to use the common sense the Good Lord gave him.

Everyone talked about Terrel's chances but Angela, whom everyone ignored. She hovered around the edge of the group, her bloodshot eyes rimmed with tears. "She is what she is," I thought, "and the one to save today is Terrel." For the first time, I felt anger toward her. Her son was the one being punished, for acting out his anger at her negligence.

When the bailiff called Terrel's name, we filled every seat in the small hearing room. Terrel, in his light-green county-issued jail suit, looked like a child in pajamas. Every person in the room holding power over Terrel was white: judge, defense attorney, prosecutor, probation officer, clerk, and bailiff. That's not always true, of course, but it often is, and I expected Terrel would remember it.

In the back of the room, we were solidly integrated, seven black people, five white people. I wished we had a little sign: "People who care about Terrel."

The judge read the file while we sat, quiet. I watched Terrel, tense in his chair, being squeezed by the adult world with its jail cells and all the rest.

Again it was a dreamlike moment for me. When I was a teenager, being a girl, I hadn't exploded. But when I imploded instead, running away, trying to kill myself, getting pregnant, I ended up in a "home for girls." As with Terrel, I was the one who was punished, while my parents acted as if they were sitting in the audience. I can't remember the name or face of a single adult who tried to help me back then.

The judge, a blond woman about forty, started to question Terrel. He admitted to the gun. He said he got it from "a friend." Dondi squirmed. "*Where* were you when you got it?" the judge asked. Terrel said, "My mom's house." The judge asked Terrel if Angela knew he had it. Angela sat motionless, looking at her lap. Unable to tell the real story, Terrel hesitated, then said, "I don't know." The judge looked disgusted. The DA made his case, and it was convincing: a loaded gun on a public bus must be punished. The judge threatened to keep Terrel locked up.

The defense attorney then showed that Terrel had not been in trouble before, had been attending high school, was getting good grades and working in the garden project. There was no mention of the family's conditions; apparently, that was a given. When Terrel's attorney asked for his release, the judge said, "I'm not inclined to do that."

There was a pause, and absolute silence in the room. In my work, I've witnessed sentences in many courtrooms — even death sentences. In that long pause before the pronouncement, it always seems to me as if the breath of history blows through the room. And if the defendant is black, I imagine the wind in the sails of slave ships and all the rest that has brought us to one of these moments when the destiny of a young man is turned forever. The judge looked out at all of us. In her shoes, I thought, seeing all these people here, I'd take a chance on this kid. And that's what she did.

Angela signed, and the judge ordered Terrel released on probation conditions a whole page long: go to school, curfew at eight every night, and so on. His foster family would now be official. *"I'm* the one in jail!" the foster mother lamented, reading the list of rules she would have to enforce.

We all walked around to the release door. While we waited for Terrel, several youths emerged who had apparently served their time. No one met them — they just headed across the parking lot alone, looking lost and angry, and much meaner than I had ever seen Terrel look.

When Terrel came out, dressed again in his own superbaggy clothes, he didn't even look at Angela. He went straight to his grandmother and held her for a long time. She then told him he owed his guardians an apology and a hug. Embarrassed, he tried to make an excuse: "I'm holding my book." And he was. In his hand was his textbook, *The History of African Civilization.* His grandmother took the book from him, and he hugged his foster mom and dad and delivered a sincere, "I'm sorry." Their children gathered around him and hugged him too. He extended a handshake to me, a big smile and a thank-you. Then we all lined up for hugs from Terrel's grandmother. Terrel said nothing to Angela, who stood at the edge of the group.

I suddenly thought, wait a minute. This is a little too happy, like a graduation or something. I started talking about how gun possession at fifteen would forever stay on Terrel's record. It's a sad day when a young man "graduates" to his first conviction. This is serious. Everyone agreed that high school graduation would be much better.

I dropped off Angela and told her, "I care about you and I want you to take good care of yourself." I took Dondi back to Berkeley to school and told him that anyone could focus on something for six weeks. He had no more term papers due. He had only to take his body to that school every day and they would give him a diploma. If he did it, I promised, Stan and I would come to his graduation.

I sat in the car after he disappeared into the campus, thinking about the gun. The kids could have been shot by the police when they were being arrested with it. Or they might have shot someone in a panic or melee. I indulged in a fantasy of the police donating the gun to a church group I had heard of that buried dozens of police-captured guns at the base of a sculpture for peace. Please let no gun ever come near them again, I wished.

I phoned Stan at his office to tell him all about it, and we agreed not to be attached to results. These kids might not graduate, might easily get in trouble again. Our efforts were small, and their efforts were going to have to be very great. It might be too much for them. Still, it had been a good day.

Back at home, Camille came over. She said she was scared by the gun too, and worried about Dondi, and Sam-Sam. We formed a partnership for the next six weeks to help Dondi finish school. Camille said she would let Dondi sleep on her couch and do his laundry at her mother's house. Stan and I would supply the extra food to feed him.

"I have the easy part," I told her. "It's easy to go to the grocery store. What really takes effort is living with teenagers." After a pause, I asked, "Where'd they get that gun, anyway, Camille?"

She hesitated. It wasn't cool to talk about stuff like that. Then, "That goddam Wilber gave it to them," she said, disgusted.

CHAPTER TWENTY-NINE

Stepping on a Land Mine

Mrs. Burley had lived on Alma Street for forty years. She was nearly deaf, walked with a cane, and was the matriarch of a big family. She had relatives on both ends of the law-abiding spectrum, from her hardworking daughter who owned a cleaning service in Las Vegas to her great-nephew Wilber, the drug dealer.

Mrs. Burley came to about half of our block committee meetings, and Wilber was an agenda item at almost every meeting. There was always someone who wanted to complain about him, and often it was his great-aunt Burley herself. She wanted the committee to get the police to do something about the fact that he stood in front of her house selling drugs.

Wilber pretended to fix cars, she said, but she could see that when people leaned under the hood seeming to look at the engine, Wilber sold them some crack under there. He hid crack around her yard too, and she told us she was afraid she would be sued for Wilber's actions. The police never seemed able to catch him in the act of selling drugs on Alma Street. Wilber was on parole, though, for drug sales in Oakland.

Nobody wanted to sue her, but we all wanted Wilber to stop racing his cars up and down the block endangering the children. He would zoom up to the barricade, slam on the brakes, and do a three-point turn, laying rubber. If he was behind the wheel of a car, the engine was roaring, the tires were squealing, and the radio was throbbing loud enough to vibrate my whole house.

Mrs. Burley was no pushover. She told me that when she had worked in the shipyards as a young woman during the war, her job had been scrubbing out metal forms used to mold rubber gaskets. It was dirty, exhausting work, and Mrs. Burley had asked for a typing job, but only white girls worked in the offices, and the boss refused. Mrs. Burley insisted, filed a grievance, and held her ground until she was allowed to become a typist. After the war, she had worked for years as a secretary, and she owned her home. She was very proud of her determination, but when it came to her great-nephew Wilber, she was at a loss.

Mrs. Burley and Wilber were locked into a push-pull, love-hate dance, where she would ban him from her house, and he would stand in front anyway. Sometimes she would call the police, and other times she invited him in to eat. His father had been killed when he was a little boy, and his mother lived in Texas. Wilber was, after all, Mrs. Burley's late sister's grandson, and she loved him, but, as she said, "I've never known what to do with him."

Evidently Wilber loved Mrs. Burley too; if he was shut out he would stand on her lawn and yell that he wanted in, that she didn't love him like she did her other nephews. But if he got drunk, he cursed her. I saw him drive slowly past her house one afternoon when she had banished him. He was making his car lurch by popping the clutch and yelling out the window in his loud basso profundo voice, "Fuck you, Auntie, I'm here! Fuck you, bitch! I go where I want!" Mrs. Burley was sitting on her front porch glaring at him, shaking her head, embarrassed.

Jarvis told me he knew all about guys like Wilber.

"When he's in prison he's probably the kind who sits way off in the corner of the yard with his back to the wall, too scared to move," Jarvis said. "He's a lot of noise outside and very very quiet in here. Other guys hate somebody like that if they find out they do stuff to old ladies."

Mahalia helped Mrs. Burley get a restraining order against Wilber, forcing him to stay a hundred yards from her house, which put him just about in front of my house, where he set up his "car repair" operation, draining oil right onto the pavement, leaving rags and car parts all over the sidewalk.

The police came by once in a while and gave Wilber a talking-to, but he was low on their long list of priorities. They were tired of Mrs. Burley and her on-again, off-again restraining orders.

One morning before I went to work, Mrs. Burley called and asked me to come over. It was hard for her to talk on the phone because of her deafness. She showed me her big old sedan in the driveway. All four tires were slashed.

"Wilber did this," she said, "because he's mad about the restraining order." She didn't want to call the police. "They never do anything," she said. Instead, she wanted me to find out who Wilber's parole officer was in Oakland and have whoever it was come to see her.

"I want them to put him back in prison for this," she said. "But tell them not to come in a government car. Tell them to act like they're coming to see me for something, maybe like a doctor or somebody."

With Wilber's date of birth, which she gave me, I easily tracked down the parole officer. An energetic voice came over the phone, sounding like an assertive, busy white man. I told him the situation, and he said that slashing tires would be a parole violation.

"I can take care of that dude right away," he chortled.

I asked him to first call Sergeant Terry Ross of the Berkeley Police Department, who could tell him Wilber's whole history. Then I emphasized the need to talk to Mrs. Burley and to be discreet for her sake. Wilber, I told the man, stayed someplace in Oakland, but he usually showed up in front of my house every afternoon to fix cars.

The parole officer asked me my name and address. I hesitated. I heard a Vietnam veteran once say that in the instant before he stepped on a land mine, he knew that he shouldn't put his foot down. I felt something like that just before I rattled off my name to that stranger on the phone. I knew better, but I was going too fast, and I ignored my own instincts.

When I came in from work late that afternoon, Rosemary was at home. She greeted me with a worried look and started talking fast the minute I opened the door.

"Mom, Wilber was busted right in front of the house, and the whole street is saying you did it."

Altars in the Street

So much adrenaline flowed into my heart, I dropped my briefcase and sat down on the couch and leaned back. I listened to her, and all I could say was, "Oh, my God."

Rosemary told me she had looked out the window to see Wilber being handcuffed and a whole crowd of people gathered around. Rosemary had gone out to watch, and she said two police were there with a white man in civilian clothes who told everybody that there had been a complaint from somebody named Melody.

The squatters from the Continental Mortgage house and some of the teenagers had challenged Rosemary, "Why'd your mom call the police on Wilber?"

"My mom isn't even home," she'd answered.

Wilber was taken away to jail. I called Mrs. Burley and yelled into the phone, "This is Melody."

"I know, I know what happened," she said right away. "They told me." She said she was telling her whole family that I had called because she had asked me to do it.

"They won't hurt you Melody," she tried to reassure me. "Don't you remember when Eddie got killed, and they were going to kill the guy that did it and all, and they never killed anybody. They just talk." This wasn't very reassuring, since it sounded as if somebody was talking about killing me.

For a long time, I'd been trying to be a bridge between those of my neighbors whose distrust of authority was so deep-seated that "telling" on someone is the worst crime of all, and the best-intentioned of the "authorities" who were trying to help. But now I felt as if I were falling into the gap between them.

Early in the morning, Elliott came over, and I went out to talk to him in my garden. "You don't do that," he said to me sternly. "You don't go calling somebody's parole officer on them."

"I wish we could live here without anybody ever having to call the police," I said. "But it seems like we can't. Why don't people get as mad at Wilber for disrespecting Mrs. Burley as they get at somebody who calls the police? If everybody ganged up on him for harassing her, he wouldn't do it anymore."

"That's not your business," he said. "You have a good heart, Melody, and nobody's going to hurt you as long as I'm out here, but you don't call like that ever again."

I didn't promise not to, but I wished I never had.

I called the parole officer back as soon as his office opened. "My neighbors are saying that I'm the one who got Wilber busted," I told him. "Do you have any idea how that might have happened?"

He neither denied nor confirmed, as they say. "If you have any trouble with any of these people, you just call me," he crowed, "and I'll come down there and take care of it myself." Then he added, "Why do you live there?"

"You don't have any idea what you've done to me," I told him, and hung up.

I headed straight for Mahalia's office in the basement of the police department. She listened to my story, looking more frightened than I wanted her to look. "Sometimes, Melody, I think there are things going on that we are never going to know about," she said.

"You mean like bureaucrats in the pay of drug dealers?" I asked her.

She shrugged. "Let's go upstairs," she said.

She and I repeated the story to Sergeant Terry Ross and an assistant city manager. They shook their heads. "We'll go talk to that so-called parole officer," Sergeant Terry said, "but that's after-the-fact now. The truth is, we can't guarantee your safety. There's no way to do it. Something could happen to you because of this next week, or a year from now, or never."

Mahalia had said to call her anytime. She was working that evening, so Stan and I went back to see her together, to try to figure out how dangerous Wilber might be.

Wilber was the kind of guy who only picked on people he thought were weaker than himself. I'd seen him shove old fat Skeeter really hard, knocking him up against a parked car. Wilber was in his twenties, but he hung out with kids six or seven years younger, impressing them with his show-off ways with his car, and his access to crack, money, and guns.

But between me and Wilber, the question of who was weaker was hard to answer: me, small, middle-aged, and white, versus him, big, and young, and African American. He had a lot of connections on the street, especially with other young black men who worked for him, but my whiteness held a lot of power, and Wilber knew I had connections in the police department and also a lot of people in the neighborhood who cared about me, among them his own great-aunt Mrs. Burley.

Mahalia and I both knew that nobody is good at predicting future dangerousness—all you can go on is a person's past behavior, which of course can change at any time. Wilber's record, as far as we knew, was just nonviolent drug dealing and being a supremely annoying person.

Mahalia advised against doing anything confrontational. She said to avoid Wilber as much as possible and to call the police if anything happened. Back home, Stan said, "You shouldn't have done any of this, Melody."

"I know you're angry at me," I said, "and I'm furious at myself."

"Maybe it'll be okay," Stan said. "I just wish there was something I could do to change the situation."

When Sergeant Terry called me the next day, he said two officers and the assistant city manager from Berkeley had gone to tell the "cowboy" from parole that he was unprofessional and had endangered a community activist. "That guy was really a jerk," Sergeant Terry said. "He's one of these tough-on-crime types who has contempt for people and he won't admit he made a mistake by saying your name."

The parole officer had refused to hold Wilber in prison longer than a week. "Maybe just to spite the Berkeley officers who went to see him, I don't know," Sergeant Terry said. The slashed tires weren't much of a parole violation, and Mrs. Burley hadn't wanted to press charges after all.

I sat on Libby's couch, depressed. "Well, you can't blame her," Libby said. "Mrs. Burley just can't stay mad at Wilber. After all, they are family."

"I just hope Wilber can't stay mad at me," I said.

"I think it'll be all right," Libby said. "People around here don't hold grudges that much. One day they're hopping mad but there's so much chaos, the next day they go on to something else they're mad about." That was true, I knew.

"Maybe it's good Wilber isn't staying in prison that long," I hoped. "Maybe it'll all blow over, no harm done."

The whole block committee heard all about me and Wilber of course—no secrets on Alma Street. Pearl was incensed. "I think that parole man is a drug dealer," she said. "He has to be, him doing you that way. It's terrible. Didn't I tell you," she carried on, "the government is behind all this crack?"

Louis the bus driver tried to comfort me in his kidding way. "Next time I'm in LA I'll buy you one of those riot T-shirts," he offered.

"What do they say?"

"Thank you for not killing me." Everybody had to laugh, even me.

When I next went to San Quentin, Jarvis said, slowly, incredulous, "You gave out your name to some cop you don't even know?"

I felt defensive. "Look," I said, "I'm going to make mistakes, okay?"

"I think you guys should definitely think about moving," Jarvis said. He explained what I already knew: all Wilber had to do to get me hurt was to say to some youngster who wanted in on his drug business, "See that white lady right there? You do something to her, and you're in."

Jarvis wanted to cook up a plan to get me out of what inmates call my "snitch jacket." "Melody, maybe you could wait for sometime when you know the cops are coming—sometime when somebody in your committee has called them—and then run out the door and tell Wilber and his homies they better leave because somebody just called you and told you the cops are on the way."

"How does this help me?" I wanted to know.

"They'll think you're on their side, that you don't want them to get busted," he said helpfully.

"Jarvis, this is a great plan maybe for a prison yard. This is just little old me, remember? And anyway, the message we need on Alma Street is that if you are doing what you ought not to do, the police *will* be coming."

"Okay, okay, you're right. I'm just trying to think of something here," he said.

"Well, you take care of inside, and I'll take care of outside," I told him, feeling grumpy.

That morning at San Quentin the visiting cells were cold. Thin sunlight barely filtered through a cold haze that hugged the surface of the bay when I crossed the bridge to San Quentin. I was tired, and I wanted to get out of prison as early as possible to buy groceries and go home.

I finished talking to Jarvis and then interviewed one other man. I was about to leave, but a lawyer called me over to be introduced to my newest client, a man who had been sent to death row for supposedly killing two people right in Berkeley, at the Marina, where I loved to walk with my dog Alaska.

I was sorry now I'd agreed to work on the case; I wasn't interested in my favorite walking place turning into just another crime scene to me. I'd been reading the files about the woman found floating in the water at the edge of the park. The man's nickname was "Dodge," and Dodge was a skinny white man, with a square face and a beard.

He stood close to the cell bars and spoke to me briefly: "I'm glad you'll be working on my case."

"Thank you, I'm glad to meet you," I told him, and made my escape.

At the grocery store I decided to buy food for Amina's household too. Just in case there's no food in San Francisco, I teased myself. I bought two big bottles of olive oil, one for her house, one for ours, and two pounds of garlic in a net bag, and lots of marinara sauce in cans.

Maybe if I make sure she eats well, she won't end up floating face-down like Dodge's victims, I thought. And then I shook my head to wake myself up. I don't *think* this way usually, I thought. I'm losing my nerve.

No one was home when I carried the groceries into the house, just Alaska, watching me go up and down the stairs. She leaped up when I changed into my running shoes, but I didn't have the heart to go out of the house again that day. I told Alaska we weren't going to the Marina, and she flopped down again, dejected.

I set the burglar alarm and, keeping Alaska inside with me, I nervously cleaned out my purse, just to tidy one small place. I threw out tissues, scraps of paper, took out my checkbook and wallet and shook the lint out of the bag over the wastebasket, thinking what folly it was these days to carry a purse.

I looked out the window at the sidewalk. All I could see were two bodies lying there—Ian Freedman's and Marcus's—two bodies I'd really seen in the dark out there, but I saw them now, in the coldly slanted winter afternoon sunlight.

These are intrusive thoughts, I diagnosed myself. I'm having trauma flashbacks. I called Elyse.

"My stress level is getting just too high," I told her. "I can't sleep through a night, I can't stop thinking about violence."

"You're having a normal reaction to an abnormal situation," she said. "You need a break from it."

When Stan came home from work, I told him I felt as if I wouldn't be able to stand being awakened by squealing tires that night. I was exhausted, and I needed a good night's sleep to get some perspective. He suggested I call Lil and go over there for a night. Stan dropped me and my sleeping bag at Lil's house on a nice quiet street.

"Right now I feel like the whole world is nothing but crime," I told Lil. She put me in her guest room and brought me a cup of calming tea. I slept long and deeply. In the morning, having tea with Lil in her kitchen, I felt better. But when she asked me, "Melody, what are you going to do?" I could only say, "I don't know."

Wilber didn't come back to Alma Street right away. A couple of weeks later, I looked outside and saw him in his usual place in front of my house, the hood of a car open, some guys gathered around.

When I walked out the door, Wilber didn't say anything, but for an instant he made eye contact with me, and he made an obscene gesture with his mouth—opening it wide and making a lewd licking motion with his tongue—that totally unnerved me. I pretended I hadn't seen it.

After that, Wilber continued to harass me with behavior that he couldn't get arrested for but that made my life miserable when he was around. He purposely poured motor oil on the sidewalk in front of my house and sometimes splashed it on the hedge.

Standing in my living room behind the lace curtain, watching him, I remembered something my first Buddhist teacher Eric had said: "A bodhisattva is not a Buddha. A bodhisattva is a person who turns her face toward Buddha. A bodhisattva is someone who sees Buddha in everyone she meets."

That means everyone, I thought, sighing apprehensively. Wilber too.

Once I walked out to my car and Wilber and two other guys I didn't know were waiting for me, lined up along my hedge. Just as I pulled out of the driveway, they all three took out their penises and peed together into the hedge, laughing at me when I turned my face away.

I took to walking out my side door when Wilber was outside and bending low to sneak past my hedge to my car. Pam came over and listened to the whole story. "That's no way to live," she said. "Can't you sue that parole agent for something?"

"For what?" I asked. "I'm scared of people like him. Just think, if I lodged a complaint with his boss, what he could do to me, or have done to me. I'm more afraid of men like that than of Wilber. In a really repressive society, people like that parole guy get on top and somebody like me gets wiped out. He has popular opinions—tough on crime, hates everybody in a neighborhood like this."

Pam and I stood together looking out through the lace curtain at the guys fixing cars in the street. "You just tell Wilber that if he lays a finger on you, there isn't a prison in this state that he could do time in, because there are people in all of them who love you," she suggested in a kidding voice. "Plus, he's going to have to answer to *me*."

"Thanks." I hugged her. "I'll tell him to talk to you."

"But Melody, I really think you and Stan should try to move," she said.

"We're talking about it," I said, "but neither one of us ever *does* anything about it. The kids keep telling me that I wouldn't believe how different my life would be if I didn't live here."

"They're right," Pam said.

I was participating in the winter practice period at the Zen center as much as my job would allow. Sitting evening zazen in the darkened zendo, quiet except for the faint sound of people breathing around me, I felt safe and cozy in the warm yellow light of the kerosene lanterns whose flames cast the altar Buddha's shadow onto the white wall.

I had tea with the head student, and I mentioned that I was struggling with worries about violence in my neighborhood. Instead of telling me some Zen story, he answered with a story of his own. He said he lived in Oakland, and he had heard automatic gunfire one night in his street.

When he looked out the window, he saw the silhouette of a man hold-ing a long gun, running.

"If that happened twice," he said, "or three times, I don't know. Maybe I'd have to move away."

Everybody has a war story, I thought, driving home, and everybody is becoming inured to the violence.

At a party at Lil's house, I found myself talking to a writer who lived in the quiet literary village of Bolinas up the coast. I told him a little about the neighborhood, and he asked, "What would you say is the per-centage of people who are really causing all the trouble?"

"Maybe one percent," I answered, "maybe less," thinking about the few like the Jackson brothers and Wilber. I told the writer about my problems with Wilber.

"I know what I would do," he said. "I'd get a gun and kill that guy." I left the party feeling as if I were standing almost alone on a shrinking little island of middle ground.

Wilber completely ignored Stan, never even looked his way. When I was with Stan, Wilber didn't dare hassle me. We hypothesized that Stan was too powerful a figure for Wilber.

I never thought of a way out of my problems with Wilber, but a way came. Passing by Mrs. Burley's one day, I saw her standing in the door of her house holding a tiny baby wrapped in a blanket. "He's Wilber's," she said, pulling the blanket back. I looked into a diminutive face, long lashes curling onto tiny brown cheeks.

"Wilber's!" I gasped.

"Wilber Junior," she said, stroking his head. "His mother ran off and left him—she was on that stuff, and Wilber found him. He'd been alone maybe two days, and Wilber brought him over here to me."

"Is he okay? Did she take drugs while she was pregnant?" I asked.

"Born full of 'em," she answered, shaking her head. "He's going to make it, though. He's a good strong baby."

"Do you have what you need for him?" I asked.

"Well, hardly," she said. "I just got him today in what he's wearing."

It happened that Amina had a big plastic bag full of boy's baby clothes Liam had outgrown. There was a mobile too, for an infant to look at. When I left the things with Mrs. Burley, she let me hold the baby for a minute.

"I hope being a father can turn Wilber's life around," she said.

"I hope so too," I said, looking down at the baby. "If anybody can do that, this little guy could."

"Wilber's not really bad, Melody," she said. "He just feels like because he's been in prison, there's nothing he can do now." She said she would tell Wilber I had brought the clothes.

The next time I saw Wilber on the sidewalk, he looked at me and I looked at him. We didn't speak, but I could feel a change, maybe a truce. I tried nodding at him, and he nodded back.

CHAPTER THIRTY

Just One Woman

About a mile away from Alma Street, in an old building owned by the school district, was a place called the Drop-In. It had been there for years, a place where homeless people, many of them mentally ill, could get off the street during the day, have a meal, and watch TV. Many of the Drop-In's clients ate the free lunches at Reverend Clara's church, and I often saw them, ragged, sometimes deranged-looking men and women, walking through the neighborhood on their way to and from the church.

Mahalia told our committee that the school district had decided it needed the space, and the Drop-In's director, a sweet woman I had met a few times, had rented an empty storefront right on Lorin's main commercial street. Everybody reacted with horror when Mahalia announced the plan. "This is going to cause a whole lot of strife!" Louis the bus driver predicted.

We heard that the Drop-In clientele sometimes gathered before it opened, slept in the bushes near it, hung around after it closed, and used people's yards as toilets. If so, they would deal a final deathblow to our already sick main street.

"Why don't they just put up a wall and shove every undesirable thing behind it onto our end of town?" asked Libby bitterly.

Lorin's merchant's association voted unanimously against allowing the Drop-In to move in. The association's president, Kenesaw Smith, a black man who owned an antique shop, asked, "Who is going to come here to shop if they have to share the sidewalk with the Drop-In people? The Drop-In wasn't on a commercial street before, and it's inappropriate to put it in the middle of the only black-owned business district left in the city."

Mahalia was in a moral quandary. We had worked together for years on the principle that no person deserves to be thrown away. "But I hate to see this community that is overwhelmed already be given something else to take care of," she said.

The droppers-in would come to us with every deficit: housing, medical care, nutrition — "You name it, they need it," Mahalia said, "and the Drop-In is underfunded and understaffed."

I wished the whole issue would just go away. I wanted the city to find another place, but I was busy with Strong Roots, and I took no action myself.

But privately I decided it came down to equity. Lorin already had most of the low-income housing in Berkeley. How about some other neighborhood opening its arms to people with multiple needs?

Every crime watch committee in Lorin voted with the merchants against the Drop-In. Reverend Clara also thought it would negatively impact the church. People collected hundreds of signatures on a petition that Stan and I signed. There was no voice *for* the move.

Maudelle, our city councilwoman, though, was against us. Her position was, poor people should be helped, many of the Drop-In clients were disabled, and they had rights. I winced. That was all true.

"What about the impact on the businesses?" I asked her. The city's own plan for Lorin mandated developing and protecting our business district. She told me, "That business district is a goner anyhow."

A dozen neighbors showed up at a zoning board meeting I didn't go to. Libby told me that the Drop-In item was pushed to last on the agenda, and was heard, unbelievably, at three o'clock in the morning, when the commission voted to approve the Drop-In's move to Lorin's main street.

People appealed, and I did go to the next hearing, held at a reasonable hour. Lorin's speakers talked about equity, they talked about democracy, all to no avail.

"We are not saying, 'Not in my backyard!' " Libby said. "It's just that our backyard is already FULL!"

When one of the merchants suggested that the Drop-In be located instead on the north side, right in Berkeley's famous gourmet ghetto, the commissioners laughed out loud at such a preposterous idea.

"Over there Berkeley eats," Louis the bus driver called out. "On our end of town it shits!"

As we left, I said to Libby, "I wonder where the boundary is—what the exact address is where they no longer care?"

The city council refused to hear the matter, letting the commission's decision rest. So much for democracy. The Drop-In would move in right away.

Stan said, "This is how society benefits from a ghetto—it acts as a pressure valve. Lorin's a sacrifice zone."

"Well, if they're going to create ghettos, they better build the prisons to go with them," I told him, preaching to the choir.

Libby and I sat slumped on her couch watching Aurora play. "That was all the political power we could muster," she said. "If we can't keep out the Drop-In, that tells me nothing good is coming our way either."

"That's what I'm afraid of too," I said. "I'm just glad this whole nasty struggle is over. Maybe things will be worse, but at least now we can get on with life."

"I feel like we should put up a sign like the Statue of Liberty—'Give us your tired, your poor, your huddled masses yearning to be free,' " Libby said. "They're here now, and we might as well start trying to get along with them."

"You're right," I said. "After all, everybody has to be someplace."

Libby went over to the new Drop-In and put flowers in the planter boxes on either side of the front door as a welcoming gesture. I went by the antique store. "How's it going?" I asked Kenesaw.

"The Drop-In's a problem," he said, depressed. "Just like we thought." He talked about the increased litter and panhandling. "And they do have bathroom problems," he added. "I don't know how long I can hold on here."

A few of the Drop-In's more functional clients started to come to our block meetings, and they turned out to be perfectly nice people. A soft-spoken black man in his thirties with the beautiful name Paris Senegal told me he had had a breakdown after he was shot. He showed me a scar under his eye and said that the bullet was still in there. "I know you didn't want us here," he said, "but we're trying to be good neighbors."

"Paris, I want you to understand that I felt like I couldn't take on any *more*," I said, "and I know you do understand that feeling."

"Yes, I do," Paris said.

Meditating, I asked myself why I had wanted to reject the Drop-In people, and looking more honestly at myself, I realized that I hadn't wanted their "craziness." Maybe my neighborhood was the place where the poor people and the addicted people lived, but I wanted the crazy people to stay away. Unless they were our *own* crazy people we already loved, like Ruth.

The truth was, there was a crazy little corner of myself that held the feeling that I couldn't cope at all, a place I feared I might not be able to climb back out of, if I dropped into it.

When I told Elyse about it, she said, "First of all, you're one of the sanest people I know. But your stress level is so high, no wonder you're afraid you can't cope. We all tend to reject people who represent our greatest fears about ourselves."

A few weeks after the Drop-In struggle, Pearl came over to sit in my kitchen over coffee and told me, "I'm going, Melody. I'm just too scared to stay here anymore." She had been talking about leaving for a long time, but it was hard to believe she had made arrangements. She showed me the application forms for an apartment a few miles away, and she asked me to help her fill them in. "I never did get to go to school much," she said, embarrassed. I phoned the landlord of the new apartment and gave her a glowing reference. She would be able to move in once the place was painted.

"You can't go now!" Mahalia teased Pearl at our next meeting. "I got that streetlight installed in front of your house just for you!"

"I'm going to feel lonely without you," I told Pearl, "but I'll be happy to see you in a safer place."

Then one day Reverend Clara called. She said she had something to tell me. She sounded reluctant. "Melody, I've decided to take a job elsewhere," she said, sounding sad. In the fall, she was leaving for a suburban parish in Southern California.

"It's for the sake of my daughter," she said.

"I understand," I said. "Clara, it's so much because of you that I've been able to hold on to my home. I thank you."

"I'm sorry, Melody, I just can't do this anymore."

"I know," I told her. "You have had enough violence, losing your son."

"Melody," she said, "I want you to think about yourself. God wants us to take care of others, and God also wants us to take care of ourselves."

"Clara, I am just one woman. There's only so much I can do," I said.

The Timsons had already sold their house and gone. Saul Schwartz had moved too. Hiram was gone and Pearl was going. Now Reverend Clara. In the face of all of this, what were Stan and I to do?

CHAPTER THIRTY-ONE

Mother's Day

The month of May was beginning, and as Skeeter said, "There's a long, drunk summer ahead."

Still, it was a beautiful spring, and warm enough for me to take my tea out into the garden every morning. A mother robin had built a nest in one of the climbing roses near the top of the trellis. If I stood on a garden chair, I could peek in and see her four blue eggs when she was off the nest. I had started a new practice: no reading the newspaper the first thing in my day. Instead of filling my head with the suffering of the world as I was waking up, I chose a book from our shelf of Buddhist teachings and took it into the garden with me. After all, the suffering would come to me soon enough.

On one of those first mornings in May, a shaken Carolina found me in my garden to tell me some frightening news. A woman named Michelle Williams, an eight-months-pregnant crack addict, had been found murdered two blocks away, her mutilated body stuffed under an abandoned house.

"We haven't had any killings like that—a pregnant woman," Carolina said.

I hunched my shoulders up and squeezed my eyes shut for a moment. "It makes me scared for Ruth," I said, "running around out at night all the time."

"Oh, I know," Carolina said. "I wish somebody could make her stay inside."

When I called Reverend Clara, she had already heard about Michelle Williams' death. We had vowed to try to respond to every killing, and Reverend Clara had already set up a meeting with Michelle's mother, who lived nearby, and several other neighborhood women.

At the meeting, Michelle's mother, a light-skinned, freckled woman with reddish hair, spoke quietly about Michelle. "I lost my daughter a long time ago," she said, "to crack." Michelle had been living on the streets for the past couple of years, she said, and she had been raising Michelle's son, seven-year-old Jonah.

The women at the meeting decided to ask the city council to offer a reward for information leading to the arrest of the killer or killers. We also decided to start a fund to help Michelle's son Jonah, and an African-American woman who worked at a bank volunteered to set up an account.

Sergeant Terry said the police could not release the details about how Michelle was killed. He would only say that she had not been shot. "But it had to have been more than one person to have done what they did," he said. "The officers who found her are still very upset."

Sergeant Terry doubted that a reward would catch the killers. "We've tried that before, but no one has come forward," he said. Nevertheless, he asked the city council to set up the reward, $10,000. At the next meeting of the group trying to support Michelle's mother, Mahalia had a stack of leaflets, showing Michelle smiling in her high school graduation gown.

An article in the newspaper listed my name as a contact person for donations to the fund for Michelle's children, and one day I got a call from a woman who said she was head of the PTA at little Jonah's school.

"I never imagined there could be a child in my son's class whose mother was using crack," the woman said. "I feel so sorry. I think Jonah's mother was doing the worst thing a woman can do—taking drugs that were hurting her baby—but still I'm sad she was killed, and I want to help. What can the PTA do?"

"Thank you. Thank you," was all I could say for a moment.

I had written so many grant applications and letters, made so many phone calls, and here was a woman I didn't know, calling *me* with simple words; "What can we do to help?"

She told me that Jonah's teacher had said he wasn't openly grieving. He was always a quiet child, but now he was hardly saying a word at school, and he hadn't mentioned his mother at all. We talked about the idea of the PTA arranging counseling for Jonah, if his grandmother agreed. Also, they would take up a collection for our fund.

The PTA chair never once asked me, "Why do you live there?"

For a month before Michelle's murder, our committee had been planning a Mother's Day block party. The idea didn't originate with the committee. Suleiman and the other musicians who lived at the Blues Band House were working on it. Suleiman had asked me to get a permit from the city, and I had agreed. "Let's do something for all the mothers," he had said. Now, a mother and baby had been murdered, right before Mother's Day.

Suleiman was not the easiest person to work with, since he wasn't always sober. The block committee's party leaflets traditionally said, "Alcohol- and drug-free event." When I suggested that phrase for the leaflet Suleiman was making for Mother's Day, he refused. I had gotten him at a bad time, when he was pretty drunk himself, and he was rude to me.

"Don't tell me how to put on a party," he snarled. "We are the ones who know how to party! We are the original party people!"

"I'll catch you later, Suleiman," I told him.

Before noon one morning, I went over to the Blues Band House when I saw Suleiman outside working on his car and tried again.

"How about a compromise, Suleiman?" I suggested. "It wouldn't be good to have intoxicated people around the children on Mother's Day. We don't want it to end with a fight and the police coming and all that."

"But if we say no alcohol, believe me, Melody, a lot of people will feel *dis*invited."

"Okay, I see that." I nodded. "We want everybody to feel welcome. What are we going to do?"

"We'll keep the drinking behind the Blues House fence, how about that?"

"Okay, that's our agreement," I said, but I had my doubts.

On Mother's Day the Blues Band set up their speakers and microphone in the middle of the street, equipment so rickety that they probably couldn't even have pawned it. The tunes had a scratchy, tinny sound that made the music sound homey and oddly comforting. Amina, with Liam in her backpack, set up a card table with paper and pens and helped the kids make cards for their moms. It was fun to watch them writing, "I love you mommy," and sticking hearts and flowers on their cards, and then running to their mothers before the glue was dry to get a hug and kiss and smiles.

Next to the food table loaded with donated chips and salsa, salads and beans, Rosemary and Pearl stood at a card table serving sugary cake with thick white creamy frosting. People had been so scared by Michelle being killed that I decided what I really wanted for Mother's Day was to give each and every one of us a big, comforting slice of cake. Rosemary and I had bought two enormous cheap cakes at the discount bakery, each one about two feet by three feet, frosted with the word "Mother" and red roses all around the edge.

I watched Wilber strut around greeting people. He accepted a piece of cake politely from Rosemary, while Pearl pursed her lips and turned her head away.

People danced to the band, and little kids rode their tricycles around among the dancers. Libby had put up a leaflet at the Drop-In, and quite a few of the clients came. Some moved to the music with that stiff free-form style lithium and Thorazine can give to a dancer.

I sat watching the party on a lawn chair with other mothers, talking to Carolina, Libby, and Camille. Carolina's daughter Sheila, out of jail and looking very ill, sat on the curb holding Raven. Both mother and child were too thin and lacked light in their eyes. Sheila nestled her face in Raven's neck and Raven smiled. "She loves her baby," I thought, "and Raven loves her."

Ruth, looking scruffy but composed, sat close to Dondi in the scant shade of a street tree. Sometimes I heard her deep laugh, but I couldn't hear what she was saying over the music.

Just as he promised, Suleiman, acting as bandleader, reminded the drinkers, as if his words were part of the music, "Take it behind the fence," and they obeyed him. I peeked back there and saw a second party that flowed in and out of the bigger party with no trouble. Even Ruth was doing her drinking discreetly.

During a break, Suleiman gestured to me to come to the microphone, and I made a short speech: "This party is dedicated to the memory of Michelle Williams, a mother who was killed in our neighborhood a few days ago," I said, "and to all of the mothers and the grandmothers, doing our best to raise our children."

"Amen," came the answers.

Then Suleiman introduced Sister Jolene, a young African-American lay preacher from Oakland dressed all in white, who looked and sang like an angel.

Sister Jolene rejected the scratchy microphone in favor of her strong voice. She sang "Amazing Grace," and then she preached about how she had once been a crack addict and a prostitute.

"I was out here in these streets," she said. "I found my life by giving my life away to Jesus." There were a lot more fervent cries of "Amen."

Sister Jolene the Angel of Hope was followed up by Alvin, a skinny old dude who lived at the Blues House and whose stage name was the Tennis Shoe Pimp. He sang the same mournful song he always sang about the woman who shot her lover to get one more hit of crack. Between the two singers the full range of possibilities was drawn in the air before us.

Not long after Mother's Day, men with an assault rifle fired into a crack house, killing one young man and wounding others. As the gunmen sped away, they fired at a man in a car, wounding him too.

Next, an old man who had lived in Lorin for years was found shot to death sitting in his car behind his house. Skeeter said he had been "the drugstore man," not a crack dealer, but a man who sold prescription drugs like codeine and valium by the pill.

Then an eighteen-year-old was shot to death in a drive-by at a busy intersection in Lorin which thousands of Berkeley residents drove past every day. His mother was a city employee, and his funeral was scheduled for the same day Shyaam and I were going to be interviewed on the local morning radio show about Strong Roots.

"That's five murders in May," I told Shyaam, "if we count Michelle's unborn baby."

We had half an hour on the radio show, and we talked fast. Shyaam told about his trip to South Africa, where, he said, "people are having a discussion about resources and how they will be shared. Maybe it's easier to see the inequities in a place like South Africa where some people have no drinking water and other people have swimming pools. But here, we aren't even addressing the inequities except to blame the poor."

We told what we were trying to do with Strong Roots, giving youths alternatives to violence, and then I told about the funeral for the eighteen-year-old young man that afternoon.

"How scary!" the interviewer exclaimed, looking at me. "It could have been you!"

After the radio show I thought long and hard about her comment, turning it over every which way in my mind. "It could have been you!" is so much like, "Why do you live there?"

It *could* have been me, but it was so much more likely that it would be a young black man, and sure enough, it had been him. Wasn't it close enough that the young man lived in Berkeley? Wasn't it close enough that he went to the junior high where my kids went and that he then went to Berkeley High? Wasn't it close enough that his mother lived in my neighborhood and worked for the city, and that the radio interviewer and I were both probably acquainted with someone going to his funeral that day?

In all those ways, it *was* something that happened to me, and to the interviewer.

At the end of our May of murders, Stan was certain he wanted to leave Lorin. "If even one news item indicated that things were going to turn around, it would be different," he said. "But everything in the papers says nothing is on the way but health care and education cuts and more prisons. Melody, staying here is flying in the face of reality."

"I feel like I have whiplash," I said, trying to change the subject.

"After the election I really thought *some* help was on the way. But no."

"Why are you surprised?" Stan asked me. "The election was a contest for the suburbs."

I called Libby, and something about the way I said, "Hi, Libby," made her answer, "You're leaving, aren't you?"

Then she said, "Melody, I know I haven't been helping as much lately." She was pregnant and hadn't been coming to meetings as often. "I'll help more, I promise, if you guys can stay."

"I don't know, Libby," I said. "I'm not sure what to do."

I hung up the phone and walked through the house. I ended up on the couch in the living room, sitting in the narrow stripe of sun that first came into that north-facing room every year around the end of May, when the sun returned after winter. I knew the light in all the rooms of my house, in all the seasons of the year.

Sitting there, I could see the carved top of a post that held up the front porch outside the living room window. Above my head on the wall in its frame was the little girl's handwriting book I had found in the attic sixteen years before. "I belong here like that book does," I thought. "I'm not going to leave my house."

CHAPTER THIRTY-TWO

Juneteenth

When Camille's son Sam-Sam was a little boy, his heart's desire was a skateboard. He never got one, and then it was "Bike, bike, bike," but before he got one of those, he was old enough to want a car. Yet Sam-Sam was far too scared to be a drug dealer and get one.

Even his own grandmother made jokes about Sam-Sam being dumb, because he didn't say much. He was always on the edge of the group of kids, but I noticed that he quietly stayed out of trouble, hiding out within his "dumbness."

He was lost in the shuffle at school, dropped out at sixteen, and grew depressed and withdrawn.

At twenty, Sam-Sam stopped to talk to me out on the sidewalk. Teetering on his beat-up bike, his eyes red from marijuana, he told me, "I'm too young to just be *out* here like this, with nothing." At that point, he was sleeping and eating with various relatives and trying, as always, to stay out of trouble. I wished he could work at Strong Roots, but he was too old for those federal summer jobs.

Sam-Sam talked to me about an auto mechanic school he'd seen advertised on TV, and he wondered if I could phone them and find out about it. I made the call and found out they had openings, and loans, but it was a forty-minute drive away, over an hour's ride on the subway, and I doubted that Sam-Sam could get all that organized.

I hated to discourage him, though, and when he asked me to go with him to check it out, I agreed. "Is it okay with Camille if I take you?" I asked.

"Yeah, she knows," he replied. So we drove out there and found a big warehouse of a building.

"I swear," Sam-Sam vowed, "if I could go here, I'd get up real early every day."

We sat waiting in the lobby watching office workers bustling around, and occasionally we got a tantalizing glimpse through a big swinging door of the auto shop floor. I was sobered by Sam-Sam's lack of basic reading skills when he asked me to help him fill in some forms. Finally his name was called. I was planning to read a magazine, but he asked me to come in with him. As soon as we were seated in front of a Filipino woman, Sam-Sam, looking queasy, asked, "Do you have a rest room, please?" He bolted through the door, leaving me and the woman to sit chatting aimlessly, me thinking about Sam-Sam's lack of social skills.

When he came back, the lady explained that someone would have to sign for a tuition loan and allow the company to attach their wages to pay it. Sam-Sam and I both knew this was hopeless. Camille with her low-wage job would not be able to sign, and Stan and I could not get financially entangled with the neighbors. Sam-Sam and I went with the lady on a tour of the shop anyway. We saw men, mostly much older than Sam-Sam, working on cars up on racks. It occured to me that they were laid-off workers being retrained. Sam-Sam looked longingly at everything.

When I dropped him off, a downcast Sam-Sam said, "Thanks anyway, Melody."

The second summer of Strong Roots, Shyaam and I decided to make the garden we had dreamed of under the billboard. The police had done a major crackdown around Bob Bradford's lot, and it seemed quieter there.

We had a new crop of Strong Roots kids. Fifteen-year-old Jesse had signed up with the program hoping for a carpentry job, but he was assigned instead to our garden. He seemed uncertain about dirt.

"This is *nasty*," he told Flora, our main senior mentor. Jesse was a little shaky too, because his older sister's boyfriend had just been murdered, and he carried a little frown between his eyes.

Another of our gardeners, Ambrose, sixteen, was new to the neighborhood, having just moved with his mother from Mississippi. We were worried about how he would get along with the other kids. He won everyone's respect quickly, not just because he was a good basketball player, but because he was the only one who was already a natural with plants, having worked on his grandfather's small farm.

"But I was getting into trouble down South, so my mom brought me out here," he told us.

"Most kids go the opposite way," Jesse said. "They get in trouble here and get sent to their grandparents down South."

Ambrose told us all about how crack, guns, and gangs had come to Mississippi too.

Shyaam planned a big event to launch the new garden. In one day of hard work, as rain threatened but never really came, a practically elbow-to-elbow crowd of nearly a hundred people dug up the whole billboard lot into neat oblong plots and planted most of them with vegetable seedlings. When I came driving around the corner to deliver lunch, all those people looked like my dream come true.

Ambrose and Jesse came running over to help me unload, and they caught me choked up with happiness. "Have you ever heard of tears of joy?" I asked them. "That's what these are."

Sam-Sam, still unemployed, still wishing to be an auto mechanic, leaned on his bicycle against the fence watching, not joining in, looking depressed. But he told me, "This is really nice, Melody."

Strong Roots' next event was a booth at the Juneteenth celebration on Lorin's main street. Juneteenth celebrates the days after the Civil War in the second week of June 1865, when the news that slavery was over reached slaves on remote plantations.

Kenesaw, the antique dealer who was chair of the merchant's association, was on the Juneteenth committee, and he walked around with a clipboard full of papers, checking off the various groups: there were African-American crafts, foods, bookstores, clothing, and above all, music, coming from the sound stage.

Our young gardeners had a photo display of the Strong Roots gardens, and they were selling T-shirts and raffle tickets for a donated mountain bike. The youths, who had to deal every day with the nervous, averted eyes of people who passed them on the street, sat soaking up smiles.

"You guys are great!" people kept saying. "What a wonderful project!"

I was in the back of the booth folding up T-shirts when a young white woman approached to ask the kids to sign a petition. She said she was a university student trying to save affirmative action.

"What is it?" a kid with the nickname Shaker asked her.

For a second she was at a loss. How to explain affirmative action to a fourteen-year-old who had never heard of it? She opened her mouth to try when Shaker decided to take a guess.

"Is it three strikes you're out?" he asked.

"No," she cried, horrified. "No, no, no."

The youths listened respectfully as she launched into an explanation, using phrases like "preferential hiring" and "admissions for minorities." The kids frowned, trying to understand. "Are you saying this is something *you* want?" Ambrose asked.

"No—well, yes, I want to *keep* it," she said.

"They already have it?" Shaker asked.

"This *is* like Juneteenth," I thought. "Word reaches people months, even years later."

The youths, who rightly felt they had almost no chance of finding any kind of job, could not believe that there had been a system of preferential hiring for blacks, which, whatever it was, was now about to end. A man in his fifties in a wheelchair had rolled up to listen, and he took over the kids' education.

"Affirmative action was the booby prize!" he told them. "You should know that too, young lady," he told the student. "When I came back from Vietnam, black people wanted good schools, good jobs, we wanted to control our own communities. Affirmative action was what they gave us instead, after they killed off our movement."

We all signed the young woman's petition. "What the hell," the vet said. "Affirmative action is all we got, so we might as well keep it."

I admired the youths' selling technique. They made eye contact with people coming along the row of booths, walked up to them, and politely said, "Excuse me, will you please support our garden project?" All day long, their enthusiasm never flagged. One dollar at a time, they raised money for Strong Roots.

Jarvis loved hearing about Juneteenth, but he couldn't understand why more young people weren't trying like the garden youths.

"Why isn't there a movement, a big nonviolent movement like Mandela had?" Jarvis asked me. "Why are people letting everything get worse?"

"Well, you know that old movement chant, 'The People, United, Will Never Be Defeated'?"

"I've heard of it."

"Well, Lil told me she heard another version."

"What?"

"The people, united, will sometimes win and sometimes lose."

Jarvis laughed. "We still have to work on seeing things as they are. But Melody, I'm asking you for real," he persisted. "Why don't the high school kids march for a good education? I saw on TV the black kids in South Africa refused to go to school until the schools taught what they needed to know."

"That's exactly what should happen," I said. "I hope they do march someday."

CHAPTER THIRTY-THREE

Ruchell Gets Arrested

One day I was at home alone, talking on the phone about one of my cases, when my doorbell rang. I opened it with the phone in my hand, and a five-year-old boy was standing on the porch.

"Come out, Melody," he said.

"Just a sec, sweetheart, let me get off the phone, okay?"

I walked outside a minute later to find a small crowd gathered in front of my house. In the middle was Cherie, a woman I knew only slightly. Her son Ruchell was in the garden group, and I knew Cherie as a drug user I had seen around for years. The only time I had talked to her was when I had given her some photos of Ruchell I had taken on a garden field trip. Cherie seemed to be very drunk, and she was talking about the police taking away Ruchell. As I walked out my front gate, Cherie immediately turned on me and yelled, "I know you're the one who called the police! The police looked right at your house while they were putting the cuffs on Ruchell."

Ruchell had not, as far as I knew, been in trouble before. My strongest memory of him was in the kitchen on one of our farm trips, cutting potatoes for french fries. I'd told him, "You're a really good cook Ruchell," and he had beamed at me.

"Why was Ruchell arrested?" I asked the group of people in general, but nobody answered me.

"You had the phone in your hand! You're the one!" Cherie yelled.

"I did *not* call the police," I said. "I don't know anything about this. I was on the phone, but not with the police."

Cherie appeared to completely lose control, screaming at me, "Snitch!" and "Bitch!"

I put my feet a little farther apart and stood my ground, telling myself to keep breathing. A dozen people, half of them teenagers, were encircling me and Cherie, who was getting more and more agitated. Everyone ignored my denials—no one would even look at me when I tried to say something.

Cherie was yelling, her alcohol-reeking breath right in my face. "Ruchell didn't do *nothing* bitch!" she yelled, jabbing an index finger at my chest. I was convinced she was about to slug me.

I was afraid to retreat. If I stepped back, or turned around to go inside, I was sure Cherie would hit me. All I could think of was to face her and keep saying, "Cherie. Cherie."

Suddenly Carletta, who lived in the Continental Mortgage building, shoved Cherie away from me, pushing hard on both of Cherie's big shoulders. "*You're* going to jail for sure if you hit this woman!" Carletta yelled right into Cherie's face.

Cherie was quiet for a second, and I said, "I did *not* call the police on Ruchell. I don't even know why he got arrested. If you want me to, I'll call Shyaam and find out where Ruchell's been taken."

Carletta pointed at me and yelled, "I believe her! I believe her! She's telling the truth!"

I raised my voice to Cherie: "Do you want me to call Shyaam?" I asked in a demanding tone.

"Yes," she said.

"Okay," I said, as if obeying her. "I'll be right back, and let you know where Ruchell is." As soon as I got inside I dialed Shyaam's beeper number, entered my phone number, and hung up. I stood holding the phone, peeking out through a crack in the curtain, watching the crowd of people still milling around Cherie, who was crying and yelling again, and pointing at my house.

To my relief, the phone rang, and it was Shyaam. "Shyaam, can you come over to Alma right now? Ruchell's been arrested for something and there's a bunch of people in front of my house saying it's all *my* fault."

"I'll be right there," he said, and when I saw him drive up I went back outside.

Shyaam mediated between me and Cherie while the crowd watched. We went back and forth with "she called," and "I didn't call" for a while, and slowly, the story emerged.

It seemed that some guys had stolen a car and gone racing around the neighborhood in it, crashing into two other cars, causing injuries to people, and then they ditched the crippled stolen car and ran off. Somehow, talking on the phone in my kitchen, I had completely missed the commotion. One of the injured victims had apparently identified Ruchell to the police as a passenger in the stolen car, and he had been arrested in front of my house. The driver of the stolen car had gotten away.

"Cherie, no one needs to *call* the police when stuff like that is happening," Shyaam said. "The police are going to *come*! If I was here, and I saw all that go down, crashes and everything, people being hurt, *I* would damn sure call the police!"

Cherie stuck to her guns. "*She* must have called," she said, pointing at me, "because the cop looked right up at her windows." I stood there reminding myself that it makes no sense to talk to drunk people.

Carletta piped up with a racial theory: the cops who had arrested Ruchell had apparently been black. "They got him because he's mixed," she said. "He's light, and you know the cops hate people that's light."

Shyaam rolled his eyes. "That's right," he said. "That's why the prisons are filled with light people."

There was a sense in the conversation of Ruchell having been snatched up by aliens and taken to Mars, where no one knew how to ever contact him again. With luck, the Martians would spit him back out, but it seemed as if there was nothing anyone could do. Whatever my clients' skin color, their families often had that same extraterrestrial attitude toward the system. Sergeant Terry, talking about the police, had told me, "We're the *blue* people! We're not considered black or white or even human. We're *blue*!"

In the end, Cherie got into Shyaam's car to go to the police station to see what was happening to Ruchell, and I went back into my house. Over the next few weeks, Shyaam took Ruchell to his juvenile court hearings. Apparently Ruchell was wrongfully accused, and I was glad when he was let go. But no one from Ruchell's family would say hello to me again. Every time I saw any of that family, which I did several times a day, all I got was an intense look of hatred.

Shyaam told me he tried to convince Ruchell that I had nothing to do with his arrest, but my snitch status had become a legend. Ruchell completely dropped out of the garden group after the whole episode. Every time Shyaam or I saw him, he was with Wilber. If Wilber's hair was braided, so was Ruchell's; if Wilber's was combed out, ditto Ruchell's. Shyaam said that was a sure sign that Ruchell was "up under" Wilber, as the other youths called it. In only half a year, the sweetness of that boy cooking french fries had gone inside, and anger glowered out of his eyes.

"So often after a kid goes to juvenile hall," Shyaam said, "they'll just say to themselves, 'Okay, if you tell me I'm bad, I'll just *be* bad.' It's a shame."

One night I was driving up the street after dark and I saw a small group of men. As my car drew close to them, I recognized Ruchell with his back pressed to a wall. Three older men were facing him, and their bodies had angry, aggressive postures. I couldn't see their faces, but I saw Ruchell's, and he looked scared to death but defensive at the same time.

"What are they doing to him?" I wondered, alarmed. For a crazy second I thought about stopping the car, but I drove on. I called Shyaam at home late that night to tell him what I had seen, and he said he would try to talk to Ruchell. Later, Shyaam told me, "He's one we're losing, Melody—at least for now."

The garden group met regularly at the senior center with Shyaam. "You know what they asked me, Melody?" he said. "They wanted me to find them a place where they could live together away from Alma Street. Isn't that something?"

"What did you say?" I asked him.

"I told them they're only fourteen and fifteen years old and nobody's going to let them live on their own. It made me sad, though."

I was in my car leaving to go to work one day when Skeeter flagged me down. I stopped, and he came over and leaned in my car window.

"Melody, I heard some kids talking about how they were going to do something to you, because they heard you was some kind of investigator."

All of the garden group knew what my job was — in fact, on our way to field trips, I had pointed out San Quentin to them, and told them about Jarvis inside.

"I am," I said. "I'm an investigator for the *defense*, Skeeter. I *defend* criminals, not prosecute them."

"Well, *I* know that," Skeeter said, "but there's no explaining anything to these people high on drugs. They're crazy."

I walked out to my car one day and saw that it was spray-painted with graffiti. The sidewalk in front of our house was "tagged" too. I couldn't tell what the cryptic letters meant, and the police youth gang expert couldn't identify them when I drove the car down to the station. He said it looked as if a whole group of individuals had each signed my car. Shyaam hadn't seen that graffiti before either, and he knew a lot of the gang tags in South Berkeley.

Camille's husband Elliott looked at the car and went to get some rubbing compound he had. "Look, this comes off easy," he said, making a circular motion with a rag. "This is nothing, it's just kids. It's bullshit. You're going to be okay."

Not a week later, Skeeter came by with the gossip that Elliott was back in prison. "Oh, no," I said. "I thought he was waiting for that bakery warehouse to call him about a job."

"Well, maybe he was," Skeeter said, "But he got caught breaking into a car, stealing a stereo, and he's gone."

I went to see Camille. "How are you getting along?" I asked her.

"I don't know," she said, her eyes full of tears. "I don't know what's going to happen to my kids, Melody. I only hope I can be here for them."

"Well," I said, "the government's spending twenty thousand dollars on prison this year for Elliott. I'm sorry your family can't be helped by any of it."

To Stan I added, "I feel a lot less safe around here with him gone."

Elyse called me to say that she had heard a story about an Oakland neighborhood activist who had been attacked. I decided to find out the details. I called the aide to the city councilwoman for that Oakland district and heard the story: The woman had been trying to clean drug dealing out of the park across the street from her house. Two men had kicked in her front door in the middle of the night. They had walked boldly through the house, past the rooms where her children slept, past some guests asleep in another room, into her bedroom where she was in bed with her husband.

One of the men had hit her, hard, on her head with a metal bar. They didn't hit her husband, they didn't take anything, or say anything, or hit her again. They just left. It had been a warning. She wasn't badly hurt, but it had been a message, and she'd gotten it. The next day, she and her family had moved out. Later, they had sold their house.

I developed a completely stiff neck, and I went to see my acupuncturist. I'd seen her for years off and on, but I'd never talked to her much. I always dozed during acupuncture, listening to the classical music piped into the room. This time I told her a little about my problem.

Like everybody else, she had a story: she and her husband had renovated a Victorian in West Berkeley and had loved their home, but after years there, their fifteen-year-old son had been mugged on the street in front of their house.

"We never slept there again," she said. "We moved in here. We actually slept in my office until we found a place. You don't need acupuncture, Melody," she said, pulling out the needles. "You need to move!"

I told these stories to Stan, and he said, "Shall we move before, or after, someone gets hurt?"

CHAPTER THIRTY-FOUR

The Woman Who Dug up Her Heart

In early June, as the Central Valley in California heats up, the ocean fog is pulled inland and cools the coast. On a chilly night, shouts woke us.

A loud, mean, ugly male voice outside screamed, "I'm going to kill your fat ass." I lay frozen in bed while Stan got up and cautiously went to the window. Two men outside were yelling curses back and forth.

Stan peeked out, moving the curtain just a millimeter to one side. He saw a tall man standing in the street silhouetted against a streetlight behind him. The man held a gun in one hand, and Stan whispered it was square looking—an automatic. Stan couldn't see the other man, but his voice sounded closer to our house. "I'm going to kill YOU."

It was about to happen again. Our muscles clenched, we waited for the shots. But they never came. Stan saw the gunman get into a big white car and drive off. It was three in the morning, and everything was quiet.

We didn't even call the cops. I could hardly believe that we didn't, but why call and say, "A man was here with a gun and now he's gone?"

After a while, Stan fell back to sleep, but I knew I would lie awake unless I could read a book to calm myself. I left our bed, all nice and warm, went into the other room, and turned down the covers on the cold single bed next to the bookcase.

Before I turned on the reading light, I went to the window, knelt down, and looked under the bottom edge of the curtain. I saw no lights shining in any of my neighbors' windows.

I knew few people on the block had slept through the shouting, it had been so electrifying. Yet the cops had never come, hadn't even cruised by slowly fifteen minutes after the shouts. No one had called them. In all those darkened houses, people like us had reasoned the same way we did. There was no point, nothing could be done.

I lay there, never going back to sleep. I didn't read, didn't try to curl up to get warm, didn't turn on my side or stomach. I lay flat on my back, staring at the ceiling, my mind, which usually races through sleepless early morning hours, hardly thinking. There was just the sensation of coldness spreading up slowly from my feet, while something died inside me.

Sometime during those hours, I imagined Malcolm X coming into the room to tell me, "A small number of people can spark a change."

"I know that's true," my mind said. "But maybe not here, not now."

Buddhism, teaching me compassion and nonjudgment, had up to now helped me to stay, trying harder. Now, Buddhism talked to me about the wisdom of knowing when to go.

"I give up," I thought toward dawn, my legs by then like lead, my stomach cement. "All right. I give up."

For a long time, Stan had wanted to make a careful plan to go, and I had resisted even talking about it. Now at least we were on the same side, and the work of leaving could begin.

After Stan went to work, I called Elyse at her office at the junior high. She instantly offered to come over on her lunch hour and hold my hand, if necessary, while I called a realtor.

"Thanks, but I think I can do it," I told her. "I'm going to hang up the phone and dial the number right now."

I made the call. Then I went into the garden and weeded, as I had on this piece of earth for sixteen years. Mindlessly, obsessed, I dug, flinching at every sound from the street, unable to get the image of the man with the gun out of my mind, even though I had not actually seen him myself.

The sun was burning off the morning fog, and I was kneeling in a rocky place in the warmest corner of the garden, a spot planted in succulents and cactus, when my hand brought something up from the hardened soil. Attached to nothing came a fist-sized piece of root burl, wood swirled into the exact shape of a human heart.

I turned it in my fingers, astonished, unbelieving. If a sculptor had carved this wooden heart, it could not be more perfect. I sat in the dirt holding it in my two palms. "I've dug up my own heart from this garden," I thought. "It's no longer in the soil here. Now I can go."

CHAPTER THIRTY-FIVE

Into the River

For years, Stan and I had divided our dilemma between us. We were both ambivalent about whether to go, but Stan owned going, while I owned staying. As soon as we were both on the same side, we completely lost our balance.

There were a thousand decisions to make, big ones and small ones, and it seemed as if all we could do was fight. We didn't know where to start. Should we house hunt? Or put that off until the house sold? And where to look? We tried to discuss moving to the country and commuting back to work in the city, or moving to a smaller house, but where? Oakland? Richmond? I felt I couldn't get ready to go until I knew at least something about where I was going.

The idea of putting my hands on every single object we owned and making a decision about it made me dizzy. Walking into the basement made me nauseous—the shelves stuffed with children's school mementoes, art supplies, the electric train, the boxes of books we'd meant to sell, the fabric I'd planned someday to sew. What about the darkroom equipment we'd always meant to set up, my old teaching materials, and Stan's sixties music on reel-to-reel tape?

"Do you realize," I asked Stan, "that starting with the babies' plastic ring set and going through the tricycle and badminton, the weight-lifting set and the skis, everything a person needs for recreation from birth to age fifty is in our basement?"

I found myself picking things up and holding them, then putting them back down.

One day, as Stan and I stood on opposite sides of the dining room arguing about one of the millions of things we seemed to disagree about, he turned and walked out of the house. I grabbed one of our dining rooms chairs by its carved wooden back and threw it against the wall as hard as I could.

I burst into tears and distractedly tried to smooth out the dent in the wainscoting with my fingers. Then I lamented the chair. One leg was snapped off just below the seat. We had six chairs that matched, and they all matched the table. We had bought them ten years before from Kenesaw, the antique dealer I'd gotten to know better during the Drop-In struggle and Juneteenth.

I cried wildly, trying to fit the leg back onto its stump, but both broken ends were splintered. I picked up the chair, tucked its broken leg under my arm, slung my purse over my shoulder, and practically ran out of the house. I knew a furniture refinisher who lived in Richmond, twenty minutes' drive away. I felt I *had* to get the chair fixed immediately. I had to be able to fix *something* right away.

I remembered where the furniture man lived. I had once had him reglue an old desk, and when he returned it we talked of houses and gardens. He was a bearded man, a little older than I and graying, one of those people who seemed to have all the time in the world to talk. He loved antiques, he said, and books and cooking. Driving up the freeway, I felt relieved: at least *this* problem I could solve.

When I pulled up in front of his house, the furniture man was mowing his lawn. It was a neighborhood of smallish stucco homes painted pastel shades on the edge of the industrial city of Richmond. The repairman acted as if emergency furniture calls were no surprise to him at all. I opened the back of my station wagon, and he examined the damage. He shook his head.

"No, I can't fix this, it's too splintered. The only way would be to make a whole new leg, and it's not worth it for these chairs. It's a shame, though—they are nice." He looked at me. "What happened?"

"Well," I said. "I could lie and say it was an accident, but the bald-faced truth is, I threw it against the wall."

His next words were, "Is this something to do with your neighborhood?"

"Are you psychic?" I asked. "How did you know? We've decided to move, and it's so much stress, I'm just freaking out."

"I don't know why I guessed that," he said. "When I came to your house with your desk, it seemed like a tough area, and my wife and I are facing the same thing."

He told me that drug dealers were in the park around the corner from his house, and that the week before, someone had driven down their street firing a gun and had shot out fifteen car windshields, including his wife's.

"We don't know where to go," he said. "We've invested everything we have here." He wished me luck selling the house.

"Next time, grab an old kitchen chair, okay? Try to spare the antiques."

Driving home, I remembered a famous Zen story about a woman who became enlightened when she dropped a bucket of water and realized the impermanence of all things. I didn't become enlightened, but somehow the spell of the house broke with that chair. There was a gap now in the circle of chairs around the table, and that empty space started me on the sad task of breaking up my home.

Stan and I stopped fighting and cried a lot, mostly in the basement. "Look at this," one of us would say, and we would get weepy over the tiny moccasins I had stitched for Amina, or a pamphlet Stan's commune had written about Vietnam. We sorted everything, giving away, selling, storing, boxing, throwing out.

I gave the kids an ultimatum—"Come and get your aikido suit, your slides of France, your Barbie suitcase, or kiss it all good-bye." I decided I had one criterion. I'd look at something and ask it: "Do I want to die owning you?" If not, it went.

At my last block committee meeting, Libby chaired, and there was the usual agenda about "problem properties." Everyone had already heard that Stan and I were going, but the surprise came when Louis the bus driver announced that he and Manuela were leaving too. "It's because of our son," Louis said in a pain-filled voice. "We can't let him out of the house to play." Continental Mortgage's squatter house next door to them had never improved, and Louis and Manuela couldn't take it anymore.

Libby and Jim were staying, at least for now. "I love my friends here just too much to go," she said. "I don't know if things will get better, but we're hanging on." She gave me a going-away gift: a book about the 1870s when the Native American people and their way of life were dying.

"Is this how you feel about *these* times?" I asked her.

"In a way," she said quietly. "But the book's not all depressing. The people have faith that their knowledge will be passed down, and that someday, people will learn it again."

Dondi had remembered my promise to come to his graduation if he made it, and he gave me a ticket to the ceremony. I found a seat at the top of the Greek Theatre at the university, and after searching the graduates' faces, I finally picked out Dondi in the front row. I ran down and took photos of him in his bright red gown as he crossed the stage, and afterward Shyaam and Stan and I gave him a party. Dondi invited some of the other garden youths and chose the restaurant, a big lively Mexican place.

I told him he deserved a special award, the Overcoming Adversity Prize, and he grinned. The waitresses led us in singing "For He's a Jolly Good Fellow" as Dondi cut a big cake that said "Congratulations." I smiled, and snapped more photos, but inside my heart ached. Where was Dondi going? And where was I going?

Like ants carrying bread crumbs, Stan and I struggled out of the doors and into the station wagon with our surplus belongings until the house was pristine. The day came at last when we were ready for what our realtor called a "walk-through," where a couple of dozen realtors come and price the house. Before they arrived, on an impulse, Stan got out the camera, and we took photos of each other in every room, posed beside the bare and shining surfaces, the vases of flowers. We had made a display on the dining table of photos of the garden in fall and in spring. It was summer, and outside the apricot leaves were big and green, almost-ripe fruit peeked out among them, and the yellow roses were rampant on the trellis.

Suddenly many cars drove up at once, and we heard car doors slamming and people laughing. They explored the garden first. "My God, a person could get married here!" I heard one of them exclaim. When Stan opened the front door, he stood aside to let in a troupe of smiling people, all of them in a hurry.

I hadn't known what to expect from a realtor's "walk-through." At least twenty men and women were everywhere at once, opening every door and closet, peering and commenting. They ignored us, or gave us quick little smiles and hurried along, nosing into every corner. "A real pantry," one said. "Look at this old-fashioned laundry chute," I heard. I wanted to grab our realtor by the arm and tell her, "Get these people out of my house, I've changed my mind." But I stood still in a corner of the kitchen during the invasion, trying to understand that my home was not to belong to me anymore.

As soon as the realtors left, I got a call from Jarvis's attorney, telling me that Jarvis had been moved, as some kind of arbitrary punishment, to the worst part of the prison, the section of death row where those with severe mental illness were kept. I was alarmed, but there was absolutely nothing either the lawyer or I could do.

That evening, Stan and I were collapsed on the couch, dully watching television, when my chest started to ache, and then my arms. Within a few minutes, I had trouble taking a deep breath. We called a nurse friend, and she said to wait twenty minutes. By the time we called her again, I felt as if a large man was sitting on my chest. I could hardly breathe. "I think you guys should go to the emergency room," she said.

At the big emergency hospital in Oakland, no one could tell if I were having a heart attack or not. I had some of the classic symptoms, so they admitted me. It was late by the time I was settled in a bed with a heart monitor on, and Stan asked the nurse if he could stay with me through the night.

"That's fine," she said, "as long as you don't threaten to kill us."

"What?" Stan said. "What are you talking about? Why did you say that to me?"

"I'm sorry, I shouldn't have said that," she apologized. "It's just that we've had so many people in here lately who have threatened the staff. It seems like people can't cope with anything anymore without a gun."

Stan stretched out on the empty bed next to mine, and we both slept fitfully. Elyse came in early in the morning with a cup of good coffee for Stan. Lil arrived too, and half-seriously she said, "Quick, tell me where you put your heart-shaped root. I think I should bury it again before anything worse happens to you."

When all the test results were in, I was found to have a perfectly healthy heart. The doctor said I'd had an anxiety attack. He said I'd probably been hyperventilating, maybe for hours without noticing myself doing it, and that had constricted my chest muscles and caused the pain.

"Some of us react more to stress than others," he said soothingly. "Is there any way that you can take it easier?"

"Enough is enough," Stan said. We decided to rent a place and leave as soon as possible, even though it meant paying our mortgage too. If the house didn't sell quickly, we had no idea what we would do next.

"It's no longer a question of how much money we might lose," Stan said. "Right now it's a question of how much we're willing to pay to get to a safer place."

The last night we spent on Alma Street, I was awakened by Ruth, outside in our driveway. She often hung out near our fence at night, and I thought she did so to come close to us for safety, knowing we would be there if she needed help. I looked out and saw her come walking out past my car. A man I'd never seen before was following close behind her, and she was laughing in her deep voice, and flailing her arms about in a way that looked disjointed. The man was almost a head shorter, and skinny, and Ruth was easily warding off his ineffectual advances by slapping at him with her hands. It was a comical scene, except that when Ruth disappeared around the corner, the little man panting after her, I was scared to think of where she might be going.

A friend found a house for us to rent, and without telling most of the neighbors, we moved our camping pads and sleeping bags and a few clothes into it and started to sleep there just a few nights after I got out of the hospital.

Our rented house was on a street so quiet that at night you could hear the slightest sound. There was a nectarine tree in the backyard covered with ripe fruit, and occasionally one would fall to the patio flagstones with a soft "plop." My nerves were so raw that every time a nectarine fell, I would awaken with a start, terrified, adrenaline filling my blood.

Toward morning, for weeks, I dreamed of men with guns.

I went to talk to Abbot Mel Weitsman at the Zen center. I told him about moving, and feeling helpless.

"Sometimes I think that I've been trying, on death row and in my neighborhood, to gain some control over the violence in my life," I told him. "As a child, I was completely helpless in the face of violence. I try to realize that I can't control anything, but I don't want to accept that I'm a refugee from violence in my own country. I don't want that to be okay."

"It's not *okay* that you've lost your home to violence," he said. "But it is what is," he said.

"Sometimes, I feel so bad that I forget Stan and I still have a home at Zen center," I told him.

"Yes," he said. "You have a home here."

I hadn't seen Jarvis for weeks. When I finally made it to San Quentin, Jarvis, looking thinner and tired, told me about life with the mentally ill inmates. Some hallucinated that insects were crawling on them or that other people were in their cells. Some could not clean themselves, or refused to eat, convinced they were being poisoned. Someone was always yelling. It was impossible for Jarvis to get any real sleep.

"Really, it's not that hard to live with them," he reassured me.

"They're so crazy, it's impossible to get mad at them. The main thing is, I'm glad your heart's healthy, and you finally moved."

"I think you should move to a better neighborhood too," I said. That got a smile.

I had brought along an article about James Baldwin's visit to San Quentin not long before he died. Jarvis hadn't seen him; no one on death row ever was allowed to go to an event like that. The article quoted Baldwin, who had written that he had faith in "the few relatively conscious black people and the few relatively conscious white people" who could bring us through the fire next time.

"That's right," Jarvis said. "Our allies are the black people and the white people who think racism and poverty are a problem."

"Who do you think the enemy is?" I asked him.

"Violence," he answered.

Ordinarily at the end of a visit, Jarvis smiled and said good-bye while he turned his back and stood with his hands behind him, holding them close to the portal in the metal door so that the officer could reach through and ratchet cuffs onto his wrists. This time, when Jarvis had to go, he didn't smile. It was obvious that it was hard for him to go back to his cell. I didn't know what to do except to stop and stand an extra second holding my legal papers, waiting for him to go.

Every two weeks our realtor held an open house. After only six weeks, the house was bought by a group of young women who for months had been looking in cheap areas for a huge house to share. They had been living in apartments above shops in a tough part of San Francisco, and to them, the house with its garden felt like moving to the country.

"Trees! Birds! Compost!" they exclaimed.

Stan and I had written a disclosure statement about the neighborhood that would make anybody's hair stand straight up on end, but their hair, spiky and dyed with Day-Glo colors, was already sticking up. They were full of energy and the right combination of cynicism and optimism. They had no children, and they were streetwise city artist types. We fell in love with them. They had hardly any money, so we gave them a second mortgage ourselves to help them finance the house.

"Maybe if I were their age, I'd buy our house all over again," I told Stan.

"Well, we're not their age," he said. "It's time for us to move on. Don't think of it as giving up, sweetie. Think of it as retirement."

I didn't have the heart to teach the new owners about the garden, so Stan explained Jarvis's magnolia tree, Ti's Norfolk pine, the little gingkos in their cages out on the street, and all the rest.

As I drove up to our house to get one of the last loads, Skeeter met me on the sidewalk, and he pointed up to the big front window. It was shattered, and inside I found a rock the size of a brick on the rug. Skeeter sat on the stairs and watched me sweep up shards of glass.

"Why do they bother to break my window now, Skeeter?" I asked him. "I'm *going*. Isn't that enough?"

"Now they're mad at you *because* you're going," he said.

All I could do was sigh and shake my head.

"You don't have to go," Skeeter said. "You don't have to be so scared."

"I'm sorry I'm going, Skeeter. I'll come back sometimes, to see you."

"No, you won't," he said, leaning his elbows on his knees and looking at his shoes.

"Right now, I can't believe that this is the last time you and I will see each other, Skeeter, after all these many years. But maybe you're right. I don't really know where my life is taking me," I said. "We'll just have to both wait and see what I do."

Skye's big house had put up with sixteen cycles of our birthdays and Christmases, with the laughter of parties and the cries of grandbabies, the noise of our slammed doors and pounding feet, the weight of children swinging on the doorknobs and people throwing themselves face-down onto the beds to cry. Now the bare rooms of the house felt as if they slept, and the sound of my shoes did not wake them as I passed through and closed the big front door for the last time. I turned and locked the door on our jokes and songs and arguments, the quiet times of talk, all part now of the house's past.

My last load was a pile of red-brown clay pots I found under the back stairs, half full of soil and sand, saved for next spring's plants. As I pulled away, they grated and clanked in the back of the car. I passed Ruth as I drove off. She had her little son riding up on her shoulders, and she was happy, walking along, looking normal except for the fact that she was barefooted. I cringed, thinking of the broken glass that was always lying around. She waved at me and swung the toddler down into her arms and kissed him.

The next day, I went to visit Pearl at her new place. She had moved at the same time we had. Young men from her church had arranged everything in her new apartment. Even her pictures of Kennedy and King were hung up over the couch.

"It looks like you've lived here two years, not two days," I told her. On Alma Street Pearl had had to sit on her cement stairs right next to the sidewalk to give her parakeets and herself some sun. Here, she had a chair on a little porch with some flowering plants on the railing. I admired everything for a few minutes. Then Pearl said she'd just had a call from someone on Alma.

"Ruth died last night," she said.

I looked down at my feet, planted in their sandals on the piece of bright green artificial grass Pearl had on her porch. Then I was standing on a bath mat right after I got out of the shower in my apartment in Oakland when my sister Naomi opened the bathroom door and said, "Melody, Skye's dead."

On Pearl's green artificial grass, my feet looked bigger, as if they had come closer to my eyes, as if Pearl's words had made me shorter. I imagined Ruth murdered, her tall, solid body crumpled up somewhere like people had said Michelle Williams' pregnant body had been. I said softly, "No."

"They said she had a stroke," Pearl said, "but I don't know . . ." Pearl's gravelly voice trailed off uncertainly as we both considered the numerous possibilities for truth that could underlie any version of an Alma Street story.

"It's so sad," Pearl concluded, "but at least it's over. But her kids . . ."

"How could a thirty-seven-year-old woman have a fatal stroke? It must be drugs. Or a stroke caused by drugs," I argued to myself, searching for a reason while, in my imagination, Ruth flew west, sailed past Pearl's porch and through the Golden Gate, out over the ocean, to where the Ohlone people believed that the spirits of the dead reside.

The story of Ruth's death, as I heard it from Libby, was that she had walked miles, barefooted, carrying her baby, to her sister's house in Oakland, had handed the baby to her sister and told her she was going to die. The sister had tried to reassure Ruth and had gotten her to lie down to rest. When the sister came back into the room, Ruth was dead.

Ruth's funeral was held on a day when Shyaam and I were working at the Strong Roots garden, and we both took a few hours off to attend. It was held at a ramshackle little church in West Oakland. Curiously, I saw no religious picture or statue inside. There was just a table with some plastic flowers at the front of the room, and on the wall above it, a broken electric clock that advertised a mortuary. In front of the table, there was a simple casket, the lid open. Ruth's children sat in the first row of folding chairs with their grandmother, Dondi holding his littlest brother on his lap. Shyaam sat in front facing the congregation with our city councilwoman Maudelle Shirek, our social worker Herb, and the old man minister of the church.

I took a seat on a folding chair between Mrs. Burley and Carolina. Mrs. Burley looked stoic, but tears streamed down Carolina's face, and I held her hand. The Blues Band people were all there, and Ruchell and Cherie, Wilber and many of the garden youths.

The congregation never seemed to settle; people kept getting up and disappearing into a kind of cloakroom at the back. It took me a while to realize that there must be some drugs back there keeping the addicts going.

After the opening prayers, Councilwoman Maudelle Shirek gave a speech about the need for a national health care system, with drug and alcohol treatment and mental health care, ways we might have helped Ruth, she said. An election was coming up, and she urged us to vote. I agreed with every word she said, but the speech seemed out of place. As she sat down, Skeeter rose and to my amazement he walked to the front. He was pretty drunk, as were quite a few others.

"This is no time for politics," Skeeter pronounced. "This is time to pray and to say good-bye to our sister."

Many agreed, calling out, "Amen."

The preacher took as his text part of the book of Job: "This life is few of days and they are full of trouble.

"Ruth was a woman who felt the pain of the world very keenly," the preacher said. "Now she has gone on, to a better place."

Nearly every speaker echoed his words, saying Ruth had at last been released from this life to go where things were better. A young black woman came forward who said, "Ruth always had a loving word for me." The young woman told the congregation that she herself was HIV-positive, and that she wanted to live the rest of her life with joy. "I have learned to suffer," she said, "and when I suffer, I will gain eternal life. When I see Jesus, it will be over."

"Life is suffering," I thought, but I didn't want the only better world to be the next one.

When people broke down crying, they leaned against the person next to them and those around them fanned air onto their faces with their programs or their hands, a ritual gesture of care that looked very old to me, as if it had been done in climates much hotter than Northern California, and passed on, funeral to funeral, for many generations.

When Shyaam spoke, the tone changed. He addressed the young men: "The women are bearing too much of the load," he said. "We men must take it up and do our part. You must BE men," he said, looking at Ruchell and Dondi and Wilber, and the others, "and don't let yourselves be snared by the traps that are out there."

As an older woman sang a hymn of life's eternal bondage, we all rose to walk past Ruth's casket. As we shuffled forward, the line of mourners halted as Dondi, a dozen people ahead of me, turned away from his mother's body and fell to the floor. People fanned him, and picked him up, and helped him to walk outside, looking ill, his head lolling back.

As I drew even with the foot of Ruth's casket, I could see that her cheeks and lips were rosy with rouge, and she was dressed in an old-fashioned powder-blue satin dress, making her look as if she had fallen asleep on her way to a long-ago prom. I stepped closer and looked into her face. Her skin, in life a polished coppery brown, was faded now and fragile, like cocoa-colored silk. She looked asleep but tired. "Good-bye," I whispered. Looking at her for the last time, I too longed for Jesus, or for a left-behind God or a God gone away to come back now. I wanted to have faith that Ruth was at home.

I had plans for a vacation, but first I found Mahalia in the basement of the police department. "I couldn't bear to go to the funeral," she said. "I can't accept yet that we weren't able to help Ruth." She paused. "A lot of endings, a lot of changes for Alma Street," she said.

"I never wanted to give up, Mahalia," I told her.

"Sometimes it's our dreams that are our burdens." She sighed. "Have you ever heard of that? The burden of dreams?"

We sat quiet for a minute.

"I always look for the healing, Melody," Mahalia said. "Your healing was that you learned not to avoid the painful reality but to try to look right at it. If we look and continue to look, maybe we can find the answers."

"I'll be a sojourner now, Mahalia," I said. "You and Shyaam work with the kids in Lorin without living there yourselves. I will too. I'll stick with the garden project."

Mahalia raised her eyebrows and nodded her head emphatically just once. "Good," she said, and smiled.

I left for a long weekend of white-water rafting with a group of women. At first I was sad, and tense, feeling separate from the women. No longer from Lorin, I no longer knew who I was. Gradually, I let the river soothe me, letting it teach me that if I let go, I would be taken to a new place, though never back upstream.

We stopped at a rocky beach where the women wanted to swim a big rapid in their life jackets. If you jumped in just right, extended your feet ahead of you, kept your head up, and leaned back in the water, the river would swirl you straight toward a giant rock and then sweep you past it in a high wave and around a bend into slower-moving water where you could swim to shore.

First, though, we had to make our precarious way from the rocky shore through the fast-moving shallow water out into the current. I got partway out, feeling the strong push of the water against my legs, feeling for footing on the slippery rocks, and holding myself upright with my hands on wet boulders.

Suddenly I thought, "This might be just how Mahalia's daughter Sophia drowned. Her foot got caught, and the current kept her under."

I froze, afraid to go on. But then, for Mahalia and for Sophia, for myself, and for the joy of living, I took some more careful steps, reached the edge of the deep water, and jumped into the wild rapids.

Epilogue

The neighbors I have called Potter, Mrs. Sanders, Addie and Joe Josephs, Libby and Jim, Ruth's children Dondi and Jamal, Kenesaw, and many many other good people still live in Lorin, sharing the good times there and the bad.

Mr. Howard the grocer passed away in 1992.

Carolina's paraplegic son, Marcus, died in 1994, and in 1995, Carolina herself died, of illness.

Paris Senegal was murdered on Lorin's main street in 1996.

Reverend Clara Mills is a United Church of Christ minister in Southern California.

My first Buddhist teacher, Eric Meller, died in October 1994 of a heart attack, just before his fiftieth birthday.

Jarvis Masters has become a widely published author, writing from death row at San Quentin, where he awaits the outcome of his appeals.

The new owners of Skye's house planted yet another gingko tree in front, where it keeps the faith with the two we planted.

> *Whenever I'm feeling discouraged*
> *I vow with all beings*
> *to remember how Ling-yun saw peach trees*
> *bloom after thirty long years.*
> Robert Aitken Roshi

About the Author

M elody Ermachild Chavis is a private investigator who works on trials and appeals for death row inmates. She is a youth justice advocate who volunteers with a community gardening program for youth at risk. A student of Zen Buddhism, she is a member of the board of the Buddhist Peace Fellowship. She is a mother and grandmother, and lives with her husband in Northern California.